1709

Economic beginnings of the far west /

D1236338

4815

XIV

ECONOMIC BEGINNINGS
OF THE FAR WEST

I

EXPLORERS AND COLONIZERS

ECONOMIC

BEGINNINGS

OF THE FAR WEST

BY

KATHARINE COMAN

TWO VOLUMES

I

EXPLORERS AND COLONIZERS

[1 9 1 2]

REPRINTS OF ECONOMIC CLASSICS

Augustus M. Kelley · Publishers

NEW YORK 1969

First Edition 1912

(New York: The Macmillan Company, 1912)

Reprinted 1969 by

AUGUSTUS M. KELLEY · PUBLISHERS

New York   New York   10010

Library of Congress Catalogue Card Number

67-29510

PRINTED IN THE UNITED STATES OF AMERICA
by SENTRY PRESS, NEW YORK, N. Y. 10019

THE BUFFALO HUNT ON THE GREAT PLAINS, 1855.

ECONOMIC BEGINNINGS
OF THE FAR WEST

HOW WE WON THE LAND
BEYOND THE MISSISSIPPI

BY

KATHARINE COMAN

AUTHOR OF

"THE INDUSTRIAL HISTORY OF THE UNITED STATES"

VOLUME I
EXPLORERS AND COLONIZERS

Illustrated

New York
THE MACMILLAN COMPANY
1912

PREFACE

FOR three centuries possession of the Far West, the vast unknown that lay beyond the Mississippi River, was in dispute. The maritime nations of Europe who in the seventeenth and eighteenth centuries contended for control of the north Atlantic coast and the eastern half of the Mississippi Valley, were engaged at the same time in a less dramatic but no less fateful tug of war for the great rivers, the arid plains, and the wind-swept coasts of western America. France through her fur traders laid hold on the Mississippi and Missouri rivers and the net-work of lakes and sluggish streams that stretch from the Great Lakes to the Canadian Rockies. Soon after the Peace of Paris had given Canada to Great Britain, the indomitable Scotch traders of Montreal carried their enterprises across the Rockies to the Pacific. Long before this, Spanish *conquistadores* and Franciscan missionaries had found their way over the lofty plateaus of northern Mexico to the headwaters of the Rio Grande and along the western foot-hills of the Coast Range to the harbors of San Diego, Monterey, and San Francisco. Spanish ships had already explored the coast well into Arctic waters and, while missing the key to the Northwest, the Columbia River, they had established the title of the most Christian Prince to all of the Pacific slope south of the Russian settlements. Unquestionably, Spain and Great Britain would have been engaged in an unequal controversy for possession of the richest portion of North America, but for the intervention of a new claimant. The young Republic that had wrested the eastern half of the Continent from the British empire and purchased Louisiana from France, did not long hesitate to demand the Floridas, Texas, New Mexico, California, the watershed of the Columbia River, and Puget Sound as her rightful inheritance.

As to the political and diplomatic merits and demerits of this struggle for possession, a mere economist will not attempt to decide. Our province is rather to suggest the underlying economic conditions that determined the outcome of war and treaty and race competition, and to reveal the bread and butter struggle that must ever result in the survival of the fittest, — the ablest to utilize the resources of a virgin territory. The controversies waged between the United States and Great Britain in Oregon and between the United States and Mexico in Texas and California were adjudicated in advance of diplomatic award by thronging settlers whose political and economic vision no less than their superior industrial efficiency made them masters of the coveted country. The self-employed and self-supporting farmer took possession of the land in a sense not to be disputed. The great estates of the Spanish regime, cultivated by forced labor, and the trade monoply maintained by the Hudson's Bay Company stifled normal development; but the American ideals of free land, free labor, and equal opportunity struck so deep root in this propitious soil that they could not be dislodged.

A goodly number of the men who bore an influential part in this long and complex contest left diaries, letters, or journals recounting what they saw and did. I have endeavored to tell the story as they understood it without bias or elaboration. For the completion of this task grateful acknowledgments are due to the officials of the Bancroft Collection at the University of California, of the Public Library at Los Angeles, the Oregon Historical Society at Portland, the L.D.S. Historian's Office at Salt Lake City, the Crerar, Newberry, and Public libraries of Chicago, and the Boston Public Library, who have rendered me patient and ungrudging service. I am also deeply indebted to my brother, Seymour Coman, and to my generous friend, Katharine Lee Bates, who read the proof and contributed many valuable hints as well as unfailing sympathy and encouragement.

KATHARINE COMAN.

The Scarab,
Wellesley, August 12, 1912.

CONTENTS

VOLUME I

PART I. THE SPANISH OCCUPATION

CHAPTER I

CHAPTER II

PART II. EXPLORATION AND THE FUR TRADE

CHAPTER I

CONTENTS

PART IV. THE TRANSCONTINENTAL
MIGRATION

PART V. FREE LAND AND FREE LABOR

CHAPTER I

LIST OF ILLUSTRATIONS

VOLUME I

LIST OF ILLUSTRATIONS

PART I

THE SPANISH OCCUPATION (1542–1846)

NEWHOUSE'S BEAVER TRAP

ECONOMIC BEGINNINGS OF THE FAR WEST

CHAPTER I

THE EXPLORERS

THE men who undertook to carry the Spanish flag into the vast unknown that lay to the north of Mexico were handicapped by certain prejudices or mental obsessions. The store of precious metals discovered in the realms of Montezuma and of the Incas rendered every less evident form of wealth unattractive to them. The search for Cibola, for Quivira, for California, was abandoned when they became convinced that the fabled riches were not there. The lure of gold had blinded the eyes of the *conquistadores* to the far greater wealth to be derived from the fur-bearing animals, the schools of fish, the forests, the fertile soil, the latent mineral resources of these unexploited lands. Moreover, the Spaniards, while a maritime people, were not successful navigators. The Spanish ships that explored Pacific waters (to say nothing here of the Atlantic) had for pilots, and sometimes for commanders, Italians and Portuguese or even Greeks. Spanish adventurers preferred *terra firma*, and their most important discoveries were made by overland expeditions. Inured to the saddle, they made extraordinary marches across stretches of desert that would have appalled another people, but they rarely took to boats. To them a river was an obstacle, not a guide, and thus they missed the most feasible routes into the interior.

A lasting handicap on Spanish colonization projects was the short-sighted policy that reserved all New World revenues to Spain and her immediate representatives. The commercial legislation promulgated by the Council of the Indies was based on the theory that colonies existed for the benefit of the mother country. Not only must all the bullion exported be sent to Spain, but also certain agricultural products, such as coffee, sugar, dyestuffs, and precious woods. All trade must be carried on in Spanish vessels and between the ports of Cadiz and Vera Cruz. No man not of Spanish blood might engage in trade, and any colonial caught in a commercial transaction with a foreigner was liable to confiscation of property and possibly death. That the colonies might furnish a market for domestic products, manufactures and the cultivation of grapes and olives were proscribed. This was a far more oppressive system than the British Board of Trade imposed on the Atlantic coast colonies at the behest of English manufacturers. It was Spain's irreparable misfortune that there was no element of resistance in her colonial population; her ruinous mercantile system persisted, by consequence, till both mother country and colonies were exhausted. The natives suffered in silence, knowing nothing of the rights of man, and the corrupt Spanish officials were ready to connive at illicit practices in return for a share in the profits.

The government revenue dwindled year by year, until the expense of maintaining control of the dependencies was greater than the income derived. Spain's colonial empire was precisely the richest portion of the New World, but it was administered on a plan so suicidal that all the advantage of these vast possessions accrued to a few hundred indolent, selfish, and overbearing grandees. The processes of decay received a temporary check at the hands of Charles III and his far-sighted premier, Florida Blanco. *Laissez-faire* economics found a hearing at court, and the policy of the mercantilists was abandoned. The monopoly by which a few merchants of Seville had absorbed all the profits of the trans-Atlantic trade was broken up, and ten open ports competed with Cadiz for this privilege. The registered fleet sailed down the Guadalquivir for the last time in 1778, the year of the "free trade" edict. This law did not accord to the colonies absolute freedom of trade, but the number of their open ports was increased, the duties levied in legitimate commerce were reduced, and freer play was given to colonial enterprise.

No less destructive of colonial development was the practice of granting great estates to Spaniards and requiring forced labor of the natives. It was an undemocratic custom that promoted individual wealth, but sapped the springs of general prosperity. Spanish enterprise was restricted to agriculture, mining, and such primitive manufactures as could be carried on by peons. Industries that demanded zeal and intelligence languished wherever undertaken.

Finally, the quality of the migration from Old and New Spain must be taken into account. It was peculiarly non-economic. There was a notable lack of the merchants and artisans who shaped the industries of New England. In the Spanish social order, the soldier and the priest far outranked the breadwinner. The wisest of the viceroys and governors recognized the importance of establishing colonies of small farmers, men with families to provide for and homes to defend; but there were few such citizens in New Spain. The mother country sent to her American possessions soldiers, administrators, friars, adventurers and grandees, but not laborers.

Throughout the sixteenth and seventeenth centuries, Spain was the leading European power in North as in South America. Cortés and his successors subjugated the Aztecs of Mexico with astonishing rapidity and imposed the Spanish language, religion, and a feudal aristocracy upon the realm of Montezuma. Within the present area of the United States, Spanish explorers had to do with the regions most difficult to penetrate. The Colorado Desert, the arid plateaus of New Mexico and Arizona, the *llanos estacados* of Texas, presented obstacles that would have seemed insuperable to men of Anglo-Saxon origin; but to adventurers from the Iberian peninsula, desert and mountain and sandy waste were familiar and unterrifying phenomena. The Spanish occupation was practically coincident with that portion of the United States which is most comparable to Spain in rainfall, vegetation, and climate.

Section I

The Route to the Orient

To explorers sailing under the Spanish flag, Europe owed its earliest knowledge of the vast ocean that divides America from the Orient. Their achievements tore apart the veil of mystery that enveloped the "South Sea" and revealed to the soberer enterprise of Holland, France, and England a vast continent. Belief in a sea-to-sea passage that should give Europe direct access to the Indies survived the theory that the New World was a mere archipelago. Gaspar Cortereal, the Portuguese navigator, professed to have sailed through such a strait somewhere above Labrador (1500), and his vaunted discovery found place on the earliest maps of the New World as *Fretum Anium*. Early in the seventeenth century, credence in this and like traditions was revived by the report that a Greek pilot, Juan de Fuca, sailing under commission from the viceroy of Mexico, had explored a channel on the north Pacific coast which opened into a wide sea dotted with islands wherein he cruised twenty days without reaching the bounds of it, and that he had finally found his way through to the Atlantic. This notable discovery rested on the unsupported testimony of an English merchant, Michael Lock, who published the story (1619) as he got it from the old pilot and who petitioned Queen Elizabeth to furnish him with an outfit with which to follow up the clew. No record of such an expedition has been found in the Mexican archives; [1]

but the narrative was accepted by Raleigh and Purchas, and the latitude of the supposed channel and de Fuca's description of it correspond with surprising accuracy to the strait that now bears his romantic name. Cortés, Mendoza, Philip II, and Charles III were each bent on the discovery of this great commercial opportunity; but when Balboa proposed to cut a ship canal through the narrow isthmus he had crossed, the suggestion was scouted as impious by the most bigoted of Spanish kings.[2]

No sooner was Cortés secure in possession of Mexico than he began to prepare for the exploration of the west coast, being persuaded that the South Sea was part of the Indian Ocean and that the Spice Islands lay not far beyond the setting sun. He was sure that new lands equally rich in gold and silver and equally helpless against European weapons must await him there. The great *conquistador* devoted twenty years to this enterprise and sent out four expeditions at his own expense. In 1522, three years after his first landing at Vera Cruz, he set about building caravels at Zacatula, his newly established port on the Pacific coast; but the machinations of his rival, Guzman, hindered the enterprise, and not till 1532 did the first ships get under way. Mutiny, adverse winds, and the hostility of the natives wrecked this and the second expedition, but the survivors of the latter brought back intelligence of an island opposite Colima where they had anchored in a beautiful harbor and found Indians fishing for pearls. This promising discovery Cortés determined to prosecute in person, and in 1535 he marched north to Chiametla with a party of seven hundred soldiers, settlers, and priests. The colonists were shipped across to the pearl harbor (Santa Cruz) in the expectation of founding there a Spanish settlement; but the land proved rocky and barren, and the people perished for lack of food. The great conqueror was not a colonizer, and the year following he was obliged to bring away the wretched survivors. Francisco de Ulloa, who commanded the fourth and last expedition (1539), followed the coast of the mainland to the head of the gulf, then west and south along the east shore of the peninsula to the Bay of Santa Cruz, rounded Cape San Lucas and sailed north again to Magdalena Bay and Cedros Island. The vast estuary revealed by this voyage he named the Sea of Cortés, and the mountain mass which he failed to circumnavigate, he called California, in the stubborn faith that it would yet prove as rich in precious metals as the fabulous island of Esplandian.[3]

In 1540, Cortés sailed away to Spain never to return to the New World. His project of exploring the west coast to find the Spice Islands or, better still, the sea-to-sea passage that should give Spain direct access to Asia, was espoused by the Viceroy Mendoza. This powerful statesman fitted out two ships and commissioned Cabrillo, a Portuguese navigator of repute, to take possession of all discovered lands in behalf of the king of Spain. The little fleet covered Ulloa's route to Cedros Island, but, pushing on to the north, rounded Cabo Bajo and sailed into a fine harbor, later known as San

Diego. As Cabrillo followed up the coast, the mountains fell away, and he anchored in an island-girt channel opposite a fertile valley and a populous Indian village, which he called the Pueblo de los Canoas because the natives came out to the ship in rude wooden boats (Santa Barbara Canal). Beyond the low promontory at the upper end of this roadstead (Point Conception), Cabrillo's ships were caught by the northwest winds that prevail along this coast throughout autumn and winter. Beating his way in the teeth of the tempest and forced again and again to take shelter under the lea of the shore, Cabrillo finally rounded a wooded point (Point Pinos) and anchored in a spacious bay which he called Bahia de los Pinos. As it was now midwinter and the incessant storms rendered further voyaging hazardous, the hardy Portuguese turned his weather-beaten prows south at last and sought a safe anchorage in the "Canal." There on San Miguel Island the daring navigator died (1543). His task was bequeathed to his loyal pilot, Ferrelo, and he in the following spring, the winds proving favorable, returned to Bahia de los Pinos, passed Punta Año Nuevo and Punta de los Reyes, missing the estuary that lay between, and so sailed up the coast to a precipitous headland which, in honor of the "good Viceroy," was named Mendocino. Here storms overtook the venturesome explorers, and provisions ran low; but Ferrelo pressed on till he sighted Cape Blanco and then, very reluctantly, gave up the quest.

Mendoza's second project, no less far-seeing than

the discovery of the Strait of Anian and much more practical, was the occupation of the group of islands that Magellan had encountered on the edge of the China Sea. If they could be brought under subjection, Spain would attain the long-coveted access to the trade of the Orient. In the same year that Cabrillo explored the northwest coast, Villalobos was despatched across the Pacific to make conquest of the Philippines (1542). He failed, but the task was not abandoned, a seven years' war broke the spirit of the natives, and by 1573 the Spanish government was established at Manila. Soon a considerable commerce was developed between Macao, Manila, and the Pacific ports, which persisted throughout the seventeenth and eighteenth centuries and was highly profitable to the merchants concerned. Every year the Manila galleon set out from Acapulco or Callao freighted with silver. This, the staple product of Mexico and Peru, was exchanged for spices, porcelains, cottons, and other Oriental luxuries, suited to the pampered tastes of the Spanish grandees. West-bound vessels were carried by the prevailing winds and currents directly across through tropic seas, but the return voyage must be made far to the northward, in the path of the Japanese Current, until Cape Mendocino was sighted; thence the northeast trades could be relied on to waft the home-bound galleon to Acapulco. It was a long voyage, six months at best, and the storm-driven mariners were often forced to take shelter in some inlet along the coast where they might find wood and water. Wrecks were not infrequent, and

the need for a well-provisioned port at some convenient harbor became each year more apparent.[4]

This traffic, so rich and so defenceless, did not
escape the notice of Spain's sworn foes, the English
buccaneers. Drake and Hawkins and other Devon
worthies had been wont to loot towns and capture
treasure ships on the Spanish Main, but to challenge
the dons' monopoly of the South Sea was a task of
greater hazard. Drake, however, was nothing loath.
In his little frigate, the *Golden Hind*, he rounded
South America, threading the Straits of Magellan
(1578–1579), and, making swiftly up the west coast,
fell upon the unfortified settlements and heavily
laden galleons of Peru and Mexico and easily
stuffed his hold with booty. Not wishing to risk
all by returning the way he came, this glorified pirate
proceeded up the California coast, seeking that open
passage to the Atlantic in whose existence every
mariner of his day firmly believed. He passed Cape
Mendocino and ran north to the forty-third or the forty-
eighth parallel; but encountering head winds and bitter
cold, he came to the conclusion that there was no
thoroughfare from west to east, since the coast "was
running continually northwest as if it went directly
to meet with Asia."[5] Turning south, the *Golden
Hind* anchored in "a convenient and fit harbor"
below the projecting headland now known as Point
Reyes, and there her commander, fully assured that
no Spaniard had ever set foot upon this shore, took
formal possession in the name of his sovereign,
Queen Elizabeth, and called the land New Albion.
Following a confiscated Spanish map, Drake then

steered across the Pacific, and so, by way of the Philippines and the Indies, returned to England (1580), having fairly won the knighthood that awaited him. The horror-struck Spaniards believed that the *Golden Hind* had come and gone through the Straits of Anian and that Britain had discovered a secret entrance to the South Sea. Their fear and wrath were intensified by the advent of other English freebooters. In the very year of the Armada, Sir Thomas Cavendish ravaged the coast towns of Mexico and even succeeded in capturing the Manila galleon.

To the masterful mind of Philip II, such adventures as those of Drake and Cavendish were intolerable, and he undertook to forestall further encroachment on Spain's monopoly of the South Sea by strengthening his hold upon the west coast. The viceroy of New Spain was therefore instructed to take measures to colonize and fortify the harbors of California. Vizcaino, the man intrusted with this important enterprise, had already (1596) and at his own cost planted a colony, La Paz, on the bay where Cortés' company had perished, with intent to prosecute the pearl fisheries. It was shortly after destroyed by the Indians; but, nothing dismayed, Vizcaino undertook, at the king's behest, a survey of the outer coast, in the expectation of finding suitable sites for colonization. His chronicler, Fray Antonio de la Ascension, records that an agricultural community was proposed, together with garrison, mission, and trading post. The Indians were to be taught to till fields of wheat and corn, domestic animals were to be introduced, and vineyards and orchards planted. An experienced pilot, he followed the course taken by Cabrillo, noting and giving the present names to the harbor of San Diego, the Santa Barbara Canal, Point Conception, the Santa Lucia range, and the Carmel River. The wide bay between two wooded points, Cabrillo's Bahia de los Pinos, Vizcaino thought might serve as refuge and supply station for the Manila fleet and named it, in honor of the then viceroy, Monterey. Here he landed his sea-worn crew and erected, under a great oak, a rude barricade and a wattled enclosure where mass was said and the ceremony of taking possession of the country performed. After laying in fresh provisions and such brackish water as the vicinity afforded, Vizcaino pursued his northward course. He anchored a few days under Punta de los Reyes in a bay indicated on later Spanish maps as Puerto de San Francisco (now Drake Bay), and then, following up the coast, he rounded Cape Mendocino and Cape Blanco, but was unable to better Ferrelo's record. Near the forty-third parallel, he noticed a passage or river mouth (Coos Bay ?) which he hoped might be the entrance to the Strait of Anian, and he named the alluring fiord Martin de Aguilar, after the lieutenant who attempted to explore it. He was forced to abandon this clew, for his crew was stricken with scurvy — that curse of Spanish explorers — terrific gales drove his vessels out of their course, and he was obliged to return without having discovered the much-desired passage to the Atlantic. Vizcaino was deeply impressed with the necessity of founding a colony at San Diego, San Bernabé, or Monterey as a halfway station for the Manila fleet, and he urged this project on the viceroy and at Madrid. Philip III sanctioned the enterprise (1606) and designated Vizcaino for its execution. But the great navigator, now an old man, died before the arduous preparations were complete, and, its master spirit gone, the statesmanlike plan was abandoned.

SECTION II

The Seven Cities of Cibola

The third of Mendoza's great enterprises was directed to the interior of the continent in search of the seven cities of Cibola and their fabled wealth of gold and precious stones. Rumors of a populous country to the north had been brought to Mexico in strange fashion. A military troop engaged in kidnapping slaves on the Rio del Fuerte in Sonora came upon four gaunt and naked men who consorted with the natives, but spoke Spanish. They proved to be the survivors of Narvaez' ill-fated voyage along the west Florida coast. They had escaped the shipwreck and, following up the San Antonio River, had crossed the wilderness of plain, mountain, and desert that lay between the two gulfs, spending eight desperate years (1528–1536) in achieving the two thousand miles. Nuñez Cabeza de Vaca, the leader of the haggard band, told how they had been befriended by nomad Indians who brought from cities in the north cotton cloth, tanned leather, turquoises, and emeralds.

Mendoza surmised that the northern cities might prove as rich in loot as the Mexican *pueblos*, and he commissioned Marco de Nizza, a Franciscan friar, to explore the country and verify the report of its wealth. Fray Marco's only companion was a negro, Estevanico, who had been one of Cabeza de Vaca's party. They succeeded in reaching one of the communal villages, probably of the Zuñi, but were not admitted by the jealous inhabitants. As the friar gazed upon the walled town from a distance, he thought it larger than the city of Mexico and doubted not it harbored as great treasure. On his return, Mendoza's emissary reported all that he had imagined and the Indians had told him of the fortified cities of Cibola. His account was seized upon by the credulous treasure-seekers and exaggerated as it passed from mouth to mouth. Wondrous tales of the wealth of the Seven Cities, their gold and silver and turquoises, spread throughout all the Spanish-speaking lands and attracted a swarm of adventurers to the quest. In 1540, Coronado, then governor of Culiacan, with the aid and approval of the viceroy fitted out an expedition, and three hundred Spanish cavaliers volunteered to accompany him. Fray Marco, who had been preaching the new crusade to enthusiastic congregations, joined the party as guide and spiritual counsellor. It was "the most brilliant company ever collected in the Indies to go in search of new lands," says Pedro de Castañeda, the chronicler of the enterprise, and it was equipped as befitted so worshipful a company. Eight hundred native allies and one thousand negroes and

Indian servants followed the cavaliers, and droves of animals, extra horses and pack mules, oxen, cows, sheep, and swine by the thousand. Two ships under Alarcon were sent up the coast carrying relays of provisions and the heavier baggage. They reached the head of the gulf and anchored at the mouth of a great river which Alarcon called the *Buena Guia* (good guide), in the hope that it might guide him to the Seven Cities. Learning from the Indians, however, that the land party was thirty days in advance, he turned back to Acapulco with his cargo of supplies.

Coronado, meantime, was driving his unwieldy caravan across leagues of desert. The party sent forward to reconnoiter the country returned after an exhausting march and reported that they had seen nothing but sand. Fray Marcos, however, assured the doubters that there was booty enough ahead "to fill every man's hands," and courage was restored. The difficulties of the march were enhanced by the aristocratic pride of the grandees. "Mendoza would have liked very well," says Castañeda, himself a foot-soldier, "to make every one of them captains of an army, but the whole number was so small, he could not do as he would have liked." [6] Jealousy and insubordination weakened the effectiveness of Coronado's force from start to finish. It took some time for these titled gentlemen to learn how to adjust their packs and firmly cinch the load to the mule's back, and many valuable things were abandoned on the road. "In the end necessity, which is all-powerful, made them skilful, so that one could see many gentlemen become carriers, and any one who despised this work was not considered a man." The first signs of hostility proved terrifying to the novices. "Some Indians in a safe place," says Castañeda contemptuously, "yelled so that, although the men were ready for anything, some were so excited that they put on their saddles hindside before; but these were the new fellows. When the veterans had mounted and ridden around the camp, the Indians fled."[7] On the edge of the desert they halted at Chichilticalli, which proved to be a ruined pueblo, "summed up in one tumble-down house without any roof."[8] Coronado "could not help feeling somewhat downhearted," for he knew that his faith in the riches of the Seven Cities depended wholly on what the negro and the Indians had said.

Arrived at the goal of his great enterprise, Coronado found Cibola "a little crowded village, looking as if it had been all crumpled up together." "There are ranch houses in New Spain that make better appearance at a distance."[9] The disappointed treasure-seekers turned on their unlucky prophet. "Such were the curses that some hurled at Fray Marcos that I pray God may protect him from them." The good father abandoned the expedition at this point "because he did not think it safe for him to stay in Cibola, seeing that his report had turned out to be entirely false, because the kingdom that he had told about had not been found, nor the populous cities, nor the precious wealth of gold, nor the precious stones which he had reported, nor the fine

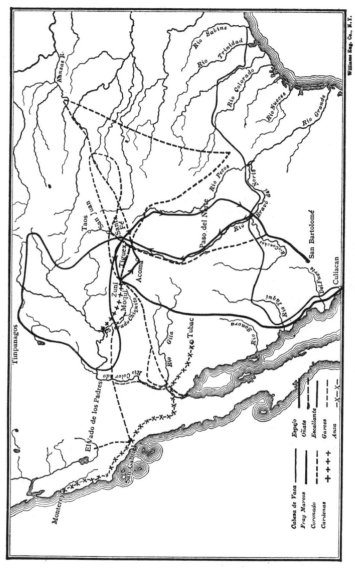

ROUTES OF THE SPANISH EXPLORERS.

Tinpanangos

Rio Sabine

Rio Trinidad

Rio Colorado

Rio Nueces

Rio Grande

Khasaa R.

Taos

San Juan

Santa Fé

Tiguex

Acoma

Zuni

Moqui

Colorado Chiquito

Rio Pecos

Paso del Norte

Rio Bravo del Norte

Rio

Rio Conchos

San Bartolomé

Culiacan

Rio del Fuerte

Rio Mayo

Rio Yaqui

Rio Sonora

Rio Gila

Tubac

Rio Colorado

El Vado de los Padres

Monterey

San Gabriel

Cabeza de Vaca
Fray Marcos
Coronado
Cardenas
Espejo
Oñate
Escallante
Garces
Anza

William Eng. Co., N.Y.

clothes, nor other things that had been proclaimed from the pulpits." [10] Cibola was in fact a communal pueblo, three or four stories high, just such as may be seen in Arizona or New Mexico to-day. Built of stone and adobe with solid exterior walls and narrow, tortuous entrance, the pueblo-dwelling was as difficult of access and easy of defence as a fortress. At sight of the Spaniards and their horses, the Zuñi took refuge within the walls, and Coronado's little force proceeded to storm the place. It was defended by two hundred warriors who hurled stones with considerable effect from embrasures cut for this purpose; but they were eventually overcome. Once within the gate, the Spaniards searched for treasure, but they found only a little unpalatable food. This was, however, thought Castañeda, "the thing they were most in need of."

Meantime the bulk of the army, with the pack trains, was making its way slowly across the desert. No serious difficulties were encountered save that the Indian allies were incapacitated by the cold and had to be carried on horseback, and that the Spaniards suffered from severe headaches brought on by eating the prickly pear preserves offered by the natives. Our chronicler opined that by this beverage "the natives might have done much harm to the force if they had wished"; [11] but fortunately for the fate of the expedition there was more wholesome food to be had. "The country is so fertile that they do not have to break up the ground the year round, but only have to sow the seed, which is presently covered by the fall of snow, and the ears come up under the snow." "In one year they gather enough for seven."[12] Forced requisition on the neighboring pueblos secured *tortillas*, salt, corn meal, and *piñons* (pine nuts), and "a large number of cocks with very big wattles" (the American turkey). The "Quires" had a little cotton cloth, too, and excellent blankets, well-tanned deerskins, and the hides of an animal new to the Spaniards.[13] They judged from the pictures drawn on the skins by the natives that this was a kind of cow (buffalo), but the "hair was woolly and snarled so that we could not tell what sort of skins they had."[14] A sufficient supply of food and clothing was thus available, for refusal to contribute to the necessities of the conquerors was punished by hanging the offender. The terrified people made little resistance. Rumors of the horrible strangers "who travelled on animals which ate people" spread throughout the region, and presents were sent in to placate the mysterious powers. At Cibola, Coronado heard of a great river, twenty days' journey to the westward, and he sent Cárdenas to explore it. The party discovered the Colorado of the West, which they called the Tizon or Firebrand River. The description Castañeda gives of the Grand Cañon is quite as accurate, though perhaps less picturesque, as the descriptions of modern travellers.[15]

The approach of winter suggested the necessity of ampler quarters than Cibola afforded and a new base of supplies. Tiguex, a pueblo lying some distance to the east on the Rio del Norte, was determined on, and the whole army marched thither.

"As it was necessary that the natives should give the Spaniards lodging places, the people in one village had to abandon it and go to others belonging to their friends, and they took with them nothing but themselves and the clothes they had on." [16] Various outrages, including the burning of a village, finally nerved the long-suffering inhabitants to expel their unwelcome guests. The Spaniards laid siege to the pueblo and displayed such strength as induced the defenders to surrender on promise of amnesty. Unfortunately for Coronado's reputation among them, a captain who had not been informed of the peace pledges put two hundred of these prisoners to death. The natives, convinced that the intruders were not to be trusted, retreated again to their houses, determined to resist to the uttermost. The siege lasted fifty days and, although its result was a foregone conclusion, the loss of the Spaniards was severe. Many were killed by stones and arrows shot from the parapets, and all suffered from lack of food and shelter. Nearly all the Indians were killed. They were shot down by the soldiers or were drowned in the attempt to ford the river, or, having succeeded in escaping the doomed town, perished miserably of cold and hunger. Coronado was at great pains to reassure the people of the neighboring pueblos as to the pacific intentions of the Spaniards; but the "twelve villages of Tiguez were not repopulated at all during the time the army was there, in spite of every promise of security that could possibly be given to them, nor could any pueblos be persuaded to receive a Spaniard within their gates." [17]

It was difficult to believe that the famous Seven Cities were nothing more than these miserable pueblos, and Coronado determined to press farther into the interior. At Pecos there was found an Indian slave, a native of the country towards Florida, who told marvellous tales of the riches of his tribe. "He said that the lord of that country took his afternoon nap under a great tree on which were hung a great number of little gold bells, which put him to sleep as they swung in the air. He said also that every one had their ordinary dishes made of wrought plate, and that the jugs and bowls were of gold." [18]   It was not difficult to persuade Coronado to undertake the pursuit of this new will-o'-the-wisp, the glib-tongued "Turk" offering to serve as guide.

In May of 1541, when the river was clear of ice, the army crossed the Rio del Norte and marched eastward over a "spacious level country" to find the golden city of Quivira. The rich spring herbage of the "staked plains" (*llanos estacados*) filled the Spaniards with astonishment. "Who could believe that 1000 horses and 500 of our cows and more than 5000 rams and ewes and more than 1500 friendly Indians and servants, in travelling over those plains, would leave no more trace where they had passed than if nothing had been there — nothing — so that it was necessary to make piles of bones and cow dung now and then, so that the rear-guard could follow the army." [19]   "It was impossible to find tracks in this country, because the grass straightened up again as soon as it was trodden down." Even the native Indian guides were obliged to mark their trail. "They kept their road in this way: In the morning they notice where the sun rises and observe the direction they are going to take, and then shoot an arrow in this direction. Before reaching this, they shoot another over it, and in this way they go all day toward the water where they are to end the day." [20]

There was no lack of food for the invading army. The plains were traversed by "an incredible number of cows," who fed on the luxuriant grasses and moved about in search of water and the salt that gathered on the surface of stagnant pools. "They came across so many animals that those who were on the advance guard killed a large number of bulls. As these fled they trampled one another in their haste until they came to a ravine. So many of the animals fell into this that they filled it up, and the rest went across on top of them." [21] From the Querechos,[22] the "Arabs" of the plains, the Spaniards learned how to prepare *charqui* (dried buffalo meat) to carry on their northward journey. These Indians told Coronado of a great river to the eastward, lined with settlements and thronged with canoes. A scouting party was immediately sent out to find the most direct route, but they returned shortly, saying that "in the twenty leagues they had been over they had seen nothing but cows and the sky." The pursuit of this clew was therefore abandoned.

Arrived at an eastward-flowing river (the Brazos), Coronado determined to go no farther in this direction. There was no trace of Turk's golden city, and the Querechos asserted that the real Quivira lay far to the north. It was therefore decided that the army should return to Tiguex, while Coronado with a picked escort of thirty cavaliers set out on the new trace. The perfidious Turk was taken along in chains. He later confessed that he knew nothing of the promised gold, but had been induced by the Tiguas to lead the Spaniards into the plains and lose them there — a treachery which cost him his life.

A forty-eight days' march directly north brought Coronado to the long-sought "city," a wretched collection of huts, belonging to the Wichita Indians. The strangers were peaceably received, but "neither gold nor silver nor any trace of either was found among these people, although their lord wore a copper plate on his neck and prized it highly." Some time was spent in exploring this region, and scouts were sent as far north as the Kansas River, but without the hoped-for result. The country was found to be fertile and salubrious, reminding the wanderers of Spain. Plums, grapes, nuts, and mulberries grew wild, as well as oats and flax; but the charming prospect had no promise for these infatuated treasure-seekers. Convinced at last that he had been duped, Coronado turned back to Tiguex. His Indian guides led him by a direct route along the Great Bend of the Arkansas over what later became the Santa Fé Trail.

The winter in the desert had demoralized the army. The Tiguas were irreconcilable and would furnish no provisions, the soldiers were almost

THE PRIMITIVE BUFFALO HUNT.
Before the Indians secured guns and horses.

naked and worn down with many privations, the few blankets that had been secured were the occasion of bloody strife, and the men were quarrelling with their officers over the apportionment of work and food. Malcontents began to mutter that theirs was a wild-goose chase, and that they would perish in this wilderness to no purpose. Soon after his return to Tiguex, Coronado was thrown from his horse and lay for some time at death's door. The murmurs grew louder, and the men began to petition their commander to lead them back to New Spain. When every captain had signed the petition and physician and friends urged retreat, Coronado was persuaded to abandon his search. He had a young wife and children and large estates at Culiacan, and he yearned to see home again. When his decision was announced, there was great rejoicing among the rank and file; but certain resolute souls determined to continue the quest. They begged permission to remain with sixty picked men and a suitable equipment, vowing that they would find the golden city or perish in the attempt. Alas for the honor of Spain! few soldiers would volunteer for this dangerous service, and the retreat of the whole army was finally ordered (April, 1543). Two devoted friars were the only Spaniards that ventured to stay behind. Father Juan de Padilla insisted on returning to Quivira to found a mission there, and Father Luis remained with his converts at Pecos.[23]

The return journey was a disgraceful rout. Coronado had forfeited the respect of his men when he yielded to their importunity. No sooner had the army reached Culiacan than the soldiers began to desert. When he finally arrived at the City of Mexico, he had only a bodyguard of one hundred all told. "His reputation was gone from this time on."

Castañeda found difficulty in reconciling himself to Coronado's inglorious retreat. "It was God's pleasure that these discoveries should remain for other peoples, and that we who had been there should content ourselves with saying that we were the first who discovered it and obtained any information concerning it." [24]   But not even Castañeda, with his zealous faith in Quivira, had any conception of the real value of the Great Plains or of the mighty river to the east. "As for entering from the country of Florida and from the North Sea, it has already been observed that the many expeditions which have been undertaken from that side have been unfortunate and not very successful, because that part of the country is full of bogs and poisonous fruits, barren, and the very worst country that is warmed by the sun." [25]

Other Spanish explorers, penetrating this same region from the east and seeking no less eagerly than Coronado the rich country described by Cabeza de Vaca, had no better success. Fernando de Soto, governor of Cuba, set out from Havana in 1539 and fought his way to the great river called by Piñeda (1519) El Espiritu Santo. He crossed the mighty current at a point somewhat below the Arkansas (Chickasaw Bluffs), visited the hot springs and salt lakes of that valley, and ascended the Mississippi itself to within a short distance of the Missouri.

Finding no trace of treasure cities, he returned to the Arkansas and there died (1542), a ruined man. His men, under the leadership of Moscoso, marched seven hundred miles west, up the Red River to the neighborhood of Pecos, where they found Indians who had pottery and cotton cloth and turquoises, and learned of Coronado's expedition from a slave who had escaped from his camp. Abandoning all hope of finding the treasure cities, they turned back. Once arrived at the Espiritu Santo, they built seven brigantines, launched them on the river, and made the two hundred and fifty leagues to its mouth without accident. Thus De Soto and his lieutenant Moscoso explored the lower Mississippi over a thousand miles, from the Missouri to the Gulf of Mexico, and they knew the Red and Arkansas rivers; but these discoveries had no significance for them. A river was a barrier, not an open highway, and the Rio del Espiritu Santo was abandoned and forgotten. It figures on the Spanish maps of this period as an insignificant stream.

CHAPTER II

THE COLONIZERS

THE decadence of Spain and the disintegration of her colonial empire set in with the loss of the Armada. Men of energy and devotion abandoned the service of the state for that of the church, and the nation was bereft of political leadership. Demoralized by plunder, the colonial officials appropriated to their own uses the funds destined for defence and neglected their administrative duties. The government of New Spain, intent on immediate revenue only, leased the mines and the pearl fisheries to private individuals, and converted the production of quicksilver, tobacco, and salt into profitable public monopolies. Large land grants were awarded to favored grandees, and with each estate went the right to command the labor of the native villages found upon it. The *encomienda*[1] served a triple purpose,—it enabled the proprietors to work the soil or the mines, brought the Indians under control of the political and ecclesiastical authorities, and furnished them with money with which to pay the head tax required of all adult males. The royal decrees minutely and humanely prescribed the limits of this labor requisition, but the practical effect of the system was to reduce the natives to a serfdom embittered by race antagonism and unmitigated by custom. Fray Antonio de Ascension denounced the *encomienda* as "the total ruin and destruction of all the Indians," citing Fray Bartolomé de las Casas and the misery of the Cubans in support of his contention. The whole financial burden imposed by a costly colonial administration was borne ultimately by the conquered peoples. The conquerors, Spaniard, creole, and *mestizo* [2] alike, were privileged to occupy all places of emolument, to live without industry, and to exploit the despised natives. Even the negro slave looked down upon the copper-colored man and would have felt himself degraded by work in the fields or in the mines. The Indians, unaccustomed to strenuous labor, crushed under the intolerable burden, sank into the lethargy of despair.

The heroic age was past, and the conquest of the regions to the north, revealed by the explorations of Coronado, Cabrillo, and Vizcaino, was attempted by men of far inferior calibre. The later adventurers lacked the enterprise, the courage, the perseverance of Cortés and Pizarro, while they abated nothing of their cruelty and their lust for gold. Bereft of the prospect of sudden wealth, the colonies languished, and but for the proselyting zeal of the monks and friars and their determination to plant the cross at the remotest reach of the king's dominions, Spain would have had no valid title to any portion of the present territory of the United States. When Alexander VI granted to Ferdinand and Isabella jurisdiction over all the lands that might be discovered west of the Azores, he stipulated that the Indians should be converted to the true church. For the fulfilment of this obligation, the Catholic kings were made personally responsible. It was a task sufficiently congenial to Philip II and his immediate successors. The royal treasury assumed the cost, and the three great religious orders undertook to send missionary priests to the New World. The Jesuits — Kino, Salvatierra, and Ugarte — founded the missions of Lower California. After the expulsion of the Jesuits (1767) the Dominicans succeeded to this task, while the Franciscans carried the gospel into regions hitherto unknown — New Mexico, Texas, and Upper California.

Section I

New Mexico

Great Undertakings. — Forty years after Coronado's bootless journey, an expedition to the Pueblo Indians was undertaken by a Franciscan missionary, Fray Augustin Ruiz (or Rodriguez). He and two of his brethren, accompanied by a small escort, followed the Rio Conchos to the Rio Bravo del Norte and so to the stone habitations of its upper valley. The natives seemed friendly, and their conversion to the true faith was eagerly undertaken ; but no sooner was the military guard withdrawn than Ruiz and his companions were murdered at the pueblo which they had made their headquarters, Puaray (probably identical with Tiguex). In 1582 Fray Bernardino Beltran undertook to find the lost brethren or at least to verify their martyrdom. The expedition was fitted out and commanded by Don Antonio Espejo, a wealthy Mexican then sojourning at the Santa

Barbara mines, who followed Ruiz' route to Puaray and thence made a tour of the pueblos along the Bravo and Pecos rivers. His *entrada* was far more successful than that of Coronado, though it was accomplished with but fourteen soldiers. This little band did not make so heavy requisition of corn and blankets, and their peaceful methods disarmed the suspicions of the Indians. Espejo visited seventy-four of the fortressed villages and estimated their population at 253,000.[3]

Finding the country fertile and productive and rich in mines, Espejo was ambitious to add the region, which he called New Mexico, to the dominion of Philip II. He proposed to undertake the conquest at his own cost, provided he was assured certain extensive privileges. The governorship of the new province, a title of nobility, the right to assign land grants and to make *encomiendas* of the native laborers, exemption from taxes, trade monopoly, — these were the perquisites that should reward success. Whether the king thought his demands excessive or his ability insufficient does not appear, but he failed to give the commission. It was awarded ten years later (1598) to Don Juan de Oñate, a rich mine owner of Zacatecas, who undertook to found a Spanish colony on the Rio Bravo del Norte. According to Gregg, who saw the contract in the archives at Santa Fé, "Oñate bound himself to take into New Mexico two hundred soldiers, and a sufficiency of provisions for the first year's support of the colony; with abundance of horses, black cattle, sheep, etc., as also merchandise, agricultural utensils, tools and materials for mechanics' purposes; and all at his own cost, or rather at the ultimate expense of the colonists." [4] The king was to provide arms and ammunition for the enterprise, to salary six priests, furnish the requisite church "accoutrements," and contribute $20,000 in money. As compensation for his services, Oñate stipulated for the hereditary title of marquis, the office of governor and captain-general to rest in his family for four generations, a grant of thirty square leagues of land wherever he might choose to locate it, with control of all the Indians resident thereon, permission to parcel out native laborers among his officers and relatives, the privilege of working mines exempt from the usual royalty, etc.; privileges and powers which, with the exception of the *encomienda*, were not unlike those accorded to the English proprietors who undertook to plant colonies on the Atlantic Coast.

By the offer of lands and liberties,[5] Oñate succeeded in enlisting one hundred and thirty soldier colonists with their families. These with eighty-three wagon-loads of supplies and seven thousand cattle made up an array hardly less impressive than that of Coronado. The train turned north from the Rio Conchos across the desert to El Paso del Norte, "the ford of the river of the north" discovered by Espejo, and, ascending the Rio Bravo beyond the hostile pueblos, came to a fertile valley encompassed by snow-clad mountains. There Oñate built his town, San Juan de los Caballeros, so called because of the courtesy of the natives, some fifteen hundred of whom were induced to assist in the construction of a dam and irrigating ditches. The friars who accompanied the expedition set about the conversion of the Indians, and they succeeded in prevailing upon thirty-four pueblos to accept Christianity. With the same uncomprehending courtesy, the Tiguas accepted the suzerainty of Philip II, and the ceremonies of administering the rite of baptism and the oath of allegiance were performed with due solemnity at town after town. There was more difficulty with Acoma, the rock fortress described by Castañeda,[6] and with the Moqui pueblos on the western plateau. Emboldened by the supposed impregnability of their stronghold, the Acomas killed a party of soldiers sent to obtain supplies. Oñate laid siege to the daring pueblo ; his men succeeded in securing foothold on the summit and, after three days of desperate fighting, gained possession of the place. A wholesale slaughter followed, and the remnant of the Acomas were forbidden to return to their ancestral *peñol*.

It soon became apparent that the several factors in Oñate's company represented diverse and incompatible interests. The Franciscans' sole aim was to convert the natives, and they regarded the military escort as merely a means to this end, while Oñate's prime object was conquest of the country. Ambitious to reach Quivira on the north and that mysterious sea to the west, on whose shores, according to the natives, were mines and populous cities, he proposed to use the soldiers and supplies in farther explorations. The soldiers, on the other hand, having been promised a chance to settle in the new province, wished to live at peace with the natives and to be left free to cultivate the land, and they held that the implements, cattle, and horses were intended to aid them in founding an agricultural colony. Among these conflicting purposes, those of the commander prevailed perforce, and he set out (1601) towards Quivira and the gold country, taking with him the pick of the soldiers and all the provisions collected by the pueblos during the six years preceding. As a consequence, the colonists were reduced to starvation long before the new planting came to harvest, and they had no choice between annihilation and retreat to San Bartolemé. Oñate was in high dudgeon when, on returning to San Juan empty-handed, he found the place abandoned. He sent a force to bring back the deserters and, having recovered the major part of his men, undertook an equally fruitless and even more costly expedition to the South Sea. Although he succeeded in reaching the mouth of the Rio Colorado (1605), the fabled cities proved to be only wattled *rancherias* of the Mohave, Yuma, and Pima Indians.[7] The salt sea was there indeed, but having no ships, Oñate could make no use of it. He was obliged to fight his desperate way back across the desert to San Juan.

Meantime, the conversion of the natives, according to the friars' statistics, proceeded apace. By 1617 they had built eleven churches and baptized 14,000 Indians. In 1626 they boasted forty-three churches and 34,000 baptisms; in 1630, ninety churches and 86,000 baptisms. To each Christian pueblo was assigned a resident priest, and there was much rivalry as to the size and splendor of their several temples. Each missionary was salaried by the crown ($330), but he expected his dusky parishioners to cultivate a corn-field for his benefit and to furnish such service as he might require in the building and maintenance of his house and the church, while fees for baptism, marriage, and burials were rigorously exacted. The Franciscans were for the most part devout, well-meaning men, but they had little comprehension of the people among whom they dwelt. They neglected to learn the native tongues, nor did they teach the Indians Spanish, preferring to rely upon interpreters, even for confession. The natives learned nothing of Christianity beyond the external ceremonies which they were taught sedulously to perform. They were thoroughgoing materialists and supposed the new religion would bring them more rain, better harvests, and exemption from disease. When these hopes were disappointed, their faith slackened. As the Franciscans came to realize the enormous difficulty of their task, the conciliatory policy of the early missionaries gave way to intolerance and persecution. Men were flogged for refusing baptism and enslaved, even put to death, for practising sorcery. From time immemorial these children of the desert had worshipped the sun, the god of life and death, and their fidelity to the requirements and exercises of their ancient religion withstood all the pressure brought to bear by the friars. Their catholicism was merely a veneer under which the practices and superstitions of the faith of their fathers persisted with undimmed vigor.

The Indians of New Mexico were, in reality, little affected by the Spanish conquest, and they were allowed to live on in their tribal pueblos and to cultivate their lands in peace, so long as they rendered the product and labor service required of them. They were quite the most industrious people of the province, tilling their fields to corn, beans, calabashes, and cotton, and manufacturing cloth and blankets and earthenware such as the indolent whites were glad to buy. For generations they had practised irrigation as a communal enterprise, directing the flood waters of the rivers on to their fields through artificial ditches. The Spaniards introduced many desirable improvements on this simple system of husbandry. From them the natives learned to manage such domestic animals as horses and cattle, sheep and goats. They quickly surpassed their instructors in the care of sheep, feeding great flocks upon the mountain pastures, and wool soon superseded cotton and skins as wearing apparel. Iron implements such as the hoe and axe, the laborers were trained to handle, and oxen yoked to a rude wooden plough rendered the tilling of the ground a less onerous task. Wheat and tobacco were introduced and many of the European vegetables; fruit trees, too, and grape-vines were brought to New Mexico, and the natives were taught how to plant and prune them. The Pueblo Indians were sufficiently advanced in the scale of civilization to take advantage of these gifts and to adopt many desirable additions to their means of subsistence.[8]

Misgovernment

It might have been possible for the natives and the settlers to live at peace but for the scant supply of water. Only the valleys of the upper Bravo and the Pecos with their tributary streams, the Chama, the San Juan, and the Puerco, were susceptible of irrigation. The new-comers thought themselves entitled to the best of everything, and, notwithstanding that the edicts of the king [9] set aside a square league of cultivated land to each pueblo, there was considerable encroachment upon these reservations. Moreover, the *encomiendas* imposed by the governor and other officials, and the tribute of corn and cloth required of each pueblo, while seeming reasonable and necessary to men accustomed to feudal conditions, struck these aborigines as an unwarranted infringement of their rights. Such exactions, coupled with the thousand individual wrongs committed by undisciplined soldiers, made up a sum total of oppression that finally drove the natives to revolt. In 1680 there were twenty-four hundred people of Spanish origin settled along the Rio Bravo del Norte in the midst of a population of twenty-two thousand Christian Indians. The garrison of two hundred and fifty soldiers at Santa Fé de San Francisco, the capital of the province, was the only armed force; no other was thought necessary.

Suddenly the seeming acquiescence of the natives was broken. The insurrection began at Taos, the northernmost pueblo, and swiftly spread from town to town. The Indians slaughtered the whites and destroyed the churches and every vestige of Christian worship, in their determination to revenge a century of cruelty and oppression and to drive the invader from the land. The refugees crowded into Santa Fé, but the place was besieged. After five days' desperate contest, the Spaniards were forced to abandon this stronghold and to retreat down the river to El Paso del Norte. There they made a stand and built huts for a winter camp about the mission of San Lorenzo, while reënforcements and supplies were collected for the reconquest of New Mexico. Fifteen years of obstinate fighting were required to recover the lost ground. Even so, the submission of the Indians was only feigned, and they seized every opportunity to attack the weaker settlements, carry off the cattle, and murder the missionaries. The Moqui and Zuñi pueblos of the plateau to the west, being too isolated and remote for serious attack, retained their independence.

In 1693 Vargas undertook to restore the ruined settlements. A caravan of fifteen hundred people, three thousand horses and mules, and $42,000 worth of supplies was escorted up the river. Santa Fé was repopulated, seventy families were settled at Santa Cruz de la Canada (1695) and thirty at Albuquerque (1708). There was little resistance, for the long years of war had decimated the Indian population. Most of the warriors fled to the mountains rather than submit again to Spanish domination, and their women and children were captured and

Pueblo of Taos, New Mexico.

enslaved. Intertribal dissensions and repeated failure of crops completed the disaster. When Vargas resumed control of the province, only twenty of the pueblos remained inhabited. The abandoned lands were distributed among the settlers, and the dejected remnant of the native population was reduced to a sullen submission.

The wild tribes of the mountains, the Apaches and the Utes, had long been the terror of the pueblo dwellers. They now directed their marauding expeditions against the Spanish settlements. Horses and fusils were the prime object of these depredations, but the savages did not hesitate to murder men and kidnap women of the hated Spanish race. The slender garrison at Santa Fé was entirely inadequate to the defence of villages and *ranchos* scattered from Taos to El Paso, and the settlers had to protect their families and flocks as best they could. In spite of these depredations, the white population continued to increase. The number of Spaniards, creoles, and *mestizos* was estimated at four thousand in 1750; the census of 1800 enumerated eighteen thousand, not including El Paso. The Pueblo Indians, during the same fifty years, declined from twelve thousand to nine thousand. The invaders by superior strength and guile were fast superseding them. Discouragement, poverty, and the diseases consequent on contact with the white man's civilization, combined to undermine the communal organization, — a primitive body politic that had preserved these peoples through centuries of struggle against the adverse forces of nature and the craft of their savage foes.

An intelligent and disinterested observer, Fray Juan Augustin de Morfi,[10] forwarded to the viceroy (1792) an indignant protest against the practical enslavement of the Indians by the *alcaldes*, the very officials to whom the king had intrusted their protection. In spite of all legislation to the contrary, the natives were induced to run into debt and then mortgage or sell the lands on which they depended for subsistence. From each pueblo in his jurisdiction, the *alcalde mayor* was wont to require a weekly contribution of flesh, butter, *frijoles*, and *tortillas*. The labor about his house and the tilling of his fields were performed by these unhappy dependents, who were not infrequently obliged to go a day's journey to their work, carrying with them their implements of husbandry. Two hundred *fanegas*[11] of wheat and three hundred of corn were required from each pueblo every harvest, and the women were forced to grind, for the use of the *alcalde's* household, the grain that should have been stored in the pueblo granary against a dry year. Some of these officials, whose names are given by the relentless informant, were accustomed to collect a tithe of the fleeces sheared within their jurisdiction, and to distribute the wool among the native weavers, who were required to make it up into blankets. The wretched Indians were then obliged to carry the product to a place designated by their taskmaster and to render a strict account of the quantity brought in. The men were often required to serve as *arrieros* (mule-drivers) and to care for the horses and mules of the *alcalde*, and this even when their wives and children were

HOPI PUEBLO, INTERIOR OF FAMILY DWELLING.

actually suffering for lack of food. Most of the governors sent to New Mexico regarded their appointment as an opportunity for speedy enrichment. They forced the soldiers maintained at the garrisons to labor on their private estates, and while sending the viceroy false reports of successful campaigns against the Apaches, withheld the pay of the troops, sold the powder and ammunition, and pocketed the proceeds. They imposed *encomiendas* upon the pueblos for which they had no warrant, and monopolized the Indian trade; they browbeat the friars and debauched the native women without shame. Far from laboring for the advancement of the province, the governors imposed heavy burdens upon the people and set an example of lawlessness which was readily followed by the lesser officials. Each *alcalde mayor* enjoyed the monopoly of trade within his own jurisdiction. Without fear of competition, he fixed the prices at which he bought and sold, and thus made money on every transaction. Not infrequently he compelled the Indians to purchase horses and cattle for which they had no need, thus involving them in debt, and then required them to work out their obligation with the very animals in which it originated. The natives were thus reduced to a state of peonage.

No better code of laws for the government of a subject people was ever framed than that formulated by the kings of Spain for their Indian vassals. They fully understood that there was no other labor to be had for the development of the mines and plantations of New Spain, and that the aboriginal population must therefore be conserved. The officials were directed to deal justly and kindly with the natives, to guard their rights to land and water, to observe the limitations on forced labor, and to teach them the ways of civilization. But to legislate was easy; to enforce the will of the home government upon the administrators of the law in a distant, well-nigh inaccessible province was enormously difficult. The governor and *alcaldes*, engaged in the thankless task of maintaining order on a dangerous frontier, inadequately provided with men and money, were often driven to measures of repression quite unjustifiable in a civilized land. Ill-paid and liable to peremptory recall, they were prone to take advantage of every opportunity that offered to enrich themselves at the expense of their unresisting charges. Charles III abolished the *encomiendas*, but the enslavement of the Indians did not cease.

According to de Morfi, the Spanish population of New Mexico was hardly less miserable than the natives. Living in *haciendas* (farm-houses) scattered through the country, they were unable to protect themselves or their crops against the marauding raids of the Apaches and much pilfering on the part of their white neighbors. They were more ignorant of religion than the natives, and more vicious. Too timid or too lazy to cultivate their fields, they were sunk in poverty, lacking the very necessities of life. They stored no grain against the dry years, after the excellent example of the Indians, because they never had any to spare. They were always in debt to the merchants of Chihuahua, of whom they bought extravagantly. These leeches mortgaged the growing and even the unsown crops, sometimes as much as six years in advance. There was no coin in circulation except at El Paso. A money of account served for commercial transactions, in which the dollar had four different values — eight, six, four, or two *reals* — according to the convenience of the merchant. The unsophisticated *rancheros* were tricked into buying in a dollar four times greater than that in which they sold. By means of this shrewd artifice, they were usually on the verge of bankruptcy, so that the building of a house, a journey, a funeral, was sufficient to plunge them into ruin. They were then likely to take refuge in an Indian pueblo, ousting some native from his field and tenement, while he, in turn, found an asylum among the wild tribes of the mountains.

The remedy proposed by de Morfi for the retrograde state of New Mexico was that the government should send artisans into the province to teach the people trades. Since the *mesas* were covered with cattle and sheep, clothing sufficient for the needs of the province might easily be produced if the Pueblo arts of weaving and tanning were practised by the Spaniards. The friar suggested that intelligent but not incorrigible convicts, who understood carpentry, tile-making, weaving, dyeing, hat-making, shoe-making, etc., should be sent to New Mexico to serve out their terms as instructors in their several trades. Raw material for the apprentice shops should be furnished by the government out of the tithes levied on the province. When New Mexico was self-sufficing and began to export manufactures as well as agricultural products, money would flow into the country, prosperity would return, and the inhabitants could free themselves from debt.

Chihuahua was the only commercial outlet for New Mexico, there being as yet no communication with Louisiana or California. The Chihuahua merchants imported their European merchandise by way of Vera Cruz; the Oriental and South American stuffs entered by way of Acapulco. The long overland carriage from these, the only licensed ports, doubled the costs and raised prices to a point at which only the wealthy could afford commodities in common use in more fortunate lands. Every autumn a caravan [12] set out from Santa Fé for the south, by way of El Paso, driving a great herd of sheep and carrying tobacco (a provincial monopoly), skins, furs, salt, Navajo blankets, and copper vessels. The return caravan brought cotton and woollen cloth, arms and ammunition, confectionery, some European wines and liquors and goods for the Indian trade. A guard of dragoons was furnished by the government, for the Apaches were wont to descend from the mountains and carry off animals and freight.

The Pike Expedition

The first definite knowledge of New Mexico, Texas, and the northern provinces of New Spain was brought to the United States by Zebulon Montgomery Pike, the young officer whose expedition to the sources of the Mississippi had commended him to the authorities at Washington. In 1806 General Wilkinson, commander-in-chief of the United States army, commissioned Lieutenant Pike to explore the sources of the Red River with a view to defining the watershed that divided Louisiana from the United States. With a squad of twenty men — soldiers and guides — Pike set out from St. Louis on July 15 and, securing horses of the Osage Indians, rode across the open country to the Arkansas River and followed its lead to the mountains where it takes its rise. Midway of this journey, he was surprised to come upon the traces of a considerable detachment of cavalry. The Pawnees of a neighboring village, who had scarlet coats, mules, bridles, and blankets, evidently of Mexican origin, were able to throw some light on this mystery. An expedition under Lieutenant Malgares, which had been sent from Santa Fé to intercept Pike, with orders to turn him back or take his party prisoners, had passed that way *en route* for Taos. The Spanish party was well equipped, six hundred dragoons with three times as many horses, and mules and provisions for six months, made up a force such as Pike could not hope to withstand; but he determined to follow the route taken by the Spaniards, hoping that it would lead him to Red River. From Pawnee Rock on the Great Bend of the Arkansas, he rode along the river until he reached the Rockies. The plains were covered with droves of buffalo, deer, elk, and wild horses, and food was abundant; but the Americans prudently laid in a supply of jerked meat, for winter was approaching and the game animals were all moving south. His party was ill prepared for cold weather, being lightly

clad and inadequately provisioned, but Pike had no
intention of turning back till he had reached his
goal. Arrived at Fontain qui Bouille (the St.
Charles River of Pike's Journal and the site of
Pueblo, Colo.), a breastwork was thrown up as a
defence against Indians, and Lieutenant Pike, with
three of the men, set out to ascend the "high point
of the blue mountain," the summit we now call
Pike's Peak. Deceived by the clearness of the atmosphere, they thought this would be a day's excursion, and carried neither food nor blankets. When
forty-eight hours' climb failed to bring them to the
top, they reluctantly returned to camp.

The months of December and January were spent
in a desperate search for that will-o'-the-wisp, the
source of the Red River. The thermometer ranged
consistently between freezing and zero, the mountain
passes were deep in snow, there was no game left but
a few pheasants and rabbits, the guns burst with the
cold, the horses were exhausted, and the men at the
limit of human endurance; but Pike would not give
up his quest. At the foot of the Grand Cañon of the
Arkansas (Grape Creek) he determined to build a
blockhouse and leave there, in charge of two of the
men, the horses and all the luggage that could be dispensed with, while the strongest of the party undertook
to cross the "White Mountains " (Sangre de Cristo
Range). It was a desperate venture. The snow was
deep and the cold extreme; nine of the men got their
feet frozen; the supply of food in their packs was
soon exhausted, and game seemed to have abandoned
the country. They had been four days without food

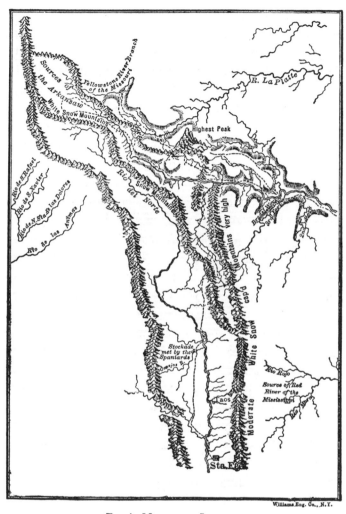

PIKE'S MOUNTAIN JOURNEY.

The source of the Red River was finally learned from the Spaniards.

"To go to Sta Fe it is best to ascend the 3rd Fork [of the Arkansas] to the Mountain, thence along the foot of said Mountain to the Pass at Taos, as was the route of the Spanish Cavalry when returning." — *Pike's Journal.*

when Pike managed to shoot a chance buffalo, and the party was saved from starvation; but he was obliged to leave three poor fellows on the trail with meat enough to keep them alive until help could be sent them. Arrived at the summit of the range, they came upon a brook that led west to a practicable pass and down into the sand-dunes of San Luis Valley, and Pike believed that he had come at last upon the long-sought boundary. He could not know that this was not the Red River, but Rio Grande del Norte, and that in crossing the Sangre de Cristo Range he was trespassing on Spanish territory. His instructions from General Wilkinson contained a warning that at the head of the river he might find himself "approximated to the settlements of New Mexico. There it will be necessary you should move with great circumspection, to keep clear of any hunting or reconnoitring parties from that province, and to prevent alarm or offence; because the affairs of Spain and the United States appear to be on the point of amicable adjustment, and moreover it is the desire of the President to cultivate the friendship and harmonious intercourse of all nations of the earth, particularly our new neighbors the Spaniards." [13]

Notwithstanding the dangers of the situation, it was necessary to make here a brief stay to recover the men, horses, and luggage left behind and to build rafts for the descent of the river. With this in view, a stockade was erected on the west bank of the Rio Grande, five miles above its junction with the Rio Conejos. The reason for choosing this site to the west of the Rio Grande, and on any hypothesis in Spanish territory, is nowhere given. Dr. Robinson, a civilian who had accompanied the expedition in the hope of reaching Santa Fé and there transacting some private business, took advantage of this delay to make his venturesome journey. A detachment was sent back to Grape Creek after the men and horses, while Pike remained at the stockade with four soldiers, two of whom were incapacitated by frozen feet.

On February 16, while the Lieutenant was out hunting, he spied two horsemen, one an Indian, the other evidently a Spaniard. Challenged as to his errand, Pike indicated that he was preparing to descend the river to Natchitoches, and asked that the governor should send an interpreter to whom he might explain in full. Having examined the miniature fort and partaken of its frugal hospitality, the unwelcome visitors departed. Ten days later, Pike was astounded by the appearance of one hundred mounted cavalry under command of Captain Salteo. Governor Allencaster's emissary brought with him two French interpreters, and the serious nature of the situation was at once apparent. Pike then learned that the source of the Red River was eight days' journey to the southeast, and that his fort was built upon the Rio Grande del Norte. He immediately ordered his men to haul down the American flag, but this did not mollify Salteo, who insisted that Pike and his men should accompany him to Santa Fé. Arguments and protests were of no avail. A guard was left at the fort to await the rescue party, while Pike and the ragged remnant of his force were hurried south.

Thus began that forced tour of the Mexican provinces which, according to some critics, was undertaken with treasonable intent. That the young lieutenant made good use of his eyes and ears during his sojourn on Spanish soil cannot be denied. He carefully studied the language, the customs, and the sentiments of the people, and when denied the liberty of taking notes or making sketches, he scrawled brief memoranda in his diary and concealed the bits of paper in the gun-barrels of his men. His *Observations on New Spain*, printed with the Journals, was derived in good measure from Humboldt's *New Spain*, but it contained many shrewd comments of his own upon the civilization of this jealously guarded land. The adobe towns of New Mexico, — Ojo Caliente, San Juan, etc., looked then, as now, mere "square enclosures of mud walls, the houses forming the walls." Within, the dwellings were ranged along cross streets, — low, one-story structures with narrow doors and small windows, unglazed for the most part, but occasionally filled with talc lights. At each village was a small stream, sufficient for watering the fields,[14] and there were water-mills where the natives made very good flour. Irrigation was carried so far that the waters of the Rio Grande were absorbed by the canals, and the lower river ran dry in the rainless season. Santa Fé was a town of four thousand souls, largely soldiers, priests, and officials. "Its appearance from a distance struck my mind with the same effect as a fleet of the flat-bottomed boats which are seen in the spring and fall seasons, descending the Ohio River. There are two churches, the magnificence of whose steeples form a striking contrast to the miserable appearance of the houses." [15] The sparse population of New Mexico was nineteen-twentieths Indian. The few Spaniards were the priests — very intelligent men and much revered — and the official class.

Arrived at Santa Fé, Lieutenant Pike, much abashed by his rags and tatters but determined to put a bold face on the situation, was received by Governor Allencaster at the Palace.

Allencaster: "You come to reconnoitre our country, do you?"

Pike: "I marched to reconnoitre our own." Pike resented the suggestion that he had been the original trespasser. "Pray, sir! do you not think it was a greater infringement of our territory to send 600 miles in the Pawnees' than for me with our small party to come on the frontiers of yours with an intent to descend the Red river?" [16]

The illogical result of this colloquy was the forwarding of Pike and his fellow-conspirators to Chihuahua, there to be examined by General Salcedo. Protests and explanations had no effect upon the courteous obstinacy of the Spaniard. A deep-seated suspicion of all Americans determined the policy of the Mexican officials — a policy that was inspired at Madrid — and a citizen of the United States crossed the boundary at his peril.

At San Fernandez, near Albuquerque, Pike's escort came up with Malgares, who was waiting to take

the prisoners to Chihuahua. Here to their joy was
Robinson, hale and hearty. The intrepid doctor
had not proceeded far on his quest before falling
into the hands of the officials. He had consoled
himself by curing several invalids, despaired of by
Spanish physicians, and by making such observations on the customs of the people as might be useful in the prosecution of a trading venture. Malgares informed the captives that his expedition had
occupied ten months and had cost the king of Spain
$10,000, and he was evidently much gratified that
chance had thrown the quarry in his way, so that
he need not return to Salcedo empty-handed. This
chivalrous warrior was ardently loyal to the king and
"deprecated a revolution or separation of Spanish
America from the mother country." Small marvel,
when he lived luxuriously at the expense of the
government. The Americans thought his "mode
of living superior to anything seen in our army.
Eight mules were loaded with camp equipage, wines,
confectionery," etc. The Mexicans, forced to serve
in the army without pay or to labor as bond-ser-
vants on the estates of the landowners, would, they
believed, tell a different story. Pike visited a wealthy
"planter" of El Paso, who owned twenty thousand
sheep and one thousand cows. In Mexico proper,
he found ranches where the number of cattle, sheep,
and horses amounted to one hundred thousand. One
such cattle king maintained a force of " 1500 troops
to protect his vassals and property from the savages," [17] who were fond of stampeding horses and
driving them off for their own use.

El Paso was the only flourishing place Pike saw. There a bridge was thrown across the Rio del Norte to accommodate the caravans and a well-built canal conducted water from the river on to the fertile bottoms. "There is a wall bordering the canal the whole way on both sides, to protect it from the animals; and when it arrives at the village, it is distributed in such a manner that each person has his fields watered in rotation. At this place were as finely cultivated fields of wheat and other small grain as I ever saw; and numerous vineyards, from which were produced the finest wine ever drank in the country, which was celebrated through all the provinces, and was the only wine used on the table of the commanding general." [18] But the methods of cultivation were very primitive. "They are, however, a century behind us in the art of cultivation; for, notwithstanding their numerous herds of cattle and horses, I have seen them frequently breaking up whole fields with a hoe. Their oxen draw by the horns, after the French mode. Their carts are extremely awkward and clumsily made. During the whole of the time we were in New Spain, I never saw a horse in a vehicle of any description, mules being made use of in carriages, as well as for the purposes of labor." [19]

Arrived at Chihuahua, the travel-worn suspects were received by General Salcedo with the words: "You have given us and yourself a great deal of trouble." "On my part entirely unsought, and on that of the Spanish government voluntary," [20] replied Pike. His papers and journals were examined and

held for farther scrutiny, while he and Robinson
were warned against indulging in conversation as to
the policy of the Spanish government, the respective

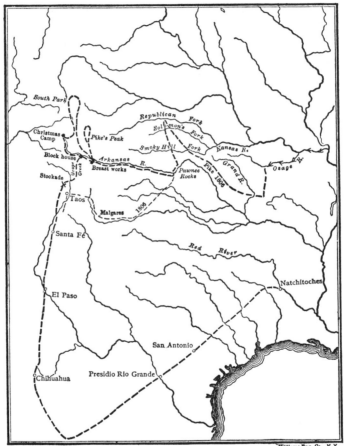

PIKE'S RED RIVER EXPEDITION, 1806–1807.

merits of republics and monarchies, etc. The lieutenant laughed at these precautions, saying "there
were disaffected persons sufficient to serve as guides,
should an enemy ever come within the country." [21]

After due consideration, Salcedo concluded that the path of prudence was to deport the suspicious Americans, and that not through Santa Fé, but by way of Texas. Pike protested this decision, although nothing could better have served his purpose had he come to Mexico to spy out the land. Escorted by a cavalry detachment, his party rode southward round the Bolson de Mapini, and then northeast along the "Grand Road" to the Presidio Rio Grande and San Antonio.

A Neglected Province

In 1812 New Mexico with other Spanish colonies was given an opportunity to send a delegate to the Cortes of the Revolution, and Don Pedro Pino, a wealthy gentleman of Santa Fé, undertook (at his own expense) to represent the needs and latent possibilities of his province at Madrid. According to his report, the population was at that time between forty and fifty thousand, fully half and by no means the least prosperous element being the Pueblo Indians. Every pueblo had land sufficient to maintain its people, and many of the ancient industries were still pursued. The Indians ground their grain into flour and manufactured pottery and copper utensils, leather, and saddles for their own use and for sale. "Many Indians know how to read and write, and all are able to speak Spanish readily and justly with a natural but persuasive eloquence. They are slow in coming to a decision, but carry through all labor with a common accord, and in their dealings are notably honorable and truthful. . . . Rarely do they suffer hunger, for their foresight causes them to accumulate for the future." [22]   The Indian trade centered at Taos, where a midsummer fair was held. Thither the Apaches, Utes, and other mountain tribes brought deerskins, buffalo robes, furs, and slaves to barter for knives, muskets, horses, blankets, and gewgaws of European make.

The only considerable Spanish towns were Santa Fé, with a population of five thousand, Albuquerque, and Santa Cruz de la Canada.   The leading products were corn, wheat, and beans — crops yielding from fifty to one hundred fold — cattle and sheep, wool, cotton, and tobacco.   New Mexico had the exclusive privilege of growing tobacco ; but the leaf must be sent to Old Mexico for manufacture, a regulation against which Pino protested as a senseless restriction on what should be one of the principal industries of the province.

The manufactures carried on by the whites were at their lowest ebb, hardly sufficient to supply them with the necessities of life.   A few hand-wrought bits and spurs were made for the *rancheros*.   Some coarse woollen and cotton stuffs, *serapes* and *ponchos*, baize cloth, serges, and friezes, neckerchiefs, cotton stockings, and table linen were the only output of the loom.   A master weaver sent in by the government had taught his craft to several apprentices in a remarkably short time, and they had woven some fine cotton goods — fine at least by comparison with what had been manufactured before ; but it was not easy to sell them, for there were foreign cloths to be had both cheaper and better, and a merchant buying domestic stuffs ran the risk of not being able to dispose of them. The only hope for the establishment of home manufactures was in the example set by certain foreign artisans : "Some Anglo-American artisans are to be found established here; and from them we may hope some improvement of the industries of New Mexico, since it is to be supposed that the *hijos del pais* [sons of the country] will get themselves taught these trades in the workshops of the foreigners, or at least will emulate them, seeing the excellent achievements of these men. Among these foreign artisans are tailors, carpenters, excellent gunsmiths, blacksmiths, hat makers, tinsmiths, shoemakers, *et cetera.*"

In the commerce with Chihuahua, the balance of trade was hopelessly against New Mexico. The exports for 1812 were $52,000, while the imports amounted to $112,000. The effect was to denude the province of coin. Until recently many of the inhabitants had never known the use of money. The country did not lack commodities for export, — peltries, wool, and salt meat; but the overland freights to the distant ports of Vera Cruz and Acapulco were prohibitive. If these articles might be shipped from Guaimas on the Gulf of California, or San Bernard (Bahia de St. Luis) on the Gulf of Mexico, the saving of nine hundred leagues of land carriage would bring down the costs to a feasible figure. Even the trade with Chihuahua was conducted at ruinous disadvantage. A good horse sold for $11 and a mule for $30, while linen cost $4 and woollen cloth $20 per yard.

The Mexican war for independence (1812–1822) found hardly an echo in this remote province. Royal Spanish officials were superseded by republican Mexican officials, and gentlemen of Spanish birth, such as the proprietor of the copper mines at Santa Rita, were sent into exile (1829); but the common people, creole, *mestizo*, and Indian alike, appreciated little change except in the more liberal commercial policy of the Mexican Cortes. All ports were now open to trade, and caravans began to come in from St. Louis, the American frontier town far across the deserts to the east. This meant the substitution of American cottons and hardware for the high-priced European goods and the still farther neglect of manufactures. Gregg, the most intelligent of the St. Louis traders, gives in his *Commerce of the Prairies* a careful résumé of the industries of New Mexico.

"The mechanical arts have scarcely risen above the condition they were found in among the aborigines. Gold and silversmiths are perhaps better skilled in their respective trades than any other class of artisans whatever, as the abundance of precious metals in former days, and the ruling passion of the people for ostentatious show, gave a very early stimulus to the exercise of this peculiar talent. Some mechanics of this class have produced such singular specimens of ingenious workmanship that, on examining them, we are almost unwilling to believe that rude art could accomplish so much. Even a bridle bit or pair of spurs it would no doubt puzzle the 'cutest' Yankee to fashion after a Mexican model — such as I have seen manufactured by the commonest blacksmiths of the country." [23]

The New Mexicans were celebrated for the manufacture of blankets, coarse and fine, which they sold to the neighboring Indians, to the southern markets, and to the St. Louis traders, as well as a coarse woollen cloth, checkered black and white, called *gerga*, the only stuff worn by the peasants. Their machinery was still of the most primitive type, a whirligig spindle, the *huso* [24] or *malacate*, which was set in a bowl and twirled by one hand while the thread was drawn out with the other, and a loom so clumsy that it could be handled only by men. A fustian coat, buckskin trousers, gayly colored *serape*, and wide *sombrero* of straw or leather was the universal costume of the men, while the women wore woollen of domestic weave. There was no flax nor hemp in the province, and the growth and manufacture of cotton was a lost art.

"Wagons of Mexican manufacture are not to be found; although a small number of American-built vehicles, of those introduced by the trading caravan, have grown into use among the people. Nothing is more calculated to attract the curiosity of strangers than the unwieldy *carretas* or carts of domestic construction, the massive wheels of which are generally hewed out of a large cottonwood. This, however, being rarely of sufficient size to form the actual diameter, which is about five feet, an additional segment or felloe is pinned upon each edge, when the whole is fashioned into an irregular circle. A crude pine or cottonwood pole serves for the axle tree, upon which is tied a rough frame of the same material for a body. In the construction of these *carretas* the use of iron is, for the most part, wholly dispensed with; in fact, nothing is more common than a cart, a plough, and even a mill, without a particle of iron or other metal about them. To this huge truck it is necessary to hitch at least three or four yokes of oxen; for even a team of six would find it difficult to draw the load of a single pair with an ordinary cart. The labor of the oxen is much increased by the Mexican mode of harnessing, which appears peculiarly odd to a Yankee. A rough pole serves for a yoke and, with the middle tied to the cart tongue, the extremities are placed across the heads of the oxen behind the horns, to which they are firmly lashed with a stout rawhide thong. Thus the head is maintained in a fixed position, and they pull, or rather push, by the force of the neck, which, of course, is kept continually strained upward.

"Rough and uncouth as these *carretas* always are, they constitute, nevertheless, the pleasure carriages of the *rancheros*, whose families are conveyed in them to the towns, whether to market or to *fiestas*, or on other joyful occasions. It is truly amusing to see these rude vehicles bouncing along upon their irregularly rounded wheels, like a limping bullock, and making the hills and valleys around vocal with the echo of their creaking and frightful sounds." [25]

Agriculture was as primitive as manufacture and the output quite as costly in labor. Pattie, a Kentucky hunter, thus describes Mexican tillage as he saw it in 1829. "Their ploughs are a straight piece of timber, five feet long and eight inches thick, mortised for two other pieces of timber, one to be fitted to the beam, by which the oxen draw, and another to the handle, by which the man holds the plough. The point that divides the soil is of wood, and hewed sloping to such a point that a hollow piece of iron is fastened on it at the end. This is one inch thick, and three inches broad at top, and slopes also to a point. Their hoes, axes, and other tools are equally indifferent; and they are precisely in such a predicament as might be expected of a people who have no sawmills, no labor-saving machinery, and do everything by dint of hard labor, and are withal very indolent and unenterprising." [26]

The scant water supply was carried to the fields of corn in the ditches originally built by the Pueblo Indians. "One *acequia madre* [mother ditch] suffices generally to convey water for the irrigation of an entire valley, or at least for all the fields of one town or settlement. This is made and kept in repair by the public, under the supervision of the *alcaldes;* laborers being allotted to work upon it as with us upon our county roads. The size of this principal ditch is of course proportioned to the quantity of land to be watered. It is conveyed over the highest part of the valley, which, on these mountain streams, is, for the most part, next to the hills. From this, each proprietor of a farm runs a minor ditch, in like manner, over the most elevated part of his field. Where there is not a superabundance of water, which is often the case on the smaller streams, each farmer has his day, or portion of a day, allotted to him for irrigation; and at no other time is he permitted to extract water from the *acequia madre.* Then the cultivator, after letting the water into his minor ditch, dams this, first at one point and then at another, so as to overflow a section at a time, and, with his hoe, depressing eminences and filling sinks, he causes the water to spread regularly over the surface. Though the operation would seem tedious, an expert irrigator will water in one day his five- or six-acre field, if level, and everything well arranged; yet on uneven ground he will hardly be able to get over half of that amount." [27]

The most profitable industry was sheep raising, for to sheep the dry climate and infrequent streams offered no difficulty, and pasture might be had the year round by shifting the herd from valley to mountain and back again with the change of season. "Nothing, perhaps, has been more systematically attended to in New Mexico than the raising of *sheep.* When the country was at the zenith of its prosperity, *ranchos* [ranges for cattle or sheep] were to be met with upon the borders of every stream, and in the vicinity of every mountain where water was to be had. Even upon the arid and desert plains, and many miles away from brook or pond, immense flocks were driven out to pasture, and only taken to water once in two or three days. On these occasions it is customary for the shepherds to load their burros with *guages* filled with water, and return again with their folds to the plains. The *guage* is a kind of gourd, of which there are some beautiful specimens with

Sheep on the Open Range, Arizona.

two bulbs, the intervening neck serving to retain the cord by which it is carried.

"These itinerant herds of sheep generally pass the night wherever the evening finds them, without cot or enclosure. Before nightfall the principal shepherd sallies forth in search of a suitable site for his *hato*, or temporary sheepfold; and building a fire on the most convenient spot, the sheep generally draw near it on their own accord. Should they incline to scatter, the shepherd then seizes a torch and performs a circuit or two around the entire fold, by which manœuvre, in their efforts to avoid him, the heads of the sheep are all turned inwards; and in that condition they generally remain till morning, without once attempting to stray. It is unnecessary to add that the flock is well guarded during the night by watchful and sagacious dogs against prowling wolves or other animals of prey. The well-trained shepherd's dog of this country is indeed a prodigy; two or three of them will follow a flock of sheep for a distance of several miles as orderly as a shepherd, and drive them back to the pen again at night, without any other guidance than their own extraordinary instincts.

"In former times there were extensive proprietors who had their *ranchos* scattered over half the province, in some cases amounting to from three to five hundred thousand head of sheep. The custom has usually been to farm out the ewes to the *rancheros* [ranchmen; in this case tenants apparently], who make a return of twenty per cent upon the stock in merchantable *carneros*, — a term applied to sheep generally, and particularly to wethers fit for market.

"Sheep may be reckoned the staple production of New Mexico, and the principal article of exportation. Between ten and twenty years ago, about 200,000 head were annually driven to the southern markets; indeed, it is asserted that, during the most flourishing times, as many as 500,000 were exported in one year. This trade has constituted a profitable business to some of the *ricos* [rich men] of the country. They would buy sheep of the poor *rancheros* at from fifty to seventy-five cents per head, and sell them at from one to two hundred per cent advance in the southern markets. A large quantity of wool is of course produced, but of an inferior quality. Inconsiderable amounts have been introduced into the United States *via* Missouri, which have sometimes been sold as low as fifteen cents per pound. It is bought, however, at the New Mexican *ranchos* at a very low rate — three or four cents per pound, or (as more generally sold) per fleece, which will average, perhaps, but little over a pound. Yet, from the superiority of the pasturage and climate, New Mexico might doubtless grow the finest wool in the world. In conformity with their characteristic tardiness in improvement, however, the natives have retained their original stocks, which are wretchedly degenerate. They formerly sheared their flocks chiefly for their health, and rarely preserved the fleece, as their domestic manufactures consumed but a comparatively small quantity.

"But the *ganado menor*, or small beasts of pasture

(that is, sheep and goats in general), have of late been very much reduced in quantity; having suffered to a deplorable extent from the frequent inroads of the aboriginal 'lords of the soil,' who, every now and then, whenever hunger or caprice prompts them, attack the *ranchos*, murder the shepherds, and drive the sheep away in flocks of thousands. Indeed, the Indians have been heard to observe that they would long before this have destroyed every sheep in the country, but that they prefer leaving a few behind for breeding purposes, in order that their Mexican shepherds may raise them new supplies!" [28]

The republican administration did even less than the viceroy had done to protect the New Mexicans against their Indian foes. Apaches raided the *ranchos* for cattle, sheep, and mules, and the proprietors were driven to the towns for protection. Gregg thought the Apaches not so good warriors as the Comanches, and these in turn were less valorous than the Shawnees and Delawares, who had opposed the advance of the English in the Ohio valley, yet the Mexican troops were afraid to encounter them. In 1837 the governor of Chihuahua offered a money reward for Apache scalps: $100 for a brave, $50 for a squaw, $25 for a pappoose. The only effect of the offer was to induce scalp-hunting expeditions against the most peaceful of the Indians, thus inciting them to revenge, and the edict was recalled in a few months. Given the backward state of agriculture and manufactures and the heavy taxes imposed on trade, it will be readily surmised that there could be no real prosperity, no rapid increase of population either by immigration or by natural growth.

Gregg estimated the population of New Mexico in 1840, including the Pueblo Indians but excluding the savage tribes, at seventy thousand souls: one thousand white *creoles*, fifty-nine thousand *mestizos*, ten thousand Pueblos. The number of naturalized foreigners was inconsiderable, perhaps twenty, and there were less than forty alien residents. On the basis of Baron Humboldt's statement that the population of New Mexico in 1803 was forty thousand, Gregg calculated that the rate of increase for forty years had barely exceeded one per cent per annum. His estimate, however, was fifteen thousand in excess of the official count for 1840, which showed the population of New Mexico to be almost stationary. Three centuries of Spanish occupation had done little for the arid land of the Pueblos.[29]

SECTION II

Louisiana

La Salle's Ill-fated Enterprise. — Meantime great changes had been taking place along the Espiritu Santo, the region that Castañeda had thought a waste of bogs. Both Cabeza de Vaca and Coronado had crossed the plains of Texas and reported the extraordinary fertility of the buffalo pastures; but sixteenth-century Spaniards thought no discoveries worth pursuing that did not lead to mines of gold and silver and the turquoise-encrusted gates of Quivira. In the first half of the seventeenth century, Franciscan friars made several attempts to reach the Tehas, the semi-agricultural Indians who dwelt near the Gulf Coast, yet the Spanish government made no move in this direction till its monopoly of the Floridas was threatened by a French explorer.

Rumors of a mighty river, the Father of Waters, had reached France through the Jesuits who carried the cross to the aborigines beyond the Great Lakes. In 1639 Jean Nicollet, a French interpreter of Three Rivers, sailed into Green Bay, crossed from the Fox River to the Wisconsin, and learned from the Indians that this water flowed southward to the sea. Little by little, the learned fathers gathered information from their converts. In 1670 Father Dablon was able to state, "To the south flows the great river which they [the Sioux] call the Messi-sipi, which can have its mouth only in the Florida sea, more than four hundred leagues from here. . . . It seems to encircle all our lakes, rising in the north and running to the south, till it empties in a sea which we take to be the Red Sea [Gulf of California] or that of Florida. . . . Some Indians assure us that this river is so beautiful that more than three hundred leagues from its mouth it is larger than that which flows by Quebec, as they make it more than a league wide. They say, moreover, that all this vast extent of country is nothing but prairies without trees or woods, which obliges the inhabitants of those parts to use turf and sun-dried dung for fuel, till you come about twenty leagues from the sea. Here the forests begin to appear again. Some warriors of this country, who say they have descended that far, assure us that they saw men like the French who were splitting the trees with long knives, some of whom had their house on the water; thus they explained their meaning, speaking of sawed planks and ships." [30]

In 1673 Count Frontenac, governor of New France, commissioned Louis Joliet and Père Marquette to attempt the voyage down the Wisconsin to the Mississippi and thence to salt water. In two bark canoes, with only five boatmen, they made their way past the Missouri and the Ohio rivers to the Arkansas. There the Indians told them it was but ten days' sail to the sea and the Spanish settlements. Fearing to fall into the hands of the Spaniards, they turned back, being convinced that they had proved that the Mississippi flowed into the Gulf of Mexico, "since its course was directly south, not east toward Virginia nor west toward the South Sea." Frontenac reported to the home government that Joliet "had found admirable countries, and so easy a navigation by the beautiful river which he found, that from Lake Ontario and Fort Frontenac you can go in barks to the Gulf of Mexico, there being but one discharge to be made at the place where Lake Erie falls into Lake Ontario." [31]

The court of Louis XIV gave little attention to these momentous findings, and the record of the daring achievement was neglected. The narrative of Père Marquette was not made public till 1681, and then by a private publisher. Frontenac had hoped that the king would take in hand the further exploration of the great river system now claimed by

France; but the project was ultimately carried out by a private gentleman, Robert Cavelier, Sieur de La Salle, then in command at Fort Frontenac, who had received a royal grant of a monopoly of the trade in buffalo hides and a commission to explore the interior. He probably learned from Joliet, *en route* for Quebec, the details of that first voyage down the Mississippi, and he may even have seen the explorer's map. La Salle was doubtless familiar with the journals of Cabeza de Vaca and Castañeda, and it was he who first divined the identity of the Espiritu Santo with the Mississippi. The commercial possibilities of a navigable river that connected the Great Lakes with the Gulf impressed him as worth developing, and he determined to prosecute the fur trade in that direction. He expected to ship buffalo skins and wool to France by an all-water route, but it was necessary first to establish intervening trading posts and to provide an adequate fleet. The difficulties and delays which La Salle encountered by reason of the jealous opposition of the Jesuits and of rival fur traders, the loss of his ship, the *Griffin*, and of his post, Fort Crèvecœur on the Illinois, need not be rehearsed here. After desertions and disappointments sufficient to discourage a man of less iron resolve, his party set out (January, 1682) from the southern extremity of Lake Michigan, crossed the divide by way of the Chicago, Des Plaines, and Illinois rivers, and finally launched three canoes in the Mississippi. A run of sixty-two days down the muddy tide brought them to the Delta (April 9, 1682) and the Gulf. There La Salle erected a cross, together with the arms of France, and solemnly took possession of the mighty river in the name of Louis XIV. Three years previous, Father Hennepin, deputed by La Salle to explore the Illinois and the upper "Mescha-sipi," had been captured by the Sioux on Lake Pepin and carried to the Falls of St. Anthony and beyond. The vast valley thus revealed was named Louisiana for the Grand Monarque, who took slight interest in the noble acquisition.

Tonti, the only officer who did not abandon La Salle on this expedition, recorded in his journal an interesting estimate of the industrial possibilities of the lower country. There were bogs and cane-brakes along the banks, but back from the river was the "most beautiful country in the world."[32]   In the rich bottom lands were corn-fields and smiling meadows, mulberry trees and grape-vines, and a great variety of fruits grew wild in the woodlands; magnificent pine forests offered an inexhaustible supply of naval stores, while lead deposits that would yield two parts of ore to one of refuse only waited the miner's pick. Beaver were rare, but buffalo, bear, wolves, and deer abounded. The trade in peltry alone could be made to yield 20,000 *écus* per year. When the Indians were trained to tend silkworms, that industry also would furnish a valuable article of trade.

In 1683 La Salle returned to France, seeking the means to plant a colony at the mouth of the Mississippi. He succeeded in enlisting the patronage of Colbert, and Louis XIV was induced to finance the expedition as a demonstration against Spain's design in that quarter.[33]   Four vessels were furnished; one from the royal navy, *Le Joly*, commanded by Captain Beaujeu, La Salle's ship *L'Aimable*, which was provided with eight guns, a store-ship *St. François*, and a bark *La Belle*, made up the little fleet. A company of two hundred and eighty colonists was collected, — soldiers, priests, artisans, and women, these last from the purlieus of the cities. La Salle's brother, the Abbé Cavelier, and his nephews, Moranget and Cavelier, were of the party.

The enterprise was handicapped from the start by a divided command. The jealous foes of La Salle had prevailed with the king to give Beaujeu equal authority with the real leader of the expedition. Moreover, on the outward voyage, La Salle displayed the harsh and arbitrary temper which so often angered his followers and dashed their loyalty. The ceremony of baptizing the novices as they crossed the Tropic of Cancer was already dear to the hearts of old salts, both because of the merriment raised and for the sake of the penalties usually paid by the cabin passengers for exemption. This harmless pastime the commander forbade, thereby forfeiting the affection of his men. The little fleet touched at Petit Goâve in Haiti for food and water, and there many of the crew deserted, and the store-ship was captured by Spanish pirates ; but La Salle laid in new supplies, and the remaining vessels proceeded along the Gulf Coast, looking for the mouth of the Mississippi. In January, 1685, they actually skirted the Delta ; but the three mouths of the river giant were concealed by shoals and fog. Suspecting his mistake, La Salle would have turned back, but Beaujeu protested, and the leader was persuaded to run on down the coast as far as Matagorda Bay. Here nothing was to be seen but sand bars and dangerous surf. Finally (February 4, 1685) Moranget and Joutel were put ashore, with a small party, and ordered to march eastward until they should come upon the river, when they were to signal the following ships. Arrived at a wide and impassable inlet, Joutel lighted a signal fire, and La Salle came ashore in the bark *La Belle* with a trusty pilot to take soundings. Having discovered a safe passage, he sent back the pilot to *L'Aimable*, to bring her into the river. But the captain refused to be directed, declaring that he knew his business. La Salle, watching anxiously from the shore, saw his ship, heavily laden with supplies, run upon a shoal. The obstinate captain immediately lowered the sails, thus destroying all chance of getting her off. Nothing but treachery could explain such disastrous tactics, and Joutel, the indignant chronicler of these events, asserts that this was done "designedly and advisedly, which was one of the blackest and most detestable actions that man could be guilty of." [34] In spite of La Salle's desperate efforts, only a fraction of the provisions was recovered. Some mischief-maker, under cover of the night, scuttled the only lighter and stove in the ship's side. By morning her hold was filled with water. Only a little flesh, meal, and grain, and thirty casks of wine and brandy were saved.

It was now of prime importance to establish friendly relations with the natives, but, unfortunately, the first encounter was hostile. Learning that the Indians had found some blankets in the wreckage and made way with them, a small party volunteered to pursue the thieves and bring back canoes as an offset. The business was badly managed. A show of force frightened the Indians, who ran away; but, returning to the village by night and finding that the strangers had taken not only the blankets but two canoes, the wily natives tracked the party and, coming upon their camp when even the guard was asleep, sent a flight of arrows into their midst. Two of the Frenchmen were killed and two severely wounded. This spilling of blood was regarded as a bad omen, and Beaujeu, making much of the disaster, determined to return to France, taking with him the malcontents. He refused to leave behind any of the stores from his ship, even the ammunition that rightfully belonged to La Salle. *Le Joly* set sail on March 14, leaving a disheartened company on this unknown coast.

La Salle resolutely set about making the best of the situation. He had a hut built and palisaded with the wreckage of the ship, where the women and provisions might be housed in safety. Leaving Joutel in command at this post, La Salle undertook an excursion into the interior (October, 1685). Left to his own devices, Joutel displayed much common sense in providing for the comfort of the one hundred men and women in his charge. He put up a second building for the accommodation of the men, and constructed an oven that they might have wholesome baked bread. Fish and flesh were abundant, and salt was discovered in the marshes of the neigh-

borhood. Every man had to serve his turn on
guard, and discipline was enforced by the ancient
penalty of the wooden horse. Only Joutel and one
trusted lieutenant had access to the ammunition, a
precaution that frustrated at least one mutiny. The
colonists would have been glad to settle here; but
La Salle, who had gone up the river and found
higher and less malarial ground, determined to build
a fort to the eastward. There being no trees convenient to this site, Joutel was ordered to make
a raft of planks from the wreck of *L'Aimable* and
haul it up the river. With great difficulty a little
lumber was transported to the Rivière aux Bœufs, so
called from the bison that came there for water,[35]
while *La Belle* carried the supplies and the women
to the new encampment. Arrived at the spot,
Joutel was amazed to find the post "so ill begun and
so little advanced." No shelter had yet been provided except for the casks of brandy. Rain was falling, and the seed, on whose harvest La Salle was
counting for food, lay rotting in the ground. Several
of the men were dead, many sick of fatigue and exposure, and all were exhausted by the task of hauling
timber across several miles of prairie without carts or
draft animals. La Salle's harsh temper contributed
not a little to the general depression. "The uneasi-
ness M. de la Salle was under to see nothing succeed
as he had imagined, and which often made him insult
the men when there was little reason for it,"[36] had
driven his people to the verge of mutiny. Within a
few weeks thirty of the men died of overwork and
discouragement, among them the head carpenter.

La Salle was thus forced to be his own master builder, to go to the forest and select the trees to be felled, shape them, and fit them to their places. The fort was completed at last, and formally christened St. Louis, a name given also to the bay which it overlooked.

In April of 1686, La Salle set out in *La Belle* to explore the coast in search of the Mississippi, and again Joutel was left in command. The equipment of this expedition had well-nigh exhausted the supplies, and there were thirty-four persons to feed; but, thanks to his careful management, they fared well. The buffalo were made to furnish not only food but shelter, for the resourceful lieutenant thatched his cabins with their hides. Of these animals, the main reliance of the Indians of the plains, there seemed to be an inexhaustible supply. "There are thousands of them, but instead of hair they have a very long curled sort of wool." [37]

Meantime, La Salle was meeting with his usual ill fortune. He had not gone far when a quite uncalled-for injury to an Indian village was revenged by a night attack on the unguarded camp, and three Frenchmen were killed. Leaving Cavelier and a small party in charge of the bark and all dispensable supplies, La Salle departed for the interior with twenty picked men. After three months of aimless wandering, he returned to Fort St. Louis ragged and worn, "his fatal river" not yet discovered. He was met by disastrous news. A boat load of men, sent off from *La Belle* to fill the water barrels, had been lost through the captain's neglect to keep the lights burning. The depleted force was not strong enough to manage the ship, and she had drifted on a shoal. Monseigneur Cavelier and his remnant had found their way back to the fort with some of the more portable goods, but the greater part was irrecoverable.

Apparently undaunted, La Salle set out almost immediately for a third excursion, taking with him another twenty men and as good an outfit as could be got together. This time he marched toward New Mexico, reconnoitring, it would seem, the limits of the Spanish dominions. He returned in August with only eight men. Four had deserted, the others were lost or killed by savages or by the alligators that infested the rivers. "All the visible advantage of that journey consisted in five horses, laden with Indian wheat, beans, and some other grain, which was put into the store." [38] Notwithstanding this calamitous failure, "the even temper of our chief made all men easy, and he found, by his great vivacity of spirit, expedients which revived the lowest ebb of hope." [39] He now proposed "to undertake a journey toward the Illinois, and to make it the main business, by the way, to find the Mississippi." [40]

La Salle's last expedition set out to northward in January, 1687. This time the faithful Joutel accompanied him, together with Monseigneur Cavelier, the two nephews, Father Anastasius Douay, Sieur Duhaut and his servant, L'Archevéque, Tessier, the pilot, Hiens, a German buccaneer, Liotot, the surgeon, La Salle's devoted Iroquois guide, his footman, and four servants. Dried buffalo meat, which they called *foucannier* in imitation of the Indian word, some grain, and the best of the remaining ammunition and camp utensils were packed on the horses, and the little cavalcade set out toward the northeast. La Salle's objective point was the villages of the Cenis, where he hoped to secure guides. He realized at last how important were the friendly offices of the Indians and was determined to "use them kindly . . . an infallible maxim, the practice of which might have been fortunate to him had he followed it sooner." [41] The route was rendered difficult by several large rivers, alligator swamps, and heavy timber. Whenever possible, they followed the buffalo trails to avoid the necessity of cutting paths through the dense underbrush, and a canoe was constructed of long poles covered with buffalo hide to carry the men and goods across the rivers, the horses being made to swim. Notwithstanding La Salle's best devices, the march was wearisome and discouraging, and the men began to grumble. A quarrel broke out between Moranget (the younger) and Liotot over the disposition of some fresh buffalo meat. Liotot, Hiens, Duhaut, and L'Archevéque fell upon Moranget and his two companions, the Indian and the footman, and beat out their brains with axes. The murderers then determined to make way with La Salle, and free themselves, once for all, of his harsh rule. Uneasy that his nephew and the others did not come up, La Salle was returning to seek them, when Duhaut, who had secreted himself beside the trail, fired and shot him through the head. The leader fell without a groan. Hiens then

stripped the body and threw it into the bushes,
some Indians who witnessed the foul deed looking on
silently, "with amazement and contempt of us." [42]
Joutel was for punishing the murderers, but the two
priests prevailed upon him to attempt no revenge;
and indeed this was the part of prudence, for they
were in the minority.   Joutel held his peace, but
he was determined to part company with the conspirators as soon as possible, and to push on to the

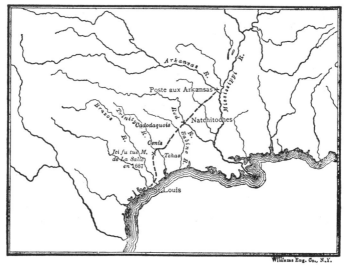

JOUTEL'S RETURN JOURNEY.

Mississippi and the Illinois country.   This was difficult, for Duhaut had assumed command of the party
and controlled the supplies. [43]

As the wanderers approached the Cenis villages,
they saw a man on horseback, dressed as a Spaniard
in blue doublet, straight breeches and stockings, with
a broad-brimmed, flat-crowned hat, and they feared

lest they should fall into the hands of the enemies of France and be carried off to serve in the mines or quarries of Mexico. To their relief, the rider proved to be an Indian who had got his horse and trappings from some Spanish settlement. The Frenchmen were cordially received by the Cenis, an agricultural people, who lived in wooden huts and made rude pottery and cane baskets. Three of the four men who had deserted La Salle on his third excursion were encountered here. They were well content with savage life, having married Indian wives and learned to hunt with bow and arrow. The new arrivals were offered the same privileges. Duhaut and his accomplices were minded to remain here, having forfeited a welcome at Fort St. Louis or in France; but Joutel had learned of a "great river, which was forty leagues off, towards the northeast, and that there were people like us who dwelt on the banks of it." [44] Thither he determined to go.

Six of the party held by Joutel; Father Anastasius, the two Caveliers, and three others who had not been concerned in the assassination of La Salle. They secured six horses and three Indian guides and, having induced Duhaut to spare them the essential supplies, pushed on to the north. The Cadodaquis proved very hospitable. Their chief was tricked out with a Spanish sword and wore a head-dress of hawks' bells whose tinklings gave him much pleasure. He invited the Frenchmen to a solemn ceremony, new to them, the smoking of the calumet, "a very long sort of tobacco pipe, adorned with several sorts of feathers," [45] and urged them to settle there and

marry into the tribe. Joutel, to be rid of his in-
sistence, promised to return with commodities for
trade. On the 24th of July they came to an eastward-flowing river and saw on the opposite bank a
great cross with "a house built after the French
fashion." Two men clothed in civilized garments
came out and fired a salute. This proved to be the
Poste aux Arkansas, founded by Henri de Tonti, the
devoted friend of La Salle, who had come thus far
with his relief expedition.

Joutel and the faithful remnant made their way
by canoe up the Mississippi and the Illinois and so
by the Great Lakes to Montreal and to France,
carrying the news of the disastrous outcome of the
great colonial enterprise. Tonti undertook to rescue
the survivors at Fort St. Louis, but upon reaching
St. Louis Bay he could find no trace of the colony.
Returning by the Mississippi, he voyaged up the
Arkansas as far as his boats would carry him and
then marched across the country to the Indian
village of Natchitoches on Red River. Ascending
this stream to the Cadodaquis, he secured horses and
again rode south to within three days' journey of
the spot where his chief had been murdered. There
his men refused to go farther, and he was forced to
abandon the search.

Such was the pitiful end of a great project. The
causes of La Salle's failure are wisely summed up
by his loyal lieutenant, Joutel. "Such was the unfortunate end of M. de La Salle's life, at a time
when he might entertain the greatest hopes, as the
reward of his labors. He had a capacity and talent

to make his enterprise successful; his constancy and courage, and his extraordinary knowledge in arts and sciences, which rendered him fit for anything, together with an indefatigable body, which made him surmount all difficulties, would have procured a glorious issue to his undertakings, had not all those excellent qualities been counterbalanced by too haughty a behavior, which sometimes made him insupportable, and by a rigidness towards those that were under his command, which at last drew on him implacable hatred and was the occasion of his death." [46]

Louisiana under France and Spain

La Salle's dream of a settlement at the mouth of the Mississippi and a commerce that should connect the Great Lakes with the Gulf was shared by Iberville, the military genius who, having demonstrated his ability in combating the projects of Great Britain on the New England coast, in the Mohawk Valley, and on Hudson's Bay, was despatched to Louisiana to defeat the encroachments of Spain. He and his brother, Bienville, arrived on the Gulf Coast with a colonizing outfit just ten years after the death of La Salle and, landing to the east of the Delta, founded Fort Biloxi on a sandy beach backed by virgin forest. In 1701 the post was transferred to a point still nearer Pensacola, Mobile, where a deep bay and navigable rivers gave harborage for vessels; but the settlement at Biloxi was maintained. The hardships of the initial years and the hot and humid climate proved disastrous to the pioneers. Twenty-five hundred colonists were sent over between 1699 and 1712, but only four hundred were living in the latter year. The monopoly of the trade of Louisiana was then granted to Anthony Crozat, on condition of establishing a colony.

During the five years of his monopoly, Crozat expended 425,000 livres on this venture and realized a revenue of but 300,000 livres. When he surrendered the concession in 1717, there were only seven hundred Frenchmen and four hundred cattle in Louisiana. In spite of these failures, the Regent was unwilling to abandon the claim to the Mississippi River and the vast valley which it drained ; the opportunity for colonial expansion was made over to the Company of the West, and Louisiana became the physical basis for the ambitious financial scheme to which John Law had converted the French court and people. The projectors secured the monopoly of trade, mines, and furs on condition that they import six thousand white colonists and three thousand negro slaves. Land was offered to voluntary emigrants, together with free transportation and sustenance until they should reach their final destination ; but it was not easy to induce men who could earn a living at home to take their chances in the wilderness, and the Company was obliged to impress colonists from the jails and almshouses and the vicious resorts of Paris. Eight hundred people were brought over in three ship-loads (1718) and distributed among the several posts, — Biloxi, Mobile, St. Louis Bay, Natchitoches, Fort Rosalic de Natchez, and the Yazoo. Bienville was made governor, and he cleared ground for a cen-

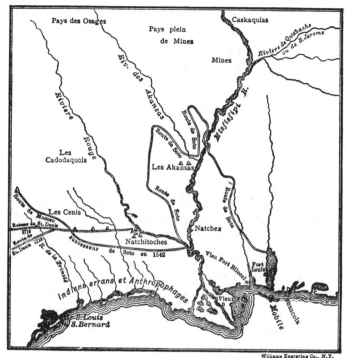

FRENCH LOUISIANA IN 1718.

tral settlement on the neck of land between the Mississippi and Lake Ponchartrain, which, in honor of the Regent, he named New Orleans (1721).

Le Page du Pratz, a gentleman adventurer who came over on the first ship with servants and implements, gives us a detailed account of the colony. His estate was at Natchez, where he found the soil very fertile and the climate salubrious; but so long as his nearest and largest market was Biloxi, there was no profit in agriculture. New Orleans promised better things commercially because the river front was deep enough for sea-going vessels, whereas lighters were necessary at Biloxi; but the ground plotted out for the town lay so low that it was inundated by the spring floods, and the river was at that season so filled with drifting timber that vessels were forced to put out into the Gulf for safety. Bienville had caused a mole three feet high and wide enough for a carriage road to be built along the water front for a distance of fifteen or sixteen leagues on both sides the river, and this served to protect not only the dwellings but the agricultural lands.

After eight years spent at Natchez, Du Pratz removed to New Orleans and was induced to take charge of the royal plantations in that vicinity. The results of this experience are embodied in some very interesting notes on methods of cultivating the most successful crops — maize, rice, watermelons, tobacco, indigo, cotton. A really serious handicap on the last-named product was the difficulty of separating the seed from the fibre, but Du Pratz invented a mill which performed this operation much more quickly than it could be done by hand. A woman from Provence, Mme. Hubert, was experimenting with silkworms, and she had succeeded in raising worms on the leaves of the red and the white mulberry that spun a silk finer and stronger than that of Lyons. Du Pratz believed that young negroes could be taught to tend the cocoons and that a profitable silk industry might be established in this warm and equable climate. He anticipated, moreover, that a flourishing trade would develop with the West Indies and ultimately with Europe. Lumber, bricks and tile, maize, beans, peas, and rice were already being shipped to the Islands, and the return cargoes of sugar, coffee, rum, and slaves were eagerly bought by the well-to-do among the Louisianians. (Du Pratz paid £55 for a negro and his wife.) Furs, deerskins, buffalo hides, and tallow were coming down from the upper river; lumber, pitch, and tar were being sent in from the near-by forests; hemp and sugar could be grown in the Delta; and there was no reason why the colony should not build its own trading vessels. "If the English build ships in their colonies . . . why might not we do the same in Louisiana?" "France has found in her lands neither the gold nor silver of Mexico and Peru, nor the precious stones and rich stuffs of the East Indies, but she will find therein, when she pleases, mines of iron, lead, and copper. She is there possessed of a fertile soil, which only requires to be occupied in order to produce, not only all the fruits necessary and agreeable to life, but also all the subjects [materials] on which human industry may exercise itself in order to supply our wants." [47]

There was no lack of energy on the part of the men who undertook to bring to light the latent resources of this rich possession. In 1718 an expedition was despatched to the Illinois Country to develop the lead deposits described by Tonti. Philip Renault and La Motte, a mineral expert, prospected the region from the Kaskaskia on the east of the Mississippi to the St. Francis River on the west so thoroughly that their numerous excavations are still visible. They opened the rich mine at the source of the St. Francis, still called La Motte, also Fourche à Renault on Big River and, with the aid of two hundred artificers and miners sent from France and five hundred slaves picked up at San Domingo, they raised and smelted a considerable quantity of first-grade metal. For twenty-five years pirogues loaded with lead were sent down to New Orleans; then the project was abandoned for lack of support, and Renault returned to France. In 1725 Bourgmont explored the Missouri as far as the Kansas, and proved that a great trade in furs might be developed with the Osages and Paducahs. In 1740 a party of traders from New Orleans followed the Arkansas to the mountains, established a trading post there (near Pueblo), and opened commercial relations with the Indians of Taos and the Spaniards of Santa Fé. These operations being reported to the Spanish authorities, the Frenchmen were seized and thrown into prison. The case was referred to Havana, and the superior court decided that, since the post was on the eastern slope of the mountains, it lay within the Province of Louisiana. The traders were promptly released and their goods restored.

Meantime the industrial experiments on the lower river were going badly. The idle and degenerate riffraff imported as colonists could not or would not work, not even food enough for sustenance would they grow, and famine and disease decimated the settlements. One hundred years before, England had proven the futility of attempting to build a commonwealth out of the "scum of the people"; but the Company of the West was bent on profits, and the places of the dead were filled by more cheap labor, — beggars, criminals, and slaves. In the first six years of its administration, four thousand and forty-four French men and women were transported to `Louisiana and fourteen hundred and forty-one Africans. The only successful farmers were some Alsatians forwarded by the canny Law to his own estates at Arkansas Post, but who later removed to the Bayou St. John (Côte des Allemands). The Canadians who came down from the St. Lawrence showed greater capacity for coping with the vicissitudes of frontier life and made excellent hunters; but the "Mississippi Scheme" was doomed from the start. The Company's feudal requisitions, their trade monopoly, and the worthless paper currency sent from France were burdens too heavy for an infant colony. When the speculative bubble burst and there was no more revenue to be had, the fictitious prosperity collapsed. The discredited company surrendered its charter (1731) and Louisiana reverted to the crown.

Bienville was continued as governor until 1743, and under his wise and efficient management, the province began to prosper. The plantations about New Orleans bore abundant crops of cotton, rice, and tobacco; salt was manufactured on Red River; naval stores came down the Mississippi in huge rafts. When Vaudreuil succeeded Bienville he found a population of thirty-two hundred whites and two thousand and thirty blacks — slaves from Cuba and San Domingo — and there seemed reason to believe that France might yet reap some profit from

Louisiana. Hoping to extend the agricultural area, Vaudreuil offered tracts of the alluvial land on the river and adjacent bayous, free of charge, stipulating only that some portion be cleared and a house built within a year and a day, and that such proprietors as held land on the river should maintain a levee and a public road along its summit and erect the necessary bridges.

When Louisiana and the Floridas were ceded to Spain (1762), the administration of the province was but little changed. Spanish officials took the place of the French, and the seat of authority and source of supplies was transferred to the City of Mexico. Land grants were given out by the Spanish governors with a more lavish hand and with less regard to the development of the country. The terms of the grants were not rigidly enforced, and the public was obliged to make good the defects in roads and levees caused by the neglect of the local proprietors. Governor O'Reilly offered to each newly arrived family settling on the river a tract of land extending from six to twelve *arpents* along the water front and forty *arpents* deep, with indefinite rights to feed cattle in the cane-brakes and cut fuel in the cypress forests beyond. Grants were conditioned on the building of levees, roads, and bridges, and the clearing of at least three *arpents* deep along the water front. If these terms were not met within three years, the land reverted to the crown. Carondelet (1795) enjoined upon the syndics that they should make a survey of the levees twice a year and require the proprietors to repair the damages wrought by floods and crawfish. If the individual planter was unequal to the work, an impressment of the negroes of the adjoining plantations was authorized, the negroes working on Sunday, their one holiday, for four *escalins* (thirty-six cents) per day. This public-spirited administrator built the canal that connected New Orleans with Lake Ponchartrain and drained the streets of the city. He provided for the lighting of the streets and arranged a force of watchmen. The cultivation of sugar, which had been abandoned since 1766, was revived by Etienne de Boré, a neighboring planter, who succeeded in granulating the molasses and producing a marketable grade.

Emigration from France ceased with the change of flag, and none but officials came from Spain, so that the population of the province was fairly stationary. The settlements made in Upper Louisiana during the Spanish régime were due to French enterprise. Maxent, Laclede & *Cie.*, merchants of New Orleans, had already secured from the French intendant the trade monopoly of the Missouri and of the upper Mississippi as far as the St. Peters, and Laclede selected as the best site for a trading post the bluff that overhangs the Mississippi just below the debouchure of the Missouri. Here a palisaded fort was erected, Auguste Chouteau, then a lad of thirteen, overseeing its construction. Laclede named his post St. Louis and thought it destined to become "one of the finest cities in America." When the Spanish governor arrived (1770), he found a town of one hundred wooden and fifteen stone houses, but the men that gathered at the post were *voyageurs*,

engageés, and *coureurs de bois,* who spent their days
in trapping and trading and had no liking for the
cultivation of the soil. To provide sustenance for
this force, Laclede had recourse to the *habitants* of
Vincennes, Cahokia, and Kaskaskia. Outraged by
the cession of the Illinois Country to Great Britain
(1763), several hundred of these loyal Frenchmen
responded to Laclede's invitation and, to be free of

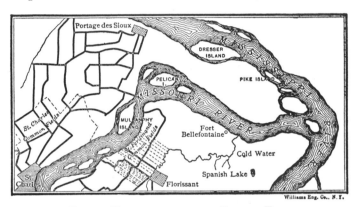

FRENCH VILLAGES WITH THEIR COMMON FIELDS.

the jurisdiction of "King George's men," crossed the
Mississippi with their families and their cattle.
They found good farming land on the bottoms at
the mouth of the Missouri, and there in a series of
agricultural villages — Portage des Sioux, St. Charles,
St. Ferdinand or Florissant — soon reproduced the
peace and plenty of the abandoned possessions.

The French villages were little communes, for the
inhabitants continued the customs they had known on
the Wabash, — on the St. Lawrence, — in old France.
Each householder had his bit of garden about his
cabin on the one street of the village, his allotment

in the plough field, his right to pasture cattle and hogs
in the unfenced land and to gather wood in the forest
back of the clearing. At Ste. Genevieve on the
Mississippi, the bottom for five miles along the
river was common field; at Carondelet, the individual
allotments, while narrow, were more than a mile and
a half in length.[48]   They were a simple, unprogressive
people, caring far more for music and dancing and
out-of-door pleasures than for industry and the
making of money. The common fields remained
undivided and were handed down from generation
to generation, and while there was no wealth there
was little poverty among them.   Loyal to church
and established authorities, with few schools and no
manufactures, the French settlers pursued a placid
and unenterprising existence under Spanish rule.
Crime was rare among them, jails were unnecessary,
and courts and lawyers had small employ.   St. Louis
was dubbed *Pain Court* by the corn-growing inhabitants, but the traders retorted by nicknaming the
agricultural villages *Vide Poche* and *La Misère* and
Petite Côtes.   At St. André, farther up the Missouri,
some thirty families from Kentucky had established
themselves and were farming the land in a fashion so
superior to that of the *habitants* as to attract the commendation of the governor-general.   On the upper
Mississippi, opposite Prairie du Chien, an enterprising
Frenchman, Julien Dubuque, had secured license
(1788) to work the lead mines he had discovered in
that district.[49]

   Laclede's trading post soon became the entrepôt
for river traffic and in 1800 boasted nearly one

thousand inhabitants, largely Canadians from Montreal and Michillimackinac. The confluence of the Missouri and the Illinois with the Mississippi gave the post increasing importance as the centre of the fur trade, and brought it into direct relation with New Orleans. Keel boats and barges laden with furs, buffalo robes, meat, and tallow were despatched to "the city," as the seaport was known in St. Louis parlance, and though the voyage of one thousand miles down-stream was quickly made, it was not without its dangers. The risk of capture by river pirates [50] was so great that in 1788 the governor ordered that no boat undertake the trip alone. Thereupon a fleet of ten keel boats was assembled by the merchants, the robbers' lair was attacked and destroyed, and the organized piracy came to an end.[51] A more persistent danger was the risk of shipwreck on the sand bars, shoals, and floating driftwood with which the Father of Floods was beset. Trees dislodged by the spring freshets floated down river and, becoming imbedded in the muddy bottom, lay in wait for the unwary navigator. Many a *bateau* and pirogue was capsized on a log or snag that rested just beneath the water, or rose and fell with the pressure of the current.

The forty years of Spanish occupation meant little for the development of Louisiana. Pursuing the traditional policy of Spanish colonial officials, the governor-general at New Orleans confined his attention to multiplying the perquisites of his post, and his example was followed by every man in authority. Bradbury, the English naturalist who made a voyage down the Mississippi to New Orleans in 1810, writes as follows of the hindrances imposed on industry: "The most depressing regulations were made to shackle the internal trade of the country; no man could sell the smallest article, not even a row of pins, without a license, and those licenses were sold at the most extravagant rates. A stranger coming into the province, and offering goods at a fair price, was certain to be sent to prison and to have his goods confiscated. All favors from these governors, all grants of land, or even common privileges, could only be obtained by bribery. . . . Under so detestable a system of government the energies of man must forever remain dormant, and the most fertile regions eternally unproductive to the world." [52]

The effect of the tolls and tariffs imposed on American goods seeking a market at New Orleans is a matter of general history. The throttling of their commerce at its natural and most feasible outlet drove the exasperated settlers along the Ohio, the Cumberland, and the Tennessee to the point of revolt. The Federal government was importuned to negotiate a treaty with Spain that should secure to American citizens free navigation of the Mississippi and rights of deposit at New Orleans. After prolonged and vexatious parleyings, these privileges were conceded (1795), but only for a term of three years. They were withdrawn in 1798, and the pioneer farmers of Kentucky and Tennessee, again threatened with ruin, addressed urgent memorials to Congress. The danger was even greater than they knew, for in this same year Napoleon was pushing to a successful conclusion his negotiations for the restoration of Louisiana to France. The transfer of New Orleans from the corrupt but unenterprising Spaniards to a ruler so ambitious and unscrupulous, was regarded with serious apprehension by the United States government. When rumors of the treaty of San Ildefonso reached Jefferson, he characterized the change of ownership as "inauspicious" and "ominous to us." In January, 1803, James Monroe was sent to France as minister plenipotentiary to assist Livingston in securing and enlarging our rights and interests "in the river Mississippi and in the territories eastward thereof." They were empowered to buy New Orleans and the Floridas for the sum of $2,000,000. After some haggling over terms, a convention was drawn up (April 30), and the Province of Louisiana was ceded to the United States in return for a cash payment of $15,000,000. The transfer of Lower Louisiana was formally made at New Orleans in December, but that of Upper Louisiana and the settlements in the neighborhood of St. Louis was delayed until March, 1804.

The extent of this extraordinary acquisition was then unknown. To the north lay the dominion of Great Britain, as yet undefined. To the west, a range of mountains, uncharted and unexplored, was believed to delimit the French province. The boundary between Louisiana and Texas was held by Spain to be the Red River, but the Americans of the Mississippi Valley were eager to extend their claim to the Sabine, to the Colorado, to the Rio Grande.

Section III

Texas

Possession contested by France and Spain. — When news of La Salle's expedition was brought to Mexico by the captors of the supply ship, *St. François*, it became evident that some measures must be taken to hold the land of the Tejas, if Spanish control of the Gulf of Mexico was to be maintained. Two vessels were despatched, therefore, to search the coast for La Salle's colony (1686–1687). The wreckage of *La Belle* and *L'Aimable* was found in St. Louis Bay, but nothing more. The overland party had the good fortune (1689) to discover the ruins of the fort and captured two of La Salle's murderers. The rest of the ill-fated colonists had succumbed to privation and disease. In 1690 the missionary occupation of the country was attempted. Three Franciscans with an escort of one hundred soldiers reached the Trinidad River and were received with delight by the natives. There the mission of San Francisco de los Tejas was built, a mere log church with barracks for the *padres*. Soon horses and cattle were sent in, and a beginning of tillage was made. The Tejas were a semi-agricultural people accustomed to the cultivation of corn, beans, melons, and tobacco, yet they declined to live in houses and, discouraged by the first failure of crops, began to steal the cattle and escape into the wilderness. Eight more missions had been projected, and that of Santa Maria was actually started among the Cenis; but the perverse character of the savages disheartened the friars, and in 1694 the enterprise was abandoned.

The grant of Louis XIV to Anthony Crozat conveying the monopoly of the trade of Louisiana indicated the Rio Grande as the natural boundary between the French and Spanish dominions. Crozat hoped to discover mines in this region and to open up a profitable exchange of products between Mobile and the Spanish settlements, San Juan Bautista and Monclova. Louis Juchereau de St. Denis was sent on a trial trip in 1714. With five canoes laden with goods he went up the Mississippi and Red rivers and, having established a trading post at Natchitoches, made his way overland as far as San Juan. He succeeded in establishing friendly relations with the *commandante*, and thus set on foot the contraband trade with Mexico that persisted for a century to come.

St. Denis' bold venture convinced the Spanish government of the necessity of taking possession of the land of the Tejas. The viceroy got together seven or eight families who were willing to risk their fortunes in this enterprise, together with some fifty soldiers and twelve friars, and put them in charge of Captain Domingo Ramon (1716). A train of pack mules and oxen with one thousand goats completed the equipment. There were no difficulties *en route*. Pursuing an easterly course through luxuriant woods and pastures, they found abundant game, — buffalo, wild turkeys, and fish. The Tejas were in friendly mood and smoked the calumet with the Spanish officers, and they allowed the friars to rebuild

the mission of St. Francisco de los Neches (Nacogdoches) and that of Purissima Conception for the
Cenis villages. Seven missions in all were founded

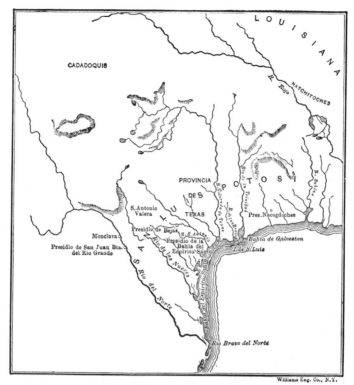

TEXAS IN 1804.

between the Trinidad and Red rivers, and one, San
Antonio de Valero, on the San Antonio River. The
adjacent *presidio* [53] of San Antonio de Bejar gave to
this position a special importance.

This brave beginning was brought to an untimely
end by the outbreak of war between France and
Spain (1719). A troop of French and Indians from

Natchitoches swept into the country, destroying the missions east of the Trinidad and the colonists were forced to take refuge at San Antonio.

Two years later, peace being declared, colonization was again undertaken. The sum of $250,000 was appropriated to the purpose, and the Marques de San Miguel de Aguayo reëntered the land of the Tejas with five hundred soldiers, thirty families, and a great herd of horses, cattle, and sheep. Additional supplies were brought by ship to Espiritu Santo (St. Louis Bay), where a fort, Bahia, was erected. The missions beyond the Trinidad were reëstablished, and a *presidio*, Pilar near Adaes, built and garrisoned to overawe Natchitoches. The *presidio* at San Antonio de Bejar was rebuilt in adobe, and a Spanish *pueblo*, San Fernando, was projected in the immediate vicinity. It was ordered (1722) that four hundred families should be brought over from the Canary Islands at the expense of the crown, while every ship clearing from Havana (1729) was to bring in twelve Cuban families. Land and full citizenship was promised, and the colonists were assured of maintenance for the initial year. In conformity with trade regulations, the immigrants were carried, not to the neighboring harbor of Espiritu Santo, but to Vera Cruz, whence they were obliged to march overland by way of the City of Mexico to their destination. Thus some thirty families were with great effort transported to San Antonio to form the Villa de San Fernando. But the immigrants proved less industrious than the natives, for they refused to till the soil, preferring to live by hunting and fishing. A similar colony, San Augustin, with a *presidio* attached, was planted on the Trinidad in 1755 with fifty families; but they, too, found it easier to live without work, and neither settlement prospered. The officials were made of no better stuff than the settlers and neglected their most evident duties; the very governor used his authority to impress the labor of the mission Indians for his own benefit and to the impoverishment of the friars.

The missionaries sent to the Tejas and the Cenis were zealous and disinterested men, and their methods were unusually wise. The native dialects were used in the instruction of the new converts, but the Indians residing at the mission were taught Spanish. The soil was cultivated in common under the supervision of the friars, and a garden lot was assigned to every man who proved diligent and capable. The government of the mission community was vested in an *alcalde* elected by the people and approved by the governor. The natives were taught agriculture, carpentering, bricklaying, blacksmithing, weaving, and other trades, in order that the needs of the mission might be supplied, and they were well fed and clothed with the double object of keeping them contented and attracting others from the savage state to this opportunity for Christian education. Adobe houses were built for their use and furnished with such domestic utensils as the people could be induced to employ. Water collected in small reservoirs was distributed over the fields by means of irrigating ditches, and corn, beans, pumpkins, and melons were grown in abundance. Sugar made from cane raised at the several missions proved especially gratifying to the sweet-toothed children of the land, and horses, cattle, hogs, sheep, and goats multiplied beyond experience, requiring only the care of a mounted cowherd.

The labor expected of the people was not thought onerous by the Spaniards. Husbandmen planted the fields, watered the crops, cleared away the weeds, and gathered in the grain. The carpenters and masons put up the adobe huts, the granaries, and the friars' dwellings. The women and children carded the cotton and spun it on *malacates*, the primitive Indian spindles, and the men who had learned the art wove this into cloth. The natives worked so slowly and carelessly, however, that it was necessary to have a Spanish overseer constantly on hand, and even so, four native laborers were not equal to one European. Each mission raised corn and beans sufficient for its own needs,[54] while the increase of cattle served for outside traffic. The friars might have developed a considerable commerce had not the settlers protested against their selling in the same market. However, cattle were sold as opportunity offered, and the secured bills received in exchange were forwarded to the superior at the City of Mexico, who laid out the proceeds in supplies for the mission, — cloth, hats, tobacco, needles, knives, pots, *metates*,[55] hatchets, crowbars, saddles, and bridles. Chocolate for the special delectation of the friars, and drugs for the restoration of the sick, together with the ornaments and sacred images and other appurtenances of the church, were furnished at cost of the royal treasury.

The Franciscan establishment in Texas never accumulated wealth, and the beautiful churches of San Antonio, San José, and Purissima Conception were built with funds subscribed by the faithful in New and Old Spain. The missions suffered very much from the raids of Comanches and Apaches and scarcely less from the depredations of the settlers and officials. The soldiers sent to guard the missions were usually their worst foes, slaughtering the cattle and debauching the neophytes without conscience, while the Indians lost their tribal virtues and became drunken, vicious, and syphilitic. In the hundred years of missionary effort the total number baptized was less than ten thousand, and there were never more than two thousand *reducidos* [56] resident at any time in the dozen odd establishments. There were two thousand mission Indians in 1732, four hundred and fifty in 1785, and no more in 1793. The secularization of the missions was decreed in 1794, the royal support was withdrawn, secular clergy were placed in charge of the churches, and the cultivated lands distributed among the converts. When Pike passed through San Antonio (1806), he visited the three missions in its immediate neighborhood and noted that while their prosperity was a thing of the past, the church buildings "for solidity, accommodation, and even majesty were surpassed by few that I saw in New Spain." He asked the resident priest at San Antonio de Valero what had become of the natives. "He replied that it appeared to him that they could not exist under the shadow of the whites, as the nations who formed those missions had been nurtured, taken all the care of that it was possible, and put on the same footing as the Spaniards; yet, notwithstanding, they had dwindled away until the other two missions had become entirely depopulated, and the one where he resided had not then more than sufficient to perform his household labor."

When Louisiana was ceded to Spain, Natchitoches ceased to be a menace; but the withdrawal of the northern garrisons (Pilar, Augustin, San Luis, 1777) worked harm to colonists and missions alike. The Comanches of the plains, waging war against their hereditary foes, the Lipan Apaches, were incited by the latter to turn their arms against the Spaniards. The settlements were attacked, priests and civilians killed, and cattle driven off, in spite of the punitive expeditions organized by the *commandante* at San Antonio. The pusillanimity of the troops only served to incite farther raids, and the settlers in despair abandoned all cultivation. The village of San Fernando was in a wretched state. There were only one hundred and forty houses in the town, more than half of them mere wooden shacks. The descendants of the Canary Island immigrants, both civilians and officials, were lazy and vicious. They would do no work, but impressed the labor of the mission Indians and stole the mission cattle for slaughter and for sale. De Morfi, who visited Texas in 1778, says of San Fernando: "This villa cost the king more than 80,000 *pesos* and to-day, if sold, would not bring in 80 *pesos*." [57] According to de Morfi's estimate, the total white population of Texas

MISSION OF SAN JOSÉ, TEXAS.

did not amount to three thousand souls (2600). The settlements at Nacogdoches and Bahia numbered three hundred each, that at San Antonio, one thousand. At the beginning of the nineteenth century the civilized population of this vast territory — Spanish and French creoles, mission Indians, and half-breeds [58] — was but seven thousand, or one to each square league. The town at San Antonio reckoned two thousand people, Bahia (Goliad), fourteen hundred, Nacogdoches, five hundred. The remaining three thousand were gathered about the smaller missions and *presidios*, while a few great landowners dwelt in feudal isolation on their *ranchos*, or cattle ranges.

The *rancheros* were a reckless, improvident race whose wealth consisted in cattle and horses. They spent the better part of their lives in the saddle, and their devotion to the buffalo hunt was a ruinous passion. Governor Cordero (1806) undertook to restrict the sport to certain seasons and required each man of family to plant a stated acreage to corn, but this legislation had little effect. It was far easier to trade horses and cattle for what was needed, since these were to be had for the taking. Pike describes the process of corralling wild horses. "The method pursued by the Spanish in taking them is as follows: they take a few fleet horses and proceed into the country where the wild horses are numerous. They then build a large strong enclosure, with a door which enters a smaller enclosure; from the entrance of the large pen they project wings out into the prairie a great distance, and then set up bushes, etc., to induce the horses, when pursued, to enter into these wings. After these preparations are made, they keep a lookout for a small drove, for, if they unfortunately should start too large a one, they either burst open the pen or fill it up with dead bodies, and the others run over them and escape; in which case the party are obliged to leave the place, as the stench arising from the putrid carcasses would be insupportable; and, in addition to this, the pen would not receive others. Should they, however, succeed in driving in a few, say two or three hundred, they select the handsomest and youngest, noose them, take them into the small enclosure, and then turn out the remainder; after which, by starving, preventing them taking any repose, and continually keeping them in motion, they make them gentle by degrees, and finally break them to submit to the saddle and bridle. For this business I presume there is no nation in the world superior to the Spaniards of Texas." [59]

The prairies teemed with horses and cattle, the progeny of the early importations, which fattened on the succulent pasture, untended and unclaimed. Great numbers were driven off by the nomad Indians and bartered to the tribes of the far north, and thousands were captured, broken, and driven to Natchitoches for sale. An edict of 1778 reserved unbranded cattle to the crown, and imposed a tax of four *reals* for each animal killed; but this measure, which should have produced a revenue of $25,000, brought but $7000 into the provincial treasury, and nothing reached the king. In fact, this province, that had cost the royal exchequer $6,000,000 all told, was on the verge of ruin. The Spanish residents were ready to abandon their property because the widely scattered and feebly manned *presidios* afforded no protection against their savage foes.

Even while the French were in possession of Louisiana, the Texans had carried on a brisk contraband trade with Natchez, New Orleans, and Mobile. Horses and cattle were driven along the "contraband trace" to Natchitoches, where they brought good prices and where merchandise was cheaper than the goods packed overland from the City of Mexico and Vera Cruz. All classes in the frontier communities — settlers, soldiers, friars, and officials — were smugglers. Even the governor had his share in the illicit profits, although he occasionally arrested French factors residing in Texas and sent them to the capital in evidence of his zeal for the public service. When Natchitoches became a Spanish town, this trade was no longer illicit, and trains of pack mules laden with West Indian and European goods followed the San Antonio road. Natchitoches was also headquarters for the Indian trade, whence agents were sent to the native villages with firearms, gunpowder, hatchets, knives, and liquor to exchange for furs and buffalo hides. The weapons and liquors quickly found their way to the nomad tribes in the interior, rendering them yet more dangerous, but there was no attempt to restrict the sale. Indeed, the Spanish governor of Louisiana favored the distribution of *ardiente* and inferior ammunition to the savages of the frontier, as a means to their speedy extinction.

The Coming of the Americans

After the peace of Paris extended the British dominions in America to the Mississippi River, the English began to cross the Appalachians in shoals, and their neighborhood became a menace to the Spanish possessions far more serious than the French. These colonizers came on their own initiative and in opposition to the royal decree that would have held the territory west of the Appalachians as a game preserve. They brought wives and children and were bent upon making homes in the wilderness of Ken-ta-kee. Flourishing settlements sprang into existence, and keel boats bearing the surplus produce of the pioneer farms began to find their way down the Ohio, the Cumberland, and the Tennessee to the Mississippi River and New Orleans. When this avenue of commerce was finally opened, the "men of the western rivers" were not slow to avail themselves of the golden opportunity. Philip II had decreed (1560) that no foreigner might enter a Spanish colony without first obtaining the royal license, and neglect of this precaution was punished by confiscation of goods and expulsion from the country. No passport held was good for longer than two years except those of the merchants, which permitted three years' residence. But as the mineral wealth of the Mexican provinces and the profits to be made in trade became known, many Americans crossed the Texas border in defiance of the law, hoping to escape detection, or in any case to obtain concessions from some venal official.

In 1800 a gentleman of Irish birth and a protégé of General Wilkinson, Philip Nolan of Natchez, who had been engaged in the Texan trade since 1785, undertook to capture horses on his own account. He entered the country with a party of twenty men, fourteen Americans — backwoodsmen from Virginia and Tennessee — five Mexicans, and one negro. Nolan had an out-of-date passport from the governor of Louisiana, but his men were unprovided. Having reached the Brazos River, they built a log camp and a corral and had succeeded in imprisoning three hundred animals when they were attacked by a party of Spanish troopers. Nolan was killed in the first fusillade, and the others surrendered on the understanding that they would be allowed to return to Natchitoches. They were carried as far as Nacogdoches, but were thence haled to San Antonio, San Luis Potosi, and Chihuahua to be examined by Salcedo, captain-general of the Interior Provinces. He referred the matter to Madrid, and the unfortunate men were held five years in prison awaiting the king's decree. When at last it was announced, the sentence proved unexpectedly severe. Every fifth man was to be hanged. As there were only nine survivors, one life was thought to be sufficient to meet the royal order, but the other men were condemned to ten years of hard labor.[60] Our first-hand authority for this adventure is Ellis P. Bean, who, a Kentucky lad of seventeen, was coming down the Mississippi to Natchez with a scowload of flour and whiskey when he met Nolan and was induced to try his young fortune in Texas. On recovering his liberty, Bean joined the revolutionary forces in the determination to strike a blow against that king at whose behest he had suffered so much.

Mexico was ripe for revolt. Three centuries of corruption and oppression had created a class antagonism that boded ill for the landowners and the bureaucracy. Pike was impressed with the contrast of riches and poverty and the general discontent prevailing in the northern provinces. The officers and grandees lived in much state, but "the mass of the people were naked and starved wretches," while the inferior clergy and the subordinate officials, usually creoles by birth, had no chance of advancement. "This had soured their minds to such a degree that I am confident in asserting that they will lead the van whenever the standard of independence is raised in the country." Pike was fully convinced that a revolution was not far distant, and that intervention on the part of his government would become inevitable. As Pike's party and its escort neared the Red River, they met a "number of runaway negroes" and some French and Irish emigrants from New Orleans. There were smugglers, too, engaged in carrying on illicit commerce with the Spaniards, "who on their side were equally eager." The trade in horses, though mutually advantageous, was once more contraband; but it was carried on, none the less, and at very great profit. All the conditions were those of an ill-regulated frontier. "The American emigrants are introducing some little spirit of agriculture near Nacogdoches and the Trinity; but the oppressions and suspicions they labor under prevent their proceeding with that spirit which is necessary to give success to the establishment of a new country." [61]

The troubled state of Mexico had not escaped attention in the United States. The settlers in Kentucky and Tennessee had their old-time grudge against the exclusive commercial policy of Spain, while Natchez, Natchitoches, and New Orleans harbored many Mexican malcontents. Even at Washington there were plots to add Texas, possibly Mexico, to the possessions of the United States. All this seething discontent and desire for vengeance centered in the projects of Aaron Burr, ex-vice-president of the United States, a man of potent personality and vast ambitions, who gathered about him a group of hot-headed adventurers, even more talkative and restless than himself. Burr had purchased a grant of 400,000 acres on the Red River from Baron de Bastrop,[62] purposing to found an agricultural colony on the Louisiana frontier and await events. At Blennerhasset Island on the upper Ohio, he was collecting provisions, agricultural implements, and boats for the descent of the Mississippi, and there a score of backwoodsmen joined him for what was, on the face of it, nothing more than a promising colonial venture. However, rumors of the enterprise reached New Spain in exaggerated form. Colonel Burr was reported to have collected two thousand men and to be contemplating an attack on New Orleans. From that base, aided by the French creoles, who had their own reasons for hating Spanish rule, he was supposed to project the invasion of New Spain and the overturn of the viceroyalty. Protests were addressed to the United States officials, and Burr's flatboats were stopped at Natchez, his men were scattered, and he himself brought to trial on charge of treason (1806–1807) by his political adversary, President Jefferson.

Meantime, stirring events were taking place on the Texas frontier. The long controversy between Spain and the American government over the navigation of the Mississippi was no sooner terminated by the cession of Louisiana, than the question of the Mexican boundary began to agitate the pioneers. The Red River, held by the Spanish government to be both the natural and the historic boundary, did not satisfy the ardent advocates of American expansion. They hungered for the fat lands of Texas, and urged that the purchase rights based on the French occupation ran to the Sabine or even to the Rio Grande. While the President and Congress were endeavoring to negotiate the cession of the Floridas, trans-Alleghany politicians were discussing ways and means of securing Texas. General Wilkinson, commander-in-chief of the United States army, General Adair of Kentucky, Andrew Jackson of Tennessee, Daniel Clarke, and the Mexican Association of New Orleans were in sympathy with the project urged by hot-heads that an expedition be organized in the western states for the invasion of Texas. The precedent furnished by Miranda's expedition against Venezuela went far to assure them that a filibustering enterprise, if successful, would not be discountenanced by the Administration. Moreover, in the event of war with Spain, which then seemed imminent, the movement would be unquestionably patriotic. The irritation of the Mexican authorities at everything suggestive of trespass on the part of their northern neighbors was extreme. The rough handling to which Pike's party had been subjected is accounted for by the excitement aroused by Burr's enterprise. Cordero had received information of Dunbar's Red River expedition as early as July, 1806, and had forwarded the disquieting news to Salcedo. Under such circumstances the arrest and deportation of Pike's party seemed quite justified. Believing that the United States government was ready to countenance invasion, the Mexican government prepared for defence. The viceroy, Iturrigaray, sent fifteen hundred soldiers to Texas, the fortifications of San Antonio and Nacogdoches were strengthened, and in April, 1806, General Herrera was sent to Arroyo Hondo (Bayou Funda, seven miles south of Natchitoches) to forestall aggression. When the news reached Washington, Wilkinson was ordered to the front to drive the Spaniards back to the Sabine. This was the opportunity hoped for by the conspirators. The West was aflame with zeal to have it out with the "dons," to drive Herrera's force beyond the Sabine, — beyond the Rio Grande, — to the City of Mexico, to expel the Spanish bureaucracy from the American Continent, to set free an oppressed people, to establish a republican government in the land of Montezuma. The creoles of Louisiana sent a volunteer force, five hundred strong, to join Wilkinson at Natchitoches; Burr's flatboats were preparing on the Muskingum; Jackson was building boats on the Cumberland for the same enterprise. But the commander-in-chief moved with great circumspection. He lingered at St. Louis for three months after receiving his orders, and did not arrive at Natchitoches until September 22. Then he entered into negotiations with Governor Cordero (then in residence at Nacogdoches) relative to the withdrawal of the Spanish troops. The governor protested that he had no authority to consider so base a desertion of His Majesty's claims. Then Herrera cut the Gordian knot by suddenly, and apparently of his own responsibility, retreating beyond the Sabine (September 29–30). His troops, less than seven hundred in number, short of food and badly munitioned, were at the point of mutiny. Moreover, he had married an English wife and travelled much in the United States, and he was not eager to try conclusions with an enemy so sure to be reënforced by popular support. His retreat was later approved both by Cordero and Salcedo, on the ground that armed conflict would have "jeopardized" the disputed territory. Instead of following up his advantage, Wilkinson delayed a full month at Natchitoches, and did not appear on the Sabine until October 29. Then he paused upon the left bank and entered into negotiations with Herrera across the river. The result was the inglorious Neutral Ground Convention by which the district between the Sabine and the Arroyo Honda was to be evacuated by both parties, the two armies retreating to their respective fortifications at Natchitoches and Nacogdoches. The details of these extraordinary negotiations have never been divulged. Burling served as go-between, and he kept his master's secrets. The indignant Westerners believed that their commander had been bribed by the Spanish government, and certainly Salcedo was well pleased with the result. He wrote to Viceroy Iturrigaray, "This treaty insures the integrity of the Spanish dominions along the whole of the great extension of frontier."

Then followed that extraordinary series of charges and countercharges, Wilkinson accusing Burr of treason against the United States, and Burr and his friends accusing the general of being subsidized by Spain, which culminated in Burr's trial at Richmond and his final acquittal. Chief Justice Marshall ruled that, while Burr had not been convicted of treason, he might suitably be indicted for high misdemeanor under the Act of 1794, which so designated the offence of any person who should, within the jurisdiction of the United States, begin or set on foot a military expedition against the territory of any foreign power with whom the United States government was at peace. Wilkinson took great credit to himself for having frustrated "a deep, dark, and wicked" conspiracy, "that would have shaken the government to its foundations," and his high-handed methods were fully indorsed by Jefferson. Only recently has the damaging fact come to light that Burling carried to Iturrigaray (January, 1807) a letter from Wilkinson, demanding that the Spanish government reward the commander-in-chief of the army of the United States for services rendered in the frustration of Burr's expedition against Mexico, to the amount of $111,000. When Burling returned to New Orleans with the information that the claim would be referred to Madrid, Wilkinson forwarded to Washington the ostensible result of this secret mission, a report on the defences of the City of Mexico, with the request that the expenses of his ambassador, $1500, be met from the United States treasury !

During the Napoleonic Wars, Spain could do little for her colonies, and they were abandoned to the misgovernment and peculation of greedy officials. Crushed under the triple burden of a shackled commerce, grinding taxation, and military service, the creole population rebelled at last (1812) and, aided by the natives, succeeded in throwing off the hated dominion. The insurrection led by Hidalgo was suppressed, but it was the signal for revolts in other parts of Mexico and a ten years' war. The viceroy had no troops to spare for the defence of Texas, and this rich frontier province lay at the mercy of free-booters and filibusters. The Neutral Ground became an asylum for criminals, both American and Mexican. Refugees from justice and desperadoes gathered in this lawless land and earned an exciting though precarious livelihood by preying upon the commerce between Texas and New Orleans. Traders along the San Antonio road, unprovided with military escort, were forced to pay tribute to these highwaymen. Moreover, Hidalgo's revolt excited among the hot bloods of the American frontier new hopes for the acquisition of Texas. In 1813 Lieutenant Magee, commander at Natchitoches, resigned his commission in the United States army and led a company of five hundred bandits, recruited in the Neutral Ground, across the Sabine. He succeeded in getting possession of San Antonio and declared for the Mexican republic, but the invaders were soon after ambushed and cut to pieces. Only ninety-three returned to Natchitoches, and Texas was well-nigh depopulated by the royalist revenge.

This unlucky expedition had no countenance in the United States, and President Madison issued a proclamation (1815) forbidding such enterprises as unlawful and seditious. By the treaty of 1819, our claim to Texas was formally surrendered in return for the cession of the Floridas, and the boundary between the United States and the Spanish possessions was fixed along the Sabine, the Red, and the Arkansas rivers to the forty-second parallel, and thence directly west to the Pacific Coast. The hope of annexing Texas to the United States was apparently thwarted.

Thenceforward Texas was a no-man's land, undefended by the Spanish government and abandoned to the anarchic elements of a frontier population. In 1816 a Mexican insurgent, Herrera, took possession of Galveston Island and set up a freebooters' republic; but a court of admiralty, with the right to issue letters of marque and to adjudicate prizes, was the principal organ of the nascent state. The sounds and bayous of the Gulf Coast furnished an ideal refuge for smugglers and pirates, and some thousand men, outlaws from the West Indies, Louisiana, and the Neutral Ground, gathered under Herrera's flag.

Twelve vessels were engaged in privateering in the
Gulf, and they captured several Spanish merchantmen and conveyed the spoils to Galveston Bay.
Slave ships bound for the West Indies were also
taken, and the helpless human cargo driven to New
Orleans for sale. In a few years Herrera was succeeded by Lafitte, a French creole driven (1814) from
Barataria, whose audacity and success won him the
title of Pirate of the Gulf. His subalterns owed
respect to no flag and dared to attack even American
vessels. The Spanish government had protested
against interference from the United States, lest that
dreaded power gain a foothold in Texas; but the
depredations of the pirate commonwealth grew intolerable. In 1821 a United States war vessel was
despatched to Galveston Bay, and Lafitte's colony
was suppressed.

Spain had been unable to colonize Texas, but any
attempt at settlement on the part of alien peoples
was instantly resented. Lallemand, a distinguished
French refugee, undertook (1818) to found a colony
on the Trinity River twelve miles above the bay.
The colonists were recruited from Napoleon's
shattered army, and they made small success as
farmers. The settlement was too weak to be a
source of danger; none the less, a Spanish force was
despatched to drive them from the land. In 1819
an expedition from Natchez, led by James Long,
who had married a niece of Wilkinson, penetrated to
Nacogdoches and induced the Americans settled
thereabouts to declare Texas a free and independent
republic. Their success was shortlived (1819–1821).

Spanish troops from San Antonio scattered Long's force and drove the Americans across the Sabine. Even men such as Barr and Davenport, who had lived in Texas twenty years and had sworn allegiance to the king of Spain, were obliged to leave the country. Nacogdoches and the ranch houses along the San Antonio road were destroyed, cattle were slaughtered, and fields laid waste. The whole region east of the Colorado River relapsed to wilderness. Bands of Apaches and Comanches, seeking horses, terrorized the isolated settlements, and Lafitte's slave gangs passed unchallenged to New Orleans. By 1830 the white population of Texas had dwindled to thirty-five hundred, and this dispirited remnant was gathered about the only remaining *presidios* of San Antonio and Bahia de Espiritu Santo.

Meantime the Revolution had been accomplished. Iturbide, the Spanish commander employed against the insurgents in the South, becoming convinced that his task was hopeless, proclaimed the independence of Mexico, and all classes, even the revolutionary leaders, flocked to his standard in support of the plan of Iguala. When it became evident that no Spanish prince would accept the proffered crown, Iturbide was declared emperor. But the republican elements were strong enough to prevent this consummation of the long struggle for self-government. Santa Anna succeeded in overturning the empire and a federal republic was inaugurated (1824). For Texas this was a bloodless revolution, accepted without enthusiasm or protest. The sparsely populated frontier province was united with Coahuila as a federal state.

SECTION IV

California

Colonization attempted. — The reign of Charles III (1759–1788) was signalized by a fresh colonizing impulse. His wise and disinterested minister, Don José Galvez, was sent to Mexico (1765–1771) as *visitador general* to correct the abuses of administration, mitigate the oppression of the Indians, and extend Spain's dominions in North America. In spite of strenuous opposition, he succeeded in ousting the corrupt incumbents and in placing honest men at the head of the government of New Spain. In the course of his five years' sojourn, this energetic and single-minded man set on foot a series of far-reaching reforms. The enterprise that most concerns this history was one that had the especial indorsement of the king, the founding of settlements on the northwest coast that should forestall foreign intervention and hold the country for the Spanish crown.

During the first half of the eighteenth century Great Britain was a menace, for her licensed privateers and even a ship of the line scoured the Pacific in pursuit of prizes. Woodes Rogers, George Shelvocke, Admiral George Anson, and other British sea-dogs whose exploits were less picturesquely chronicled, captured Spanish merchantmen, ravaged coast towns, and filled the breasts of Spanish *commandantes* with terror and dismay. Because of these depredations, every Manila galleon must needs be attended by an armed frigate, a system of defence whose cost eventually ruined the Philippine trade. But none of the privateers attempted exploration or made any pretence of reënforcing Drake's assertions of British suzerainty. They were content to conduct their prizes into Puerta Segura and there rifle them of their silver and such Oriental stuffs as might be worth carrying away. Much better founded was the apprehension of danger from the north. Exploring expeditions, sent out by Peter the Great and his immediate successors, had given Russia a foothold on the Pacific. In 1728 Vitus Behring discovered the strait that divides Asia from America; later exploration revealed the haunts of the sea-otter, and by 1760 Russian fur traders had begun operations in the Aleutian Islands. If Spain's control of the Pacific was to be maintained, it behooved her to fortify California.

Galvez proposed three frontier posts on the three known harbors, San Diego, the Santa Barbara Canal, and Monterey, and summoned the Franciscans to his aid. This order had just succeeded to the Jesuit missions in Lower California, and the new venture was organized on the plan that had proved so successful at Loreto and La Paz, that of a monastic community in which the natives were the neophytes.[63] Since the conversion of the Indians and the defence of the coast were the dominant issues, and the industrial development of the country was but a secondary consideration, the mission and the *presidio* were the important concerns, and the *pueblo* was but little considered. Few contemporary Spaniards besides Galvez realized that the perpetuation of Spanish control in Upper California depended on planting there a Spanish population. Costanzó's *Journal* (1769) states that the *visitador general* "felt the necessity of peopling the explored part of California with useful folk, capable of cultivating its lands and profiting by the rich products which it offers in minerals, grain or other fruits, and likewise capable of taking Arms in defence of their Houses whenever the occasion should arrive." [64]   But colonists of this description were not to be had. The Spaniards who came to the New World were soldiers, missionaries, and adventurers ; the peasants staid at home. It is not surprising, therefore, that the pioneer colonists of California were four officers, sixty-five soldiers, and seventeen Franciscans, with a suitable complement of servants, mule-drivers, and converted Indians. The *visitador general* succeeded in enlisting for the direction of this sacred expedition a group of singularly efficient and devoted men — Portolá, the wise and honest governor, Costanzó, the resourceful engineer, and Pedro Prat, the faithful surgeon ; but no man counted for so much in counsel or in action as Father Junípero Serra, the *padre presidente* of the missions of the two Californias. Ten years' experience among the Pamis had convinced him that if the Indians were to be civilized, they should be taught the white man's industry as well as his religion, and he hoped to reclaim the degraded tribes of the north coasts and make of them self-supporting farmers. His work for the missions of Alta California evinced strong common sense as well as ardent sympathy for the people to whom his life was consecrated.

Galvez presided in person over the preparatiôns at La Paz. Two barks, the *San Antonio* and the *San Carlos*, loaded with provisions, seeds, plants, and agricultural implements, besides bells and other church furnishings, were despatched up the outer coast. Because the sea voyage was always attended with serious risk, it was determined to send the cattle and mules, together with the major part of the people, overland from Santa Maria, the northernmost mission. At this rendezvous were collected the live stock and the generous toll of grain, dried fruits, wine, and olive oil contributed to this new enterprise by the several missions of California Baja. Two months were consumed in the toilsome traverse of the mountains, and when Father Junípero and Governor Portolá arrived at San Diego Bay (June 28, 1769), they found the ships already at anchor. The *San Carlos* had spent one hundred and ten days on the voyage and the *San Antonio* fifty-nine. Both crews had suffered terribly from scurvy — of which dread disease two-thirds later died — whereas the land party had not lost a man. No sooner were the forces reunited than the cross was raised, a mass was said, and the spiritual conquest of California had begun. The *presidio* was built upon a bluff overlooking the native *rancheria* and the bay, but the mission was soon removed from this arid spot to a fertile valley three miles back from the coast, where there was level land that might be irrigated from the river. The Indians were a brutish lot and could be enticed to baptism only by the promise of material reward. They had a redundance of food (fish and acorns), but were eager for clothing and trinkets, and they hung about the camp and the wattled huts of the mission, pilfering everything they could lay hands on.

San Diego, however, was only the initial point in the scheme of conquest. Within two weeks of his arrival, Portolá set out with such soldiers as could be spared, two priests, *Padres* Crespi and Gomez, Lieutenant Pedro Fages, and Costanzó, to seek Vizcaino's harbor of Monterey.[65] A long mule train, loaded with supplies, was driven over the rough trail prepared by a force of neophytes, armed with axes and spades. Following up the coast, between the foothills and the sea, they came into a wide valley stretching far inland. Its fertile plains were shaded by great oaks, and numerous springs, rising to the surface, kept the herbage green. Father Crespi thought this pleasant prospect "one of the marvels of this world," and opined that "ten or twenty laboring peons," [66] if set to work here, could provide sufficient grain for all the settlements. Here they proposed to found a mission dedicated to San Gabriel. Turning west, they passed up the Porciuncula River, where were "extensive swamps of bitumen," into another promising valley, Santa Catalina (later San Fernando), and over a precipitous pass (Las Casitas) into the smiling verdure along the Santa Clara River. This brought them to the shores of the Santa Barbara Canal, and here they found a tribe of some ten thousand souls who lived in comfortable wicker huts, planted grain, built wooden boats, made a rude pottery, and gave evidence of a higher state of civilization than any yet encountered. Noticing the advantages the place afforded for a future mission, Portolá pressed on across the Santa Lucia Range and into the narrow valley of the Salinas River. The country grew "more fertile and more pleasing in proportion as they penetrated more to the north," [67] there was plenty of game, and the weather was perfect. The only serious danger that attended the march, according to Costanzó, was the proneness of the great *caballada* (troop of horses) to stampede at the slightest alarm. In the first week of October, they reached a wooded point (Point of Pines) in latitude 36° 40'. Here should be Vizcaino's landing, but since the wide, open bay seemed to afford no anchorage, Portolá failed to recognize the harbor and went on to the sand dunes above Point San Pedro. There a hunting party, ascending the hills (October 31), descried Point Reyes and the Farallones, the well-known landmarks of the Puerto de San Francisco. To the north and east of the intervening range lay a broad lagoon communicating, apparently, with the sea. A reconnoitring party sent out to fathom this mystery returned after four days and reported that it was in truth an arm of the sea surrounded by swamps and level glades, where were populous Indian villages shaded by great oak trees. This was an important discovery, but Portolá did not pursue it. There were only fourteen sacks of flour remaining, and the party was subsisting on geese and ducks. The men were sick and discouraged and clamorous for retreat. After looking in vain for the supply ship that was to put in at Monterey, Portolá decided to return to San Diego.

In the year following, a second expedition, freshly provisioned, was sent to found the northern post on the roadstead now discerned to be Vizcaino's harbor. The *presidio* was placed on the "magnificent ampitheatre"[68] above the bay; but the San Carlos Mission was soon transferred (1771) to the Carmel River, south of the Point of Pines, where a heavy growth of grass indicated the "feracity of the land," and the sea teemed with fish. In the four following years, four more missions were founded at the most promising sites on the route between San Diego and Monterey — San Juan Capistrano, San Gabriel, San Luis Obispo, and San Antonio de Padua. The proselyting zeal of Father Junípero quite outran his resources in the way of funds, supplies, and military guard, and he determined (1773) to make the long and difficult journey to the City of Mexico to intercede for more adequate support in his patriotic task of securing California for the Church and for Spain.

The new viceroy, Bucareli, was an administrator of unusual energy and foresight. It required little persuasion to convince him of the importance of supplying the north coasts with loyal and zealous friars who should bring the Indians under subjection. He immediately set about refitting San Blas, the indispensable base of supplies, and under instructions from the king despatched a vessel loaded with provisions to the starving missionaries. This efficient statesman arranged for an annual supply ship, forwarded mules and cattle to each mission, at the

THE MISSION OF SAN CARLOS ON THE CARMEL RIVER, 1792.

INDIAN BALSA OR TULE RAFT ON SAN FRANCISCO BAY.
Such rafts were used by the Ancient Egyptians.

charge of the Royal Exchequer, and ordered that goods be furnished at no more than 150 per cent advance on Mexican prices. The salaries of the *padres* ($400 each) were to be paid from the Pious Fund, the endowment of the Jesuit missions, and six servants were provided for each settlement at public cost.[69] At Father Junípero's express request, two blacksmiths and two carpenters were engaged to teach the natives their respective trades. The men were under contract for one year, but were offered inducements to remain as settlers. Bucareli further ordered that four *presidios* with adequate garrisons be maintained in Alta California, one at the Santa Barbara Canal and one at the Puerto de San Francisco, in addition to the two already in existence.

Serra was bent on building a mission in honor of the founder of his order, on the port that had long borne the name of San Francisco. To this end a land party had been sent out from Monterey (1772) to explore the lagoon and discover the shortest route to Point Reyes and the best location in its vicinity. Lieutenant Fages and Father Crespi followed the east shore of the bay until they found their progress blocked by an estuary which they called Estrecho Carquines, into which flowed an "unfordable" river (the San Joaquin), dividing them from their goal. Having no boats, they found the water an insuperable obstacle and returned disheartened to Monterey. The project of a mission at this northernmost harbor was discussed in the conference between Bucareli and Father Junípero, and another effort was determined on. The viceroy ordered a more extensive survey to be prosecuted both by land and sea. Rivera y Moncada, who was intrusted with the former expedition, did not get beyond Point Lobos; but the *San Carlos*, deputed to examine the Puerto de San Francisco and ascertain its relation to the interior basin, sailed without difficulty between the two headlands and entered (August 5, 1775) the wonderful harbor, hitherto hidden from the explorers of the coast by the prevailing fogs. The *San Carlos* lay forty days at anchor under Angel Island while surveys were being made and a map of the three arms or bays (now denominated San Pablo, San Francisco, and Suisun) was prepared. Her commander, Ayala, thought he had discovered the best harbor in Spain's dominions, "not one · port but many ports with a single entrance." [70]   There were several *rancherias* along the reedy shores, and the natives came out in their frail *tule* rafts (*balsas*), bringing tribute of fish to the august strangers. Here Bucareli determined to plant not only a mission and a *presidio*, but a colony.

A young soldier, Juan Bautista de Anza, *commandante* of the *presidio* of Tubac in Sonora, had asked to be allowed to explore a route across the unknown stretch of desert and mountain to Monterey. This he offered to do at his own expense, but the advantage of overland communication with the northern post was so evident that the viceroy not only gave the desired permission, but fitted out the expedition (1774). Anza was accompanied by Father Garcés, who had crossed the Devil's Highway and the Colorado Desert three years before, but even so

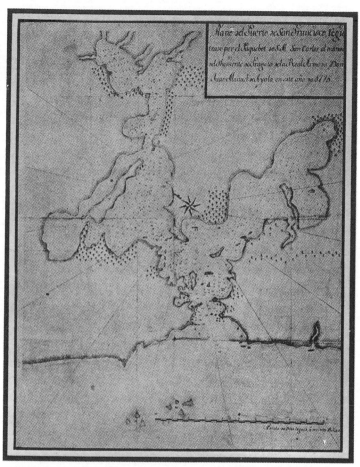

FIRST SURVEY AND MAP OF THE BAY OF SAN FRANCISCO, BY
LIEUTENANT AYALA.

From the original drawing attached to the Log of the *San Carlos*, in
the India Office at Seville. This map had been lost sight of until 1908,
when it was discovered by an agent of the Commercial Club of San
Francisco.

they found it a difficult task. Harassed by drifting sands, alkali water, scant pasturage, and the exhaustion of their animals, they would have perished but for the hospitality of the Yuma Indians and the devotion of a neophyte, escaped from San Gabriel, who served as guide. The trail ascended Coyote Cañon and, crossing the divide which Anza called San Carlos Pass, followed the San Jacinto River to the Santa Ana and so on to San Gabriel Mission.[71] From that point Portolá's route was followed to Monterey.

In 1775 the successful emissary was commissioned by Bucareli to collect a party of settlers and conduct them to the site of the proposed colony. The task was accomplished with an efficiency and despatch unusual in the officials of New Spain. Recruits were attracted by the bait of two years' pay, five years' supplies, and land of their own. The money stipend ($120) was to be paid from the date of enlistment, and the prospective settlers were fitted out with clothing. Only four civilian families were secured, but the twenty-nine married soldiers who were to make up the garrison of the new *presidio* brought up the quota of men, women, and children to two hundred and seven. The transportation of the supplies required one hundred and sixty-five pack mules, and three hundred and forty horses were provided for the people. These, with the herds of (320) cattle destined for food by the way and to stock the settlement, made an unwieldy caravan. Pedro Font accompanied the expedition as chaplain. The company set out in October, 1775, reached the Colorado (*via* San Xavier del Bec and Tucson) without difficulty and, since it was the season of low water, succeeded in fording the river. But the crossing of the Colorado Desert meant terrible suffering. It was now midwinter; rain, hail, and snow fell in dismal alternation; the north wind blew incessantly, and the nights were bitter cold. The misery of the women and children was pitiful; even the men fell ill, and many of the cattle perished with exposure and exhaustion.

Anza acted the triple part of guide, commander, and physician; his courage and patience were unfailing, while his previous experience enabled him to guard against the most serious dangers, the failure of water and pasture. The train was divided into three companies, and the leader of each was instructed to keep a day's march apart from the others so that the scant *aguajes* (water holes) might not be exhausted. Where there were no springs to be found, wells were dug in the sand, and camping places were selected with a view to shelter as well as to grass and water. When possible, wood was collected and fires built for the comfort of the sick and feeble. Eight children were born *en route*, and at each birth the march was delayed till the mother should be able to ride on. Even so, one woman died; but it was on the whole a robust set of people that Anza brought into Coyote Cañon, where water was again abundant. At sight of the snow-covered summits of the San Jacinto Range, the women wept for dread of what was to come; but Anza assured them that the cold would abate as they approached the sea, and the descent

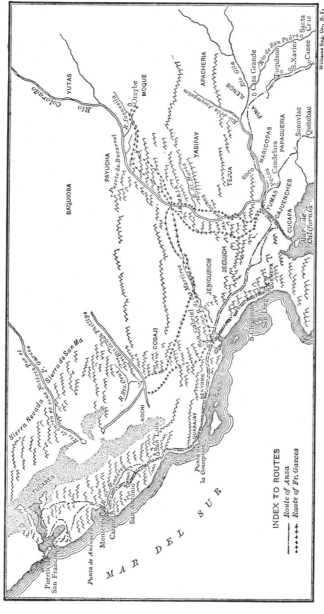

PADRE PEDRO FONT'S MAP OF CALIFORNIA, 1777.

into the valley of the San Jacinto, with its wealth of woods and pastures, cheered their hearts.

As they neared San Gabriel, a detachment was sent forward to warn the *padres* of the approach of the weary caravan.   The men returned in a few days with seventeen fresh horses from the mission herd and the news of the massacre at San Diego.[72]   Anza determined to leave his charge under the protection of the *padres* and join Rivera y Moncada, *commandante* of the California *presidios*, in a punitive expedition against the southern Indians.   During the six weeks thus occupied (January 4 to Febuary 15, 1776), the San Francisco recruits had time to recuperate their strength in the hospitable quarters of the mission.   On February 21 the march was again taken up.   The cavalcade was now on the well-worn mission road (the *Camino Real*), and there were no more hardships.   The Santa Barbara Indians brought them fish, and the *padres* at San Luis Obispo killed a fat deer for their delectation.   At San Carlos the long-expected immigrants were received with open arms. Anza was delighted with the signs of prosperity at Carmel and with the promise of greater things.   Soil and climate seemed adapted to the raising of cattle, grain, and vegetables.   Salmon ran up the river and "sardines" were cast upon the beach.   A boat and seine were all that was necessary to afford abundant food, but no one had thought fit to provide them.

An important part of Anza's commission was the exploration of the shores of San Francisco Bay and the determination of the best site for the *presidio* and the settlement.   With Lieutenant José Moraga and Father Pedro Font, a sufficient escort, and provisions for twenty days, he set out on March 23. The result was a more thoroughgoing examination of the peninsula than had yet been made. A high bluff (Fort Point), overlooking the narrowest part of the entrance, was selected as the best site for the *presidio*, and the irrigable land about Dolores Lagoon was noted as the spot best suited to a mission. Following the east shore of the bay, Anza came to that unfordable river which had turned back his predecessors. There the intrepid captain stopped. To north and south, before his baffled gaze, stretched the vast interior plain that divides the Sierras from the Coast Range, verdant and alluring; but to the desert-bred warrior the San Joaquin was an impassable barrier. Returning to Monterey, Anza gave over his charge to his trusty lieutenant, Moraga, and bade farewell to his little company. As he mounted his horse in the *plaza* and waved adieu to the people who had suffered good and evil fortune so patiently under his leadership, they crowded about him, especially the women, weeping and lamenting, more for his departure than for their own fate. In passionate Spanish fashion they poured out solicitude, prayers, praises, and regret, while the brave captain, protesting that he did not merit such devotion, assured them of the affection he had felt for them since the day of their enlistment, and praised their fidelity, saying that he had never had occasion to fear desertion on the part of the men who had given themselves and their families to this great enterprise. In his report to the viceroy, Anza called attention to their loyalty. "If I may be permitted, I will render testimony to the devotion of these people who in time will be very useful to the monarchy in whose service they have voluntarily abandoned their parents, their country, and all that they hold dear." [73]

It would have been better for this critical venture if Anza had been continued in command; but he promptly returned to his post at Tubac, and Rivera y Moncada became responsible for the future of the colony. This officer was absurdly jealous of Anza and in disgrace with the *padres*, and he set his face against the project of a settlement on San Francisco Bay. Forced by fear of a reprimand from the viceroy, he gave most grudging aid to the building of the *presidio*, not, however, at the point indicated by Anza, but somewhat to the eastward on a semicircular bay where wood and water were more accessible. He refused, however, to have anything to do with Serra's mission. It was erected, notwithstanding, and dedicated on November 7. Unfortunately the site proved unsuited to colonization. The barren hills and sand dunes of the peninsula, swept by trade winds and overhung with fogs, offered little promise for the farmer, and Anza's settlers were fain to find shelter within the adobe walls of the fort, where they spent a year in demoralizing idleness.

Bucareli died in 1779, but Filipe de Neve, whom he had appointed governor of the two Californias (1775) as "a man endowed with wisdom and love for the service," undertook with zeal and intelligence to carry out the viceroy's purpose of colonizing the north coast with Spaniards. In 1777 de Neve removed from Loreto to Monterey, thus indicating that Alta California was regarded as the more important province. On his journey north he visited the several missions and came to the conclusion that, although wheat and corn were being successfully grown at San Gabriel and San Antonio, the mission fields could probably do no more than provide for the increasing number of neophytes. If the *presidios* were ever to be provisioned from the country, California must have agricultural colonies. The Franciscans had selected the most favored locations, but the valleys of the Porciuncula and the Guadalupe were yet available, and colonists for a northern settlement were already at San Francisco. Anza's volunteers who were still idling about the *presidio* were glad to transfer their families to the more promising interior, and nine soldiers of the garrison who knew something about farming threw in their lot with the new venture. In November, 1777, a company of sixty-six men, women, and children, under Moraga's lead, took up their abode at San José de Guadalupe across the river from Santa Clara Mission. Each man was assigned a house lot about a central *plaza*, and irrigable land sufficient for the planting of a *fanega* of corn, also live stock and implements for its cultivation. He was assured support for the initial years, *i.e.* a stipend of ten dollars a month and rations. The river was dammed at public expense and a canal built to irrigate the land suited for ploughing.

De Neve carefully watched this initial experiment and apparently thought it successful, for, in 1781, he issued his famous *reglamento* fixing the conditions

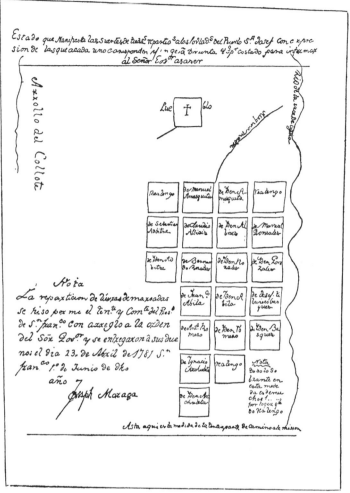

MAP OF PLOUGH LANDS ASSIGNED TO THE NINE SETTLERS OF SAN JOSÉ.

Each man received two *suertes*, two hundred varas square, and one *solar*, thirty varas square, in the *pueblo*.

"A manifest of the plow lands divided among the pobladores of Puerto San Josef with the representation of those which belong to each one [map torn] for the information of Señor Governor Fages.

"The repartition of the foregoing lands was made by me, the lieutenant and commander of the presidio of San Francisco in conformity with the order of his excellency, the Governor, and with all due attention to his desires, the 23rd day of April, 1781. San Francisco, June 1st of the same year. Joseph Moraga. All the residue in this survey is by far [map torn] therefore there remain *realenga* (royal or public lands). Up to this point is the measure of a third part of the road to the mission."

Axxollo del collote=Arroya of the Cayote. Acequeia madre=mother ditch. Rio de la saca de aguä=river from which the water was taken.

134

for all subsequent colonies. The object stated was "to make this vast country . . . useful to the State, by erecting *pueblos* of *gente de razon* (people of reason in distinction from the savages) who, being united, may encourage agriculture, planting, the breeding of cattle and successively the other branches of industry; so that some years hence their produce may be sufficient to provide garrisons of the *presidios* with provisions and horses, thereby obviating the distance of transportation and the risks and losses which the royal government suffers thereby." [74] It was hoped that "the progressive augmentation" of the population of the first *pueblos* would "provide for the establishment of other towns and furnish recruits for the *presidio* companies." The terms were similar to those that had been offered to the San José settlers. Each *poblador* (citizen) was to receive an allowance of $116 for the first two years and $60 for each of the next three,— not in money, but in supplies at cost. A soldier's pay was $220 per year; but since this was largely met in goods at 150 per cent advance on Mexican prices, the position of the colonist was not inferior. To each family was to be allotted, on condition of repayment, ample stock — viz., two mares, two cows, one calf, two sheep, two goats, one yoke of oxen, one pack mule, and a variety of tools — one ploughshare or point, one hoe, one axe, etc. Each man was furnished with two horses, a musket and a leather shield, and he must hold himself equipped to answer the governor's call for the defence of the country. The community was provided with breeding animals and with a forge and anvil and "the necessary tools for carpenter and cast work." Four square leagues of land were assigned to each *pueblo* and surveyed into village, tillage, and pasture lands. The house lots, seventy-five *varas* square,[75] were to be located about the *plaza*, and a series of plough fields, each two hundred *varas* square, was surveyed in the area deemed most fitted for cultivation. Every *poblador* was entitled to a house lot and two *suertes* of irrigable and two of non-irrigable land, the total grant amounting to about twenty-eight acres. Title was assured at the end of five years, provided the settler had in the meantime built his own house and lived in it, planted fruit trees on his land, ten to a *suerte*, doubled his original endowment of cattle and tools, and performed his due proportion of the public works.

Irrigation was a race heritage of the Spaniards. The Moors had taught them how to make good an insufficient rainfall by conducting streams on to the fields, and much of the central and southern portion of the Spanish Peninsula had been rendered productive by artificial canals. These were usually undertaken by the towns for the benefit of their inhabitants, and the common ownership of the source of supply — spring, well, or river — was the ancient Spanish usage. De Neve was therefore proposing nothing new when he made the building of dams and canals a collective obligation, and intrusted the town authorities with their maintenance and with the equable distribution of water. Other common interests were met in this same coöperative fashion. A common field (*proprio*) was set aside for the public sowing. Every *poblador* must perform his share of the common tillage, putting in one *almud* or twelfth of a *fanega* of corn, and the crop went to meet municipal expenses. The pasturing of cattle was not only an individual right, but a common obligation.[76] Two *pobladores* were delegated to the care of the large cattle, mares, asses, and cows; but each proprietor must see to the marking and branding of his own stock, and the record of the branding irons was to be kept by the town authorities.[77] The advances made to the settlers in money, horses, cattle, seed, etc., must be refunded within five years of the first occupation out of the produce of their lands and the increase of their stock. The grain and cattle brought to the *presidio* by each *poblador* were to be credited to his account at the "just" prices established by the governor.[78]

The *pueblo* on the Porciuncula, Nuestra Señora de los Angeles, was founded in 1781. With considerable difficulty twelve families were recruited in Sonora, Sinaloa, and Guadalajara, and brought across the desert to San Gabriel. They were a dubious group. Of the men, but two were full-blooded Spaniards, one was a *mestizo*, four were negroes or mulattoes, and five were Indians, while the women were Indians and mulattoes. Not one of the forty immigrants could sign his own name. The government stipend was probably necessary, yet it seems to have had an enervating effect. The men readily accepted the loan of cattle and money, but they were slow to meet the obligations involved. When the land grants were confirmed in 1786, five of the twelve

settlers were rejected because of indolence. The San
José colonists proved no better farmers. Proud of
their Spanish name and lineage, they regarded labor
as degrading, and managed to hire neophytes from the
missions for such work as might not be avoided. Both
pueblos soon degenerated into lawlessness and vice
and became harbors of refuge for broken-down soldiers
and renegade sailors, who married Indian women and
spent their useless lives in gambling and drunken-
ness. The *alcaldes* were often in league with the
lawbreakers, and the town population, far from being
the strength of the new province, became the most
perplexing problem of the government. By 1790
the number of householders in San José had doubled,
the increase being derived from the neighboring *presidios;* but they were still living in miserable shacks
with palisaded walls and sod roofs, and their crops
and cattle had multiplied but slowly. Los Angeles,
in the same year, boasted twenty-eight families, and
their wheat harvest was greater than that of any
California mission save San Gabriel. The houses
were built of *adobe,* and the town was enclosed
within an *adobe* wall.

The third and last of the *pueblos* was founded by
Governor Borica (1797) near the mission of Santa
Cruz. He besought the viceroy, Branciforte, for
whom the new settlement was named, to send practical farmers, carpenters, masons, tile-makers, tan-
ners, shoemakers, shipwrights, and sailors; but
though land and cattle, supplies and money stipend
were offered, the result was very disappointing.
Only nine families were collected. The men were of

Spanish blood, to be sure, but they were vagrants and petty criminals, not farmers and artisans, and the denizens of Branciforte soon attained a reputation for mischief-making rather than for hard work.

Borica was the last of the statesmanlike governors. He set himself to correct the vicious tendency of the *pueblos* by prohibiting the importation of brandy and *mescal* (a liquor distilled from the century plant) and by deposing the corrupt *alcaldes*. Neglect of tillage was punished by fines and, in case the delinquent proved incorrigible, by forfeiture of land. For the benefit of the oncoming generation, Governor Borica ordered that secular schools should be opened in San José and in Los Angeles, and that parents be compelled to send their children, paying a cent a day for each child.[79] The growing boys of San Diego were apprenticed to a trade, and night schools were maintained for the soldiers, one dollar being withheld from each man's pay on this account. The governor invaded even the sacred precincts of the missions, and directed that the Indians be taught Spanish, in accordance with the royal order. He sent six masons, two carpenters, and three blacksmiths, at government expense, to teach the Spanish children and the natives certain useful trades. The wages offered the weaver were $30 a month, and the governor directed that if he neglected his duties he was to be chained at night. These master workmen were under a five-year contract, and it was hoped they would remain as settlers, but they all returned to Mexico within five years. The boys and girls of the garrison families got little benefit from this instruction, but the neophytes acquired some useful arts. Borica gave assiduous attention to the industrial possibilities of the country. A flour mill was put up at Branciforte and a soap factory at Monterey, while the increase in the number of sheep, as a foundation for woollen manufactures, he made a matter of keen concern. His efforts were ill requited, for all industries languished. In 1800 the combined population of the three towns did not exceed five hundred and fifty : one hundred and seventy in San José, three hundred and fifteen in Los Angeles, and sixty-six in Branciforte. Of the one hundred families represented, thirty had been imported from New Spain, and seventy were those of retired soldiers. Field labor was for the most part performed by *gentiles* (wild Indians), who were paid in grain and blankets which the colonists could ill spare. Nine thousand bushels of wheat were grown each year, and the herds of the *pobladores* had multiplied to 16,500 cattle and horses and one thousand sheep.[80] In this same year, while at the three royal *ranchos* — San Diego, San Francisco, and Monterey — there were but 18,000 head, the eighteen missions possessed 153,000 cattle, horses, and mules, and 88,000 sheep.

Worn out by six years of arduous service, Borica retired in 1800, with the recommendation that the administration of the two Californias be divided. The enormous distances to be traversed and the vexatious delays involved in transmitting orders, the diverse industrial and monastic interests, rendered this measure necessary. The suggestion was adopted, and the first governor of California, Baja, was appointed in 1805. The southern capital was placed at Loreto, and the boundary was fixed at San Miguel.

All the statesmanlike Spaniards who had to do with California urged colonization as essential to the defence of the coast and the permanent prosperity of the province. Witness Costanzó: "The first thing to be thought of, in my opinion, is to people the country. *Presidios* to support the missions are well enough for a time, but there seems to be no end of them. Some missions have been for a hundred years in charge of friars and presidial guards. The remedy is to introduce *gente de razon* among the natives from the beginning. Californians understand this, and clamor for industrious citizens. Each ship should carry a number of families with a proper outfit. The king supplies his soldiers with tools; why not the farmer and mechanic as well? They should be settled near the missions and mingle with the natives. Thus the missions will become towns in twenty-five or thirty years." [81] De Neve was animated by a lofty public spirit, and his scheme of colonization will bear favorable comparison with that of William Penn or Oglethorpe. That he failed to bring to California a thrifty and industrious farming population was due mainly to the fact that there were few such immigrants to be found in New Spain, and the mother country was too remote to furnish colonists. The available Spaniards were, for the most part, discouraged soldiers, unaccustomed to industry, and broken-down adventurers, while the *mestizos* and mulattoes enlisted had inherited the vices rather than the virtues of their progenitors. The burden of obligation to the government was not a light one ($500 for each family imported would be a fair estimate), and the standard of achievement set was too much to expect of men who were bringing an arid soil under cultivation. The climate, moreover, was delightful but enervating, and the very ease with which food and shelter might be had, acted as a deterrent to labor. Finally, the successors of de Neve and Borica gave slight attention to industrial interests, while the *padres*, far from forwarding the growth of the *pueblos*, regarded them with increasing disfavor, disputed their right to pasturage, forbade intermarriage with the neophytes, and even withheld the religious services demanded of the only clergy in the country, until due compensation was tendered.

The colonization of California was undertaken by men of marked ability and devotion. No English colony had more far-sighted and disinterested service than was rendered by Galvez, Bucareli, de Neve, Borica, Portóla, Costanzó, and Anza; but the prime essential in colonial development, settlers of resolution and resource, was lacking, and thus all the heavy expenditure in money and in human energy came to little. Vancouver, the British admiral who visited Monterey in 1792, expressed his astonishment at the petty results of Spanish enterprise in California. "Why such an extent of territory should have been thus subjugated, and after all the expence and labour that has been bestowed upon its colonization turned to no account whatever is a mystery in the science of state policy not easily to be explained." [82]

Causes for Failure

All projects for the colonization of Texas and New Mexico had failed for like reasons. The families transported at so great cost to the valley of the Rio Grande and the land of the Tejas had neglected the cultivation of the soil and fallen into idleness and vice with fatal facility. Nowhere, in fact, did the viceroys succeed in planting self-supporting settlements. The failure of Spain to develop her American possessions shows in marked contrast to the rapid growth of the English colonies on the Atlantic seaboard. The contrast is in part to be accounted for by physical differences. The Spanish colonies were more remote from the mother country and less adapted to the method of cultivation familiar to Europeans, and the initial stages of settlement were more difficult. The population of Spain was stationary, while that of seventeenth-century England was rapidly increasing. So eager were Englishmen for the new industrial opening that farmers and artisans were shipped to the Atlantic coast by planters' associations at the company's cost, whereas the royal treasury was heavily taxed to support the Spanish colonies.

Nevertheless, the attitude of the Spanish government toward its New World plantations was the prime cause of failure. Until the last quarter of the eighteenth century, the mercantile policy was maintained with consistent thoroughness, and the several colonies were administered for the benefit of the mother country and in the interest of the merchants of Seville. Moreover, the grandees who were intrusted with colonial office were not chosen with a view to disinterested and effective service, and, with few exceptions, they regarded such appointment as opportunity for the exploitation of their subjects and the building up of their own fortunes. The same attitude characterized to a marked degree the priests and soldiers sent out to the colonies. Every man of Spanish blood thought himself above the necessity of work and expected to subsist off the forced labor of the natives. The *encomienda* was intended to prevent the enslavement of the Indians, but it led to peonage, a form of slavery which gave the proprietor all its profits with none of its responsibilities. The people imported from the Canary Islands, from Cuba, and from Sonora could not plead race pride as ground for exemption from labor, but they, too, belonged to the non-productive classes, being for the most part convicts, prostitutes, and abandoned children. Lord Bacon had early protested against the sending of such colonists to Virginia. "It is a shameful and unblessed thing to take the scum of the people, and wicked and condemned men, to be the people with whom you plant; and not only so, but it spoileth the plantation; for they will ever live like rogues, and not fall to work, but be lazy and do mischief, and spend victuals, and be quickly weary, and then certify over to their country to the discredit of the plantation. The people wherewith you plant ought

to be gardeners, ploughmen, laborers, smiths, carpenters, joiners, fishermen, fowlers, with some few
apothecaries, surgeons, cooks, and bakers." [83]

Success of the Missions

The only flourishing enterprises in California were
the missions, and here the aspiration of Pope Alexander for the conversion of the aborigines was being
realized. The proselyting zeal of the Franciscans led
them to undertake the most hazardous journeys in
search of farther fields of conquest, and they hesi-
tated at no labor and no self-denial. Their desire
to found new missions, baptize new tribes, and
thereby add to the glory and extend the power of
their Order and of the Church amounted to a passion
and transformed these friars into fearless explorers.
In 1776 Father Escallante of Santa Fé, with a brother
Franciscan and a small party of soldiers, undertook
to find a direct route across the mountains to Monterey. He ascended the Rio Grande to the rivers
that flow westward to form the Colorado, and thence
followed an Indian guide to the land of the Tim-
panagos (Utah Lake). Finding that an impassable
desert lay between this oasis and his goal, Escallante
turned south to the Sevier River. Not until provisions were exhausted and his little party became
mutinous did the resolute *padre* consent to return
to Santa Fé. The natives conducted them to one
of the few practicable crossings of the vast cañon
of the Colorado, a ford still called in memory of
this exploit, *El Vado de los Padres*. Father Francisco Garcés, who accompanied Anza on his first

and second expeditions to California, was not content with this strenuous service. Parting from the expedition at Yuma (1776), alone and on foot, he journeyed up the desolate *mesas* of the Colorado, visiting tribe after tribe, baptizing their children, and subsisting on their bounty, until he came to the Moqui pueblo of Oraibe. He had hoped to recover these apostates to the faith; but the Moquis were suspicious of all Spaniards, and after a brief experience of their inhospitality, Garcés returned to the Yumas. It was his ambition to found a mission at the junction of the Gila and Colorado rivers, and the project was approved by the authorities, for the civilization of the tribe that controlled the route from Sonora to Alta California was a matter of political importance. The outfit furnished, however, was not that of a mission or *presidio*, but that of a *pueblo*: twenty families and twelve laborers with four hundred animals — cattle, sheep, and horses — four priests and a corporal's guard of soldiers (all that could be spared from the garrisons of Altar, Tucson, and San Gabriel), commanded by Rivera y Monçada. Two settlements were planted on the west bank of the Colorado, La Purissima Conception and San Pedro y San Pablo de Bucuñer, but the outlook was ominous. The Yumas had been led to expect gifts of blankets, beads, and tobacco, as compensation for their reception of the white men. They were outraged when they found that no largess was intended, that the cattle were trampling down their scant harvests and eating the mesquite beans on which they relied for food. In the night of July 17, 1781, a concerted

Hopi Pueblos, Cañon of the Colorado River.

attack was made on the two *pueblos*, and the Spaniards were killed to a man. Father Garcés, the fearless friend of the Indian, perished, as well as Rivera y Monçada, who had small faith in the wisdom of attempting to civilize the aborigines. The authorities determined to found no more *pueblos* that could not be adequately protected.[84]

The direct route between New Mexico and California remained a dream throughout the Spanish occupation. Humboldt noted in 1803 that no traveller had yet penetrated from Taos to Monterey, and that, because of the inertness of the Spanish authorities, the trade route that would foster commerce and strengthen both provinces remained to be discovered.

The submissive Coast Indians of California offered a far more promising mission field than the fierce tribes of the interior, and the Franciscans gave their best men to the task of converting them to the faith. The progress from San Diego to San Francisco had been like a crusade. With the achievement of success and the attainment of material comfort, missionary ardor languished. The later *padres* were more zealous for the enrichment of existing foundations, the embellishment of existing churches, than for seeking out new and difficult fields of conquest.

In 1784 Junípero Serra died, worn out by thirty-five years of strenuous mission labor — fifteen years among the Indians of Upper California. Many times he had journeyed by land or by sea the entire length of his apostolate, visiting the several stations, ministering to the needs of priests and soldiers, neophytes and *gentiles*, showing equal concern for little children and powerful *caciques*. He had founded nine missions along the *Camino Real* — San Diego, San Juan Capistrano, San Gabriel, San Buenaventura, San Luis Obispo, San Antonio, San Carlos, Santa Clara, and San Francisco de Dolores — and the number of Indian converts had risen to five thousand. Substantial buildings, churches, dwellings, and storehouses had been raised at the older missions; large areas had been planted to wheat, corn, barley, and beans, and the yield of cereals was 15,800 bushels per year. The two hundred cattle supplied by the government had multiplied with extraordinary rapidity on the native grasses. There were in 1784 more than five thousand mules and cattle, as many sheep, and four thousand two hundred and ninety-four goats. The olive trees planted at San Diego bore abundantly; grapes, pomegranates, and citrus fruits throve in the orchards of San Gabriel and San Juan Capistrano, while in the rich black soil of Santa Clara cereals and garden vegetables flourished, so that the material prosperity of the establishments seemed assured. La Perouse, the French explorer, who visited Monterey in 1785, found the friars of Carmel living in great comfort off the produce of their fields. "The crops of maize, barley, corn, and peas cannot be equalled but by those of Chili," [85] while the yield of wheat was not infrequently one hundred fold.

The labor of the mission farms was performed by the Indians under the immediate supervision of the friars. The neophytes were taught to plough and sow and harvest the grain, to tend the cattle and drive the rude wooden-wheeled ox carts. The more intelligent men were trained as carpenters and masons and smiths. They shaped the adobe bricks and pressed and baked the tile and raised the churches that are still the glory of California. Indians were even found with artistic taste sufficient to execute the frescoes and paintings and the crosses of silver and iron with which the interiors were enriched. The women were taught the domestic arts; baking, spinning, weaving, and the fashioning of garments. The implements were of the rudest and the results meagre, but the whole Christian population was clothed and fed by its own industry. The *padres* had no ambition to do more. Corn was parched in bark baskets over open fires and ground between *metates*, after the primitive Indian fashion. The French explorer gave the establishment of Carmel a hand-mill with which four women could accomplish as much as one hundred with the *metate*. When von Langsdorff visited Carmel twenty years later, this mill had disappeared and no new one had been supplied. The fathers wanted no labor-saving machinery, because they had more labor than they could use, and the neophytes must be kept busy lest they get into mischief. To meet the extraordinary supply of flour required by the occasional vessels that put into Monterey, the women were obliged to work night and day.

Good Catholic though he was, La Perouse thought the régime imposed by the friars unnecessarily severe. The neophytes were allowed no free time.

Their day was portioned out to labor and prayer, as in a monastic establishment. Any deviation from a discipline that must have been extremely irksome to this primitive people was promptly and severely punished. The Frenchmen saw Indians who had been cruelly beaten, lying in the public stocks or loaded down with chains, and they heard the lashes administered to the women and shuddered at their cries for mercy. To the *padres* such punishments seemed a suitable penance and essential to the salvation of the soul that had lapsed from grace; but La Perouse thought the lot of the neophyte differed little from that of the slaves on a West Indian sugar plantation. They were compelled to perform all the labor of the mission establishment and received in return a daily dole of broth and bread and a scant allowance of clothing. No Indian was allowed to leave the premises without permission, and if he did not return at the stipulated time, a posse of soldiers was put on his trail. When caught, the unfortunate man or woman was beaten with fifty stripes. Regarding the situation through the light of the teachings of Rousseau, La Perouse exclaims: "But would it be impossible for an ardent zeal and an extreme patience to make known to a small number of families the advantages of a society based on human rights; to establish among them the right of property so attractive to all men; and by this new order of things, to induce each one to cultivate his field with emulation, or else to devote himself to work of some other kind?" [86]

De Neve believed that the Indians should be

given the normal human inducements to labor and urged that lands be assigned them. He held that the Indians would makê more rapid progress if they were less constrained, and he undertook to provide each Indian village with a tribune who should represent them before the civil authority whenever they were maltreated by the soldiers or unduly oppressed by the friars. Both de Neve and Borica (1795) remonstrated with Lasuen, the second president of the missions, against the "enslavement" of the Indians, and refused to furnish soldiers to recover the runaways. There were two hundred and eighty desertions and two hundred and three deaths — fully half the neophyte population — at San Francisco de Dolores in that single year, and the situation had become intolerable. Borica instanced as causes of this unprecedented mortality insufficient food, the filth in which the people lived, the restraints imposed on men accustomed to the largest freedom, the custom of confining the women and girls in crowded and ill-ventilated *monjas* or female quarters. Lasuen promised that a more humane régime should be introduced — shorter hours and better food, with a more generous allowance of recreation — and the number of lashes that might be inflicted for a single offence was reduced to twenty-five. Dolores was probably an extreme case, but there were serious complaints from the other missions.[87]

The isolated position of the friars and their absolute power over the neophytes, coupled with relentless zeal for the conversion of the *gentiles*, bred abuses that were little in keeping with the saintly devotion of Father Junípero. Vancouver, the English explorer, who visited the missions of San Francisco de Dolores, Santa Clara, Carmel, and Santa Barbara during his three years on the coast (1792–1794), was permitted to see little of these abuses; but to his Protestant mind the *padres* seemed engaged in a hopeless task. The Indians had profited little from the teaching given them; they were still living in frail wicker huts, filthy and squalid beyond description, and gave few signs of real progress. At Santa Clara, the fathers were then building adobe cottages, with garden ground attached, for the more promising neophytes, in the hope of inciting them to cleanliness and industry. But even here, at the most progressive of the mission farms, the tillage was of the rudest. "By the help of a very mean and ill-contrived plough drawn by oxen, the earth is once slightly turned over, and smoothed down by a harrow; in the month of November or December, the wheat is sown in drills or broadcast on the even surface, and scratched in with the harrow; this is the whole of their system of husbandry, which uniformly produces them in July or August an abundant harvest." The grain was threshed out on an open-air floor by the tread of oxen. Vancouver noted the herds of cattle and horses on the hills about the Bay and marvelled at their fecundity and the slight cost of rearing them. The Indians made excellent herders, and the fifteen head of cattle brought to Santa Clara in 1778 had multiplied a hundred fold in the fifteen years' interval.[88]

When von Langsdorff [89] visited Santa Clara in 1806, he found the Indian apprentices weaving a coarse woollen cloth sufficient for their own clothing. Besides the shops for blacksmiths and carpenters, there were soap-works and salt-works and vats for the refining of tallow, and a considerable traffic was carried on with San Blas in wool, hides, salt, tallow, soap, and butter. Von Langsdorff had seen the Kodiak thralls of the Russian-American Fur Company, and he marvelled at the excellence of the food furnished the neophytes; but he was no less astonished when he came upon a reclaimed runaway who had been bastinadoed and who hobbled about with an iron weight fastened to his foot. Kotzebue, the commander of the Russian exploring expedition fitted out by Count Krusenstern, visited Dolores mission ten years later and found the Indians housed in adobe huts, but still wretched and dirty. Both sexes were obliged to labor to the limit of their strength. The men did all the work of the fields, and the harvest was delivered to the missionaries and stored in magazines, the laborers receiving only so much as was necessary for their subsistence. Out of the thousand neophytes, three hundred died every year, and only vigorous missionary raids on the interior tribes kept up the quota of laborers. Ten different tribes were represented at this mission, speaking as many different languages, and all were but imperfectly acquainted with Spanish. They could therefore understand little more of the religious teaching than the forms. "The missionaries assured us that it was difficult to instruct them, on account

of their stupidity; but I believe that these gentlemen do not give themselves much trouble about
it." "California is a great expense to the Spanish
government, which derives no other advantage from
it than that every year a couple of hundred heathens
are converted to Christianity, who, however, die very
soon in their new faith, as they cannot accustom
themselves to the different mode of life." The unsympathetic Russian thought the fault lay in that
the *padres* "do not take pains to make men of them
before they make them Christians." [90]

Junípero Serra had hoped to make men of the
savages to whom he preached the gospel, and intended that the neophytes should be assigned land
of their own as soon as they were qualified to use it
to advantage; but the later Franciscans postponed
the emancipation of their charges from time to
time, and it was not easy to convince them that
these childlike people needed any other incentive to
labor than the arbitrary command of their superiors.
Meantime the natives, *gentile* and convert alike,
protested that they were robbed of the land that
had been theirs from time immemorial. It was
quite true that the Franciscans had no valid title
to anything more than the usufruct of the vast
tracts which were tilled and pastured under their
direction, neither had they any claim to the labor of
the Indians—the law expressly forbade the granting
of *encomiendas* to ecclesiastics — but they had forgotten the terms of their tenure. Galvez and Bucareli
had planned that the natives of California should
be led to form self-supporting communities like

those of New Mexico. Fages, de Neve, Borica, and other conscientious officials had protested that justice and the law required that every neophyte should be emancipated and placed on land of his own after serving a ten-year term. But the friars were the strongest party in the new province, and their policy prevailed. The neophytes were kept in a state of tutelage that offered few paths of advance.

Such population statistics as are available seem to show that, although subject to occasional variations, the neophyte population was practically stationary here as in Texas and New Mexico. There were twenty thousand neophytes in Vancouver's day, and Governor Sola's census for 1818 reported the same figure. According to Beechey, there were no more in 1825. The mission Indians were, in fact, rapidly dying off, but the labor force was as rapidly recruited from the wild tribes of the interior. Proselyting bands, soldiers and Indians, were sent up the Sacramento and San Joaquin rivers to bring in new converts. Since the leaders were rewarded in proportion to the number obtained, their methods were often unscrupulous. Foreign visitors heard shocking tales of these kidnapping expeditions.

The Franciscan régime was no more favorable to colonization, and the Spanish population increased but slowly. Von Humboldt's estimate for 1803 was thirteen hundred whites and *mestizos*, and he attributed the tardy development of the country to the rigid military requirements and the opposition of the friars. "The population of New California would have augmented still more rapidly if the laws by which the Spanish *presidios* had been governed for ages were not directly opposite to the true interests of both mother country and colonies. By these laws the soldiers stationed at Monterey [for example] are not permitted to live out of their barracks and to settle as colonists. The monks are generally averse to the settlement of colonists of the white cast, because being *people who reason (gente de razon)* they do not submit so easily to a blind obedience as the Indians." [91]   La Perouse thought Alta California as promising a country as Virginia, notwithstanding its remoteness from Europe. In his opinion, its progress was retarded by celibacy and despotism. Good government and freedom of commerce would, in his opinion, "speedily procure it some settlers." [92]

Commercial Restrictions

Until 1800 there was no trade between California and the outside world except that carried on by the transport which brought the annual consignment of goods ordered for the missions and *presidios*, and these were sold through the appointed agents at exorbitant prices. No commerce was permitted with other vessels, even though they bore the Spanish flag. Exception was made in favor of the Manila galleon, which occasionally put into Monterey for supplies; but only under stress of weather and necessity for repairs or shortage of wood, water, or food, was a foreign vessel admitted, and even so, aid must be refused if, after investigation, the necessity was not evident. Aliens were never permitted on shore except by express order. The transports carried back to San Blas some salt and salted meat and a few otter skins, the surplus products of the missions. Borica urged that the government send goods direct to the *pueblos*, taking grain in exchange, and the project was authorized by the crown; but through the duplicity or inertia of the officials, it failed of execution. The effect of these restrictions on industrial development was well-nigh disastrous. Missing the stimulus of a good market for their produce, the *pobladores* cultivated no more land than would supply their own immediate needs, while the heavy cost of European goods forced them to get on without the implements and machinery that would have enabled them to manufacture on their own account. A mission establishment could store its produce and await the arrival of a trading vessel, but the isolated farmer could not avail himself of such a chance. The needs of the *presidios* were met by *ranchos del rey* at San Diego and at Monterey.

La Perouse and Vancouver were cordially received at Dolores because they were engaged in scientific explorations and were therefore indorsed from Madrid. Both were liberally supplied with provisions from the mission stores, the only payment permitted being some tools, utensils, seeds, etc., which the *padres* gratefully received and utilized in the improvement of their gardens. Vancouver thought the Bay of San Francisco "as fine a port as the world affords; failing only in the convenience of obtaining wood and water." [93] He noticed that the Spanish commanders were content to take on a very inferior quality of the latter necessity, and he attributed the prevalence of scurvy on their ships to carelessness in this regard. The British navigator was astonished to find no trading vessels in this "spacious port." There was literally no craft to be seen except an old rowboat and the frail rush canoes of the Indians. Yet there was every incentive for an extensive trade in tallow, hides, and cattle, in timber and otter skins. Von Langsdorff was as much impressed as Vancouver had been with the neglect of water transportation. Here were three missions, Santa Clara, San José and Dolores, gathered about the Bay, and yet the frequent communication between them and the *presidio* was carried on by a circuitous land route. It seemed to him "incredible that, in not one of them . . . is there a vessel or boat of any kind." [94] The Spaniards preferred to go three times the distance on horseback and to transport their produce in ponderous, slow-moving ox carts. At land travel, on the other hand, they were experts. "From St. Francisco any one may travel with the greatest safety even to Chili: there are stations all the way kept by soldiers." [95] When Krusenstern came in through the narrow strait to San Francisco Bay in April, 1806, he was hailed from Fort Point [96] through a speaking trumpet and, since by this time the old rowboat had disappeared, he could not get into communication with the *commandante*, Don José Arguello, until he sent one of the launches off to fetch him. De Resanoff desired to procure a cargo of provisions for the posts of the Russian-American Fur Company, offering cloth,

THE PRESIDIO OF SAN FRANCISCO IN 1817.

leather, shoes, and iron implements — sheep-shears, whip-saws, etc. — in exchange. The monks were eager to sell their surplus products for these much-needed articles; but neither the *commandante* nor the governor nor yet the viceroy had authority to allow the trade. After much demur, de Resanoff was permitted to purchase $24,000 worth of wheat, flour, salt meat, salt, tallow, and soap from the monks, the governor consenting to serve as go-between and becoming personally liable for the transaction. The proposition that a regular trade be established between the Russian settlements and California was referred to Madrid, where it was consigned to oblivion.

Under the Spanish régime, American vessels rarely visited Californian ports because of the well-known risk of confiscation. Boston fur traders, bound for the northwest coast, occasionally put in for supplies; but they did not meet with an encouraging reception. The *Otter* (Captain Ebenezer Dorr) stopped at Monterey (1796) to leave some stowaways from Botany Bay, the first English settlers. The *Eliza* was ordered out of San Francisco Bay (1798) after securing a meagre allowance of provisions. The *Betsey* (Captain Winship) put into San Diego for wood and water (1800); but the *Alexandria* and the *Lelia Byrd*, smugglers attempting to purchase otter skins at this port in 1803, were roughly handled. Cleveland, supercargo on the *Lelia Byrd*, had circumnavigated South America, touching at Valparaiso where he narrowly escaped seizure and at San Blas where, by the special grace of the viceroy, he secured permission to sell $10,000 worth of goods. Having purchased a quantity of sea-otter skins (1600) and learning that more might be had at San Diego, the venturesome Yankee made for that port. The *commandante* had several hundred skins, confiscated from the *Alexandria*, and private individuals were eager to dispose of more. In the attempt to get hold of these, Cleveland came into conflict with the authorities and therefore deemed it best to leave the harbor. As the *Lelia Byrd* sailed out of the narrow entrance, she was fired upon from the fortification at Point Loma, but passed out uninjured. Her return fire scattered the garrison and reduced the Spanish battery to silence. The *Lelia Byrd* returned to San Diego in 1804, and other Yankee vessels followed in her wake. Captain Shaler estimated their annual purchases of furs at $25,000.

At the close of the War of 1812, Yankee traders began to frequent the California coast, and their goods—hardware, ammunition, cloth, and blankets— were readily taken by both friars and officials. The *contrabandistas* ran great risks of being captured by Mexican privateers or by the California *commandantes*, and more than one cargo was confiscated and the ship's officers thrown into prison (*e.g.* Captain G. W. Ayres of the *Mercury*, 1814; Captain Smith of the *Albatross*, 1816). But the officials grew lax as the needs of the community increased, and after 1818 foreign traders had no difficulty at any of the California ports. Governor Sola established a tariff of duties on exports and imports which he levied on his single authority.

The struggle for independence had no champions in California. The white population, being almost wholly made up of the mission fathers and the *presidio* garrisons, declared for the king, and only uncertain rumors of the far-away conflict reached their ears; but a very apparent and bitterly lamented effect of the ten years' war was the failure of supplies. The San Blas transport was captured by the insurgents (1811), the hard-pressed viceroy could send no reënforcements, and the wages of officers and soldiers fell far in arrears. Food and clothing were furnished on credit by the mission fathers, the Spanish officials thereby incurring a heavy obligation which was never repaid. Governor Sola had been loud in his protestations of loyalty to Spain and expressed unmitigated contempt for the revolutionists; but he could not defend his position. The *presidios* were quite untenable; a few undisciplined soldiers cowering behind crumbling walls, a dozen rusty howitzers and some antique muskets liable to explode when fired, made up the defences of five harbors and two hundred leagues of scantily peopled coast. When in March, 1822, a war vessel sailed into Monterey flying the Mexican colors, Sola was fain to pull down the Spanish flag and run up the tricolor without striking one blow for his sovereign.

Luis Arguello, Sola's successor, the first republican governor, was a *hijo del pais* and a man of great force and originality. In 1805, while hardly more than a boy, he undertook an expedition into the interior, hoping to find a route to Santa Fé. His horseback party rode up the Sacramento until they faced the lofty profile of the Sierras, and then, the snow-clad summits seeming an insurmountable barrier, they turned back. When this venturesome man succeeded his father as *commandante* at San Francisco (1806–1822), he wished to rebuild the ruinous *presidio*. With the aid of a carpenter deserted from a British vessel, he built a launch, trained a crew, and succeeded in towing over a raft of timber from San Rafael. This daring deed was sharply criticised by Governor Sola, who charged Arguello with insubordination and possible treason. No man could want a boat on the Bay of Francisco except for the purpose of smuggling or of carrying on illicit trade with the Russian settlements ! The launch was seized and taken to Monterey, where it proved so convenient that it was never returned. No sooner was he governor of California (1823–1825) than Arguello negotiated an agreement with the Russian-American Fur Company by which they were to turn over half the otter skins taken for the privilege of fishing in the Bay. The same untrammelled official opened a trade with Bodega, which, though illicit, had great advantages for both parties. Such a man was not likely to feel bound by trade regulations enacted by the turbulent government at the City of Mexico.[97] Foreign commerce was a necessity for California, and he welcomed the first opportunity to supply his people with the manufactures they so much needed. In 1823 the *Rover* of Boston, Captain Cooper, came to Monterey with a cargo of cottons and other New England goods, and Governor Arguello, in defiance of the law but with the full approval of the Californians, gave him license to trade. The profits on this transaction were so evident that Arguello undertook a venture on government account. He purchased the ship, loaded her with otter skins, and sent her to Canton under Cooper's command. She brought back a cargo of silks, cottons, etc., valued at $12,000. The way was open for a commerce with China that would have rivalled the old Manila trade; but Arguello was soon supplanted, and none of his successors cared to follow up the opportunity. Arguello, however, opened a customhouse at Monterey, and his example in admitting Yankee goods was imitated by his successors.

For years to come, California was provided with manufactures by Boston skippers who, having learned how to placate the officials, carried on a highly remunerative trade, exchanging groceries, cottons, cutlery, and liquors for otter and beaver skins. These last, carried to China, were sold to advantage, and a cargo of teas and silks was taken on for the Boston market. It was a round-the-world commerce that netted ten and twenty per cent on the capital invested, but the supply of furs was soon exhausted. In 1822 W. A. Gale, representing Bryant & Sturgis, a Boston firm, opened a mercantile house in Monterey. He began the collection and exportation of hides, a commodity much in demand among the shoe manufacturers of New England, and of which California had superabundance. In this same year John Beggs & Co., merchants of Lima, succeeded in negotiating a three-year contract with Arguello under which their vessels were to take all hides and tallow offered by the missions, paying in money or goods at stipulated prices. Their agent, W. E. P. Hartnell, made his headquarters at Monterey. An attempt to pack beef for a distant market was made in 1824. Learning that California cattle were killed for tallow and hides alone and the carcasses wasted, Hartnell opened a packing house. Twenty salters and coopers, Irish and Scotch, manufactured on the spot the salt and barrels needed, and several cargoes of excellent pickled beef were forwarded to Lima; [98] but the Peruvian government, having no funds, was unable to fulfil its part of the contract, and the venture failed. Hartnell resided in Monterey as the representative of Beggs & Co. and for many years maintained an enterprising mercantile establishment, selling supplies to the *padres* and shipping to Lima the tallow taken in exchange.[99] Soon the southern missions demanded a share in this commerce, desiring to find a market for their surplus stock, and new concessions had to be made. In 1829 ships chartered by Gale and Hartnell were accorded license to touch at San Diego, San Pedró, Santa Barbara, and San Francisco for cargoes. Within a few years the five ports were thrown open to all comers, and the trade in hides and tallow was well under way.

From 1825–1834, the height of its prosperity, the lion's share of the hide trade was in the hands of a few Boston merchants. Dana's full and accurate description of the traffic is so well known that no quotations need be given here. During his two years on the coast (1835–1836) there were five

FISHERMAN'S WHARF, MONTEREY.

ARGUELLO'S CUSTOM HOUSE, MONTEREY.

American "droghers"[100] engaged in exchanging goods for hides; three carried Mexican or Peruvian colors, though their owners were Scotch and Italian, and three hailed from Oahu. The handicaps on the trade were already becoming apparent. A captain had to spend two or three years soliciting at the *ranchos* all the way from San Diego to San Francisco. The weight of the hides had dwindled to half, because the *rancheros* killed the animals too young. They never took the trouble to cure the skins, so every shipload must be carried to San Diego to be salted and dried. California hides, moreover, were more difficult to tan than those from Buenos Ayres and brought less in the Boston market. When Sir George Simpson, governor of the Hudson's Bay Company, visited the Coast in 1841 there were sixteen vessels, mostly Americans, engaged in this "drogher" trade; but the annual output of hides had fallen from 100,000 (1838) to 30,000,— not enough to fill the holds of two first-class ships. The effect of the consequent competition for cargo was to raise the price of hides and the costs of the voyage.

The first British whaler put into San Francisco Bay for provisions in 1820, the Americans followed in 1823, and this harbor was for some years a favorite stopping-place on the homeward voyage. The *presidio* bay lay directly in the sweep of the tides and was not a safe anchorage. Merchant ships preferred Yerba Buena, a roadstead that offered shelter from the west winds and neighborhood to the missions of Santa Clara and San José; but the whalers made for Sausalito, because the water there was particularly good, and William A. Richardson, the ex-mate of a British whaling vessel, had a ranch near by from which they could obtain supplies. In spite of the abundant resources of the region, the whalers soon found they could provision at less cost in the Sandwich Islands. The Mexican government imposed vexatious restrictions and heavy tonnage fees, while a ship could enter the port of Oahu duty free.

Captain Beechey, of the British ship *Blossom*, visited San Francisco Bay in 1826 in the course of his explorations of the North Pacific, and was astonished to find "in a harbor sufficiently extensive to contain all the British navy" no vessel except seven American whalers come in for supplies. His ship was challenged from Fort Point by "a soldier who protruded a speaking trumpet through one of the embrasures and hailed us in a stentorian voice"; but since there was no boat belonging to the garrison, the *commandante* came out to inspect the papers by Beechey's courteous aid. The *Blossom* was allowed to anchor off "a small bay named Yerba Buena," but the nearest trading establishment was at Monterey. Provisions were obtainable from the near-by missions, — flour, beef, vegetables, and salt; but the negotiations must be carried on through the governor, who pocketed the profits. The only buildings visible were the dilapidated adobes of the *presidio* and Dolores Mission. There were no cultivated fields about the Bay, and the garrison was still dependent on the farms of Santa Clara and San José for supplies. Beechey thought it a great pity that "so fine a country, abounding in all that is essential to man, should be allowed to remain in such a state of neglect." "With the exception of the missions and *pueblos*, the country is almost uninhabited; yet the productive nature of the soil, . . . and the immense plains of meadow land, . . . show with how little trouble it might be brought into high cultivation by any farmers who could be induced to settle there." [101] On the road between San Francisco and Monterey there were but three ranch houses and these of the poorest description.

"The trade of Upper California at present consists in the exportation of hides, tallow, *manteca* [butter], horses to the Sandwich Islands, grain for the Russian establishments at Sitka and Kodiak, and in the disposal of provisions to whale-ships and other vessels which touch upon the coast, — perhaps a few furs and dollars are sent to China. The importations are dry goods, furniture, wearing-apparel, agricultural implements, deal boards, and salt; and silks and fireworks from China for the decoration of the churches and celebration of the saints' days." [102] The prices of all imported goods were high, because the supply was always short of the demand and the costs of transportation great. To the risks and delays of the voyage round the Horn must be added, not only the import duties (forty-two per cent), but the tonnage charges ($1.50 per ton) and the expense of landing the cargo. Under the vexatious navigation act devised by the Mexican Assembly, every foreign vessel must put into Monterey, present the required papers, and pay duty on all goods destined for sale. Under no circumstances might a trader put into an earlier port and break stowage. He must discharge the whole cargo at Monterey and reload for his run along the coast. Since at no place in California could a full cargo be disposed of, the trader must go from port to port, paying the heavy tonnage fees at each new entry. The commerce could be prosecuted only by evasion, and it soon became customary for a ship from the Sandwich Islands or Boston to anchor off-shore under the lea of a convenient island, while her cargo was being conveyed in lighters to the near-by settlements.

It seemed to the Englishman passing strange that the Californians did not make for themselves the articles for which the raw material was at hand. "They were actually living upon the sea-coast and amongst forests of pine, and yet were suffering themselves to buy salt and deal boards at exorbitant prices." [103] "They were purchasing sea-otter skins at twenty dollars apiece, whilst the animals were swimming about unmolested in their own harbours; and this from the Russians, who are intruders upon their coast, and are depriving them of a lucrative trade; and again, they were paying two hundred dollars for carts of inferior workmanship, which, with the exception of the wheels, might have been equally well manufactured in their own country." [104] California combined all the essentials of prosperity in climate, soil, forests, plains overrun with cattle, excellent ports, and navigable rivers. "Possessing all these advantages, an industrious population alone seems requisite to withdraw it from the obscurity in which it has so long slept under the indolence of the people and the jealous policy of the Spanish government. Indeed, it struck us as lamentable to see such an extent of habitable country lying almost desolate and useless to mankind, whilst other nations are groaning under the burthen of their population." [105]

Beechey expressed his conviction that the Mexican government must institute an economic reform, or some other power would take control of this promising province. It was "of too much importance to be permitted to remain long in its present neglected state." There was general discontent with the Mexican administration. The governor's salary was eleven years in arrears, and the soldiers' allowances had long been withheld. By way of meeting immediate necessities, a cargo of cigars had been shipped to Monterey on which the men might draw against their back pay! Under the Spanish régime, soldiers were enlisted for ten years, at the end of which term they might retire to one of the *pueblos* and be assigned a portion of land for the support of their families. This privilege was now withheld. Retiring soldiers were allowed to pasture stock on the public lands, but could acquire no permanent title, — a restriction that effectually prevented their becoming farmers.

The Mexican government was far from appreciating the value of this northernmost province and, proposing to utilize it as a penal colony, sent shiploads of convicts to Monterey and Santa Barbara to serve out their terms at public labor. These were sometimes artisans condemned for slight offences and in such case became useful colonists; but the greater part added a difficult element to the scant white population. A formal protest drawn up by the law-abiding citizens and indorsed by the territorial deputation (1829) had its effect. No more shiploads of criminals were sent from Mexico; but the soldiers furnished to the garrisons were little better, being for the most part vagabonds and ne'er-do-weels, recruited from the slums of the cities. In these same years a considerable number of foundlings and destitute children was despatched to the northern posts in the expectation that the boys would be bound out to service and the girls married to soldiers and ex-convicts. Indeed, more than one governor urged that marriageable maidens be furnished to mate with such dubious characters, as the *padres* refused to allow their Indian charges to wed.

No one of the mushroom presidents who rose and fell at the City of Mexico regarded California as a possession that was worth the cost of protection. Fully absorbed in maintaining their precarious hold on the reins of government, they could sacrifice neither men nor money to the defence of this remote territory. In 1829 the military forces of the two Californias numbered four hundred and seventy men, and this feeble, undisciplined, and badly armed garrison was divided among half a dozen *presidios*. The forts had not been repaired nor the ordnance replenished since Borica's day. In case of foreign invasion, the people would have no recourse but to retreat to the interior, carrying their portable possessions and driving their cattle and flocks before them. The weakness of the garrison rendered a political revolution a matter of astonishing ease.

The frequent changes of government at the Mexican capital, the discontent of the ill-paid garrisons in California, the rivalry of north and south fomented by the ambitious politicians of Los Angeles and Monterey, furnished frequent occasion for insurrection, and an enterprising leader with a score of followers had no difficulty in putting to flight three times the number of regular troops. These battles were marvellous displays of bluster and musketry with a minimum of fatalities. All concerned had a wholesome distaste for bullet wounds, and were accustomed to capitulate with a facility and cheer that proved them philosophers rather than heroes. California should have bred a Cervantes to record these burlesque encounters. One dominant motive is discernible throughout the complex history, — dislike of the unsympathetic Mexican officials and desire to secure the privilege of self-government.

The Centralist revolution at the City of Mexico (1834) was keenly resented in the northern states. A demand for home rule had been gaining ground, and the attempt to bring the provincials under more effective control and to impose direct taxes was met by armed resistance in all the northern provinces. In California the insurrection was led by Alvarado, a *hijo del pais*, and one of the ablest men in the country. His political ideal was George Washington, and he seems to have aspired to imitate the American revolt against arbitrary government. The parallel was not maintained. Once in possession at Monterey (1837), Alvarado effected a compromise with the Mexican government, and affairs were managed much as before. He and his relatives, the Valléjos, arrogated to themselves all the perquisites of power, but the people had the satisfaction of being plundered by men born in California.

Secularization of the Missions

The secularization of missions of more than ten years standing was ordered by the Spanish Cortes in 1813. Although this was a project of the Revolutionists, the edict was confirmed by Ferdinand VII in 1820. The order was received with submission by the *padres* of Alta California, and they declared themselves ready to withdraw as soon as secular priests were provided to take charge of the neophytes. This being as yet impracticable, the Franciscans were permitted to remain. In 1825 the secularization of the missions was undertaken by the Mexican government. Aside from the large financial considerations involved, it was believed that the Indians would be sooner civilized if they were freed from their quasi bondage and given a property interest in the land they tilled.

The *padres* were even more disaffected toward the Mexican government than the laymen of California. The decree of 1829, exiling Spaniards from all Mexican states, had removed the ablest of the Franciscans. The salaries furnished by the royal government were withdrawn, the Pious Fund [106] which had been devoted to the conversion of the Indians was turned into the republican treasury, while a tithe of the mission revenue was required in support of the civil government. The limitless cattle ranges were abridged to an allotment of fifteen square miles to each mission, and, most grievous innovation of all, Governor Echeandia proposed a gradual emancipation of the neophytes.[107] The *padres* opposed the plan, since it deprived them of their best laborers, and no Californian had much confidence in the ability of the mission Indians to take care of themselves. They had been so long under tutelage, the "nurslings" of friars, to use von Langsdorff's phrase, that they had lost the capacity for self-direction. The few men already set free from mission bondage had made unhappy use of their liberty. They would not work, but idled away their days like boys out of school. They drank and gambled and ran into debt, forfeiting their clothing and implements and even their land to sharpers who led them into temptation. The freed men became so obnoxious that the missionaries were requested to take them back, and the most incorrigible were condemned to hard labor on the wharf at Monterey. Sola thought this experiment in the civilization of the Indians a costly failure. The neophytes were "lazy, indolent, and disregardful of all authority, costing for half a century millions of *pesos* without having made in that time any recompense to the body politic.[108]

In 1833 the Federal Congress ordered that the missions of the two Californias be secularized. Curates were to supersede the *padres*, their salaries being paid out of the Pious Fund, and the mission chapel was to become the parish church. A convenient residence for the priest was provided, and the remaining buildings were to be utilized as schools, workshops, court-house, etc. The land and cattle were to be distributed among the neophytes. This could hardly be regarded as confiscation, for the Franciscans had no titles to the mission lands, and the capital invested had been drawn from the Pious Fund and from the royal treasury. If labor constitutes the best claim to possession, the mission Indians were fairly entitled to the property.

The administration of this decree fell into the hands of Governor Figueroa, an able and patriotic man, who, having Aztec blood in his veins, was inclined to do justly by the natives. He had had some experience of emancipation, having established three Indian *pueblos* (San Dieguito, Las Flores, and San Juan Capistrano) in connection with the three southernmost missions. The object of Figueroa's regulations of 1834 was to render the emancipated neophytes self-supporting citizens. The mission lands were to be apportioned to the resident Indians, each adult man receiving a plough field from one hundred to four hundred *varas* square, according to the size of his family, a building lot in the *pueblo*, the right to pasture cattle in the commons, and his due quota of cattle, implements, and seed. One-half of the cattle and other movables belonging to each mission was to be divided among its neophytes; the remaining half was left "at the disposal of the supreme Federal government." These, together with the unoccupied land, gardens, orchards, and so forth were to be worked by the Indians under direction of a major-domo appointed by the governor, and the revenue was to be applied to the payment of the obligations of the mission, the salary of the curate and major-domo, the expenses of public worship, the maintenance of police and schools. A commissioner was sent to each mission to take a detailed inventory of the property and a census of the population, to distribute among the neophytes their portion of the lands, cattle, etc., and to instruct them as to their rights and duties. Meantime the friars were forbidden to sell any produce or to kill more cattle than were needed for immediate subsistence.

The wealth of the missions had reached its climax in 1833. The live stock exceeded the possibility of numerical count, but was estimated by competent men at 424,000 cattle, 62,500 horses and mules, and 321,500 sheep, including a few hogs and goats. The annual grain crop was 122,500 *fanegas*, or double that amount in bushels. The wheat crops alone amounted to 120,000 bushels. The money income of the missions was believed to be great, but the *padres* endeavored to conceal the facts. Reckoning that one-fourth the herd was killed each year and that the value of hide and tallow would average $5 to $6 per animal, the sales from the missions herds alone must have brought in between $500,000 and $600,000 in the year 1833. The *padres*, moreover, had an assured labor force in their thirty thousand neophytes. At San Gabriel, the richest establishment in the two Californias, there were three thousand neophytes, 105,000 cattle, 40,000 sheep, 20,000 horses, and the annual grain crop exceeded 40,000 bushels. Two grist-mills and extensive workshops were kept busy. The vineyards, olives, and orange orchards more than supplied the needs of the fathers, while a ship was despatched to San Blas every year laden with olive oil, jute, and linen, and another to Lima with a cargo of soap and tallow. To the harbor of San Pedro and the "droghers," the Indians carted each year 35,000 hides. In the storehouse belonging to San Gabriel were $40,000 worth of European goods. At the beautiful mission of San Luis Rey there were 100,000 sheep and 50,000 cattle and horses, and the thirty-five hundred Indians were employed in well-developed industries, — blacksmith shops, tanneries, soap-works, distilleries, salt-works, woollen, cotton, and jute factories. Such an industrial centre may fitly be compared with a monastic establishment of mediæval Europe or with Hampton Institute. It might have been as productive for its beneficiaries but for two handicaps — the backward character of the Coast Indians and the despotic nature of the Franciscan discipline which thwarted individual development and rendered the neophyte incapable of self-direction.

The result of the law of 1834 was far from consistent with Figueroa's admirable plan. Notwithstanding the prohibition, a wholesale slaughter of cattle was begun for the purpose of converting the chief wealth of the missions into cash. One hundred thousand head were killed in a single year (1834), and the proceeds from the sale of hides and tallow was reckoned at $1,000,000. The wastes of this horrible *matanza* were enormous, and the influence of the defiance of law reacted to the injury of the *padres*. Moreover, the neophytes were quite unequal

SAN CARLOS MISSION ON CARMEL RIVER, 1830.

MISSION OF SAN LUIS REY, THE MOST BEAUTIFUL IN CALIFORNIA, 1841.

to the responsibilities thrust so suddenly upon them. Freedom from restraint gave opportunity for idleness and vice. Portilla, the commissioner of San Luis Rey, reported that his people refused to work in the common fields, neglected even their own crops, and wandered away to the mountains with their horses and mules, after having killed the cattle assigned to them. The improvidence of the Indians soon made it necessary to forbid them to sell or mortgage land or cattle and to place them under the tutelage of major-domos. In 1836, Governor Chico ordered that every Indian found absent from his *pueblo* without a license should be arrested and sentenced to labor on the public works.

The determination of the Franciscans to save something from the wreck of their vast possessions and the incompetence of the Indians were in a large measure responsible for the ruin of the mission industries; but the ultimate failure of the scheme of secularization was due to the unscrupulous greed of the commissioners. Figueroa himself was free from blame, but few of his agents neglected the opportunity to enrich themselves out of this tempting spoil. By the sale of hides, tallow, wool and other products, by sequestering cattle, horses, and tools, by contracting debts in the name of the mission, a shrewd administrator might accumulate a fortune at the expense of his trust. No one of the twenty-one missions escaped this systematic looting. "A few years sufficed to strip the establishments of everything of value and leave the Indians, who were in contemplation of law the beneficiaries of secularization, a shivering crowd of naked and, so to speak, homeless wanderers." [109]

Governor Alvarado undertook to stay the impending ruin and to conserve to California the accumulations of seventy years' missionary labor. In 1839 he issued regulations for the control of the administrators. An annual financial report was required, stating the revenues and obligations of each mission. No sales were to be made or debts contracted or paid without express authorization from the governor; no cattle were to be slaughtered except what were necessary for the support of the Indians. The horses and mules were not to be traded off for woollen goods, but the neophytes were to be induced to labor by moderate penalties, — notably in the manufacture of cloth, lest this important industry perish. A census of the emancipated Indians was required, both those occupied on land of their own and those employed by the administrator, and no white settlers or *gentiles* were to be admitted to the mission *pueblos* while the natives remained. Finally, the newer and less developed missions of the north, San Rafael, Sonoma, Carmel, Santa Cruz, Soledad, and San Juan Bautista, were brought under the immediate control of the government. In the following year, Alvarado deposed the administrators with their high salaries and indefinite powers, and appointed a *visitador general* to whom the immediate superintendent or major-domo should be responsible. He selected for this difficult task W. E. P. Hartnell, the English merchant of Monterey. Hartnell had been seventeen years in California, was a naturalized citizen, and had travelled up and down the coast many times. He took a more disinterested view of the situation than did most Californians, and his report was a melancholy recital of the cruelty and corruption of the administrators. The Indians had been deprived of their lands, their cattle were stolen, and they themselves scattered and held in a bondage far more onerous than the tutelage exercised by the *padres*. Gangs of the wretched creatures were hired out to private persons, and the major-domo did not hesitate to punish the refractory with one hundred lashes. One of the worst offenders was Alvarado's own uncle, Mariano Guadalupe Valléjo, who had managed to possess himself of the mission properties of San Rafael and Sonoma and, taking advantage of his powers as commander-in-chief of the army, ruled the country north of the bay like a feudal baron. The mission Indians whom he had taken over with the land and cattle were miserable thralls. Too dispirited to marry and bear children, they were rapidly perishing of want and disease. Valléjo, moreover, had won an unenviable notoriety by barbarous raids against the *gentiles* of the Sacramento Valley who were skilful horse thieves, and these punitive expeditions often brought back captive Indians. When Hartnell undertook to visit San Rafael, he was arrested by this lord of the border and held prisoner till he promised to forbear investigation. Pio Pico at San Luis Rey was no less defiant. The baffled *visitador general* resigned his office (1840), and Alvarado's reform project failed.

The testimony of foreigners is unanimous in condemnation of the ruin wrought. Sir Edward

Belcher, who visited San Francisco Bay in 1837, had great difficulty in securing supplies, since the missions of San José and Santa Clara had been "plundered by all parties" and were reduced to destitution. He states that the administrators had taken about two-thirds of the revenue for themselves and turned over but one-third to the government. The Indians, both Christian and *gentile*, were carrying off the horses and such other property as they thought desirable, to the mountains. De Mofras, attaché of the French embassy at Madrid and later at the City of Mexico, made a tour of the missions in 1841. He grievously lamented the ruin wrought by secularization. In the seven years of political control, the Indian population had been decimated, the cattle had been reduced to 28,220, the horses to 3800, the sheep to 31,600, and the yield of grain to 4000 *fanegas*. At San Diego, the Indian *rancheria* was extinct, and the *rancho del rey* had passed into private possession. The mission was crumbling to decay; the great olive orchard and vineyard, and a fine cotton plantation were untended for lack of laborers. The workshops and tanneries of San Luis Rey were empty. The famous fruit orchards of San Juan Capistrano had been appropriated by Señors Yorba and Nieto. At San Gabriel there were but five hundred Indians left, and the *ranchos* of San Bernardino, Chino, and Santa Anita had fallen into private hands. The Indian *pueblo* at San Fernando had been broken up by the brutality of the administrator, Valle; but Santa Barbara, which was the seat of the bishop, had not suffered so severely. The buildings of San

VINEYARD PLANTED BY THE PADRES OF SAN GABRIEL.

ADOBE RANCH HOUSE AT SAN GABRIEL.

Luis Obispo were in ruins, and all the able-bodied neophytes were fled to the mountains; yet the aged *padre* clung to the spot, refusing to take refuge in Santa Barbara, since he preferred to die at his post among the remnant of his people. Three years before, Father Sarría had perished of misery and famine at Nuestra Sonora de la Soledad, whereupon Governor Alvarado had driven off the remaining cattle and taken all the ironwork and even the tiles from the roof to build his own house. The land he had given to one of his friends in exchange for a ranch near Monterey. A popular saying, "the governor's cows calve three times a year," was a covert allusion to the source of Alvarado's wealth. Other public estates had been used to bolster up the governor's power. The *rancho del rey* belonging to the *presidio* of Monterey he gave to his brother-in-law, José Estrada. The property of San Juan Bautista had been made over to José Castro as the price of his support. General Valléjo had been allowed to devastate the missions of San Rafael and San Francisco Solano in order to fit out his ranch and the *pueblo* of Sonoma. Another Valléjo, while serving as administrator of Santa Clara, had grown wealthy in cattle and land.

Sir George Simpson, the governor of Hudson's Bay Company, condemned no less severely than de Mofras the wasteful destruction of the missions and the wreck of their industries. "In the missions, there were large flocks of sheep; but now there are scarcely any left, the Hudson's Bay Company having, last spring, experienced great difficulty in collecting about four thousand for its northern settlements. In

the missions, the wool used to be manufactured into
coarse cloth; and it is, in fact, because the Californians are too lazy to weave or spin, — too lazy, I sus-
pect, even to clip and wash the raw material, — that
the sheep have been literally destroyed to make more
room for the horned cattle. In the missions, soap
and leather used to be made; but in such vulgar processes the Californians advance no farther than nature herself has advanced before them, excepting to
put each animal's tallow in one place, and its hide in
another. In the missions, the dairy formed a principal object of attention; but now, neither butter
nor cheese, nor any preparation of milk whatever, is
to be found in the province. In the missions, there
were annually produced about 80,000 bushels of
wheat and maize, the former, and perhaps part of
the latter also, being converted into flour; but the
present possessors of the soil do so little in the way of
tilling the ground, that, when lying at Monterey, we
sold to the government some barrels of flour at the
famine rate of twenty-eight dollars, or nearly six
pounds sterling, a sack, a price [110] which could not be
considered as merely local, for the stuff was intended
to victual the same schooner which, on our first arrival, we had seen at anchor in Whalers' Harbour.
In the missions, beef was occasionally cured for exportation; but so miserably is the case now reversed,
that, though meat enough to supply the fleets of
England is annually either consumed by fire or left
to the carrion birds, yet the authorities purchased
from us, along with the flour just mentioned, some
salted salmon as indispensable sea-stores for the one

paltry vessel which constituted the entire line of battle of the California navy. In the missions, a great deal of wine was grown, good enough to be sent for sale to Mexico; but, with the exception of what we got at the mission of Santa Barbara, the native wine that we tasted was such trash as nothing but politeness could have induced us to swallow." [111]

The destruction of the missions was consummated by Pio Pico, governor during the last two years of the Mexican administration. The ruined estates of the Franciscans were sold at public auction or leased to the highest bidder with small consideration for the remnant of the friars and neophytes. [112] The state realized only sixty-seven thousand *pesos* from the sale of the best lands in California, and the purchasers, newly arrived Americans for the most part, although the names Pico, Arguello, etc., figure in the list, had every reason to be satisfied with their bargain. [113]

The Cattle Kings

Already, in 1783, the governor of California had been empowered to grant lands to private persons. Such grants might be three leagues in extent, but must not overlap the lands appropriated by mission, *pueblo*, or *rancheria*. To secure title, the proprietor must prove that he had built a house of stone and collected two thousand cattle on his holding. Several such estates were acquired, notably in the neighborhood of Santa Barbara and Los Angeles; but no more than twenty grants were ratified during the Spanish régime. The Mexican administration was more liberal, yet there were but fifty private *ranchos* in Upper

California in 1830. The secularization of the missions attracted a crowd of adventurers who managed by one device or another to get possession of some portion of the spoil, and by 1840 there were six hundred of these *rancheros*. The forced sales authorized by Governor Pico added twenty-five large proprietors to this number.

Governor Simpson attributed the lack of enterprise among the Californians to the ease of acquiring wealth and absence of "the necessity for relying upon the steady and laborious use of the axe and the plough." The *rancheros* had the proverbial indolence of a pastoral people ; with "horses to ride and beef to eat, with hides and tallow to exchange for such other supplies as they want," there was no incentive to labor. The Californians, moreover, came of a non-industrial stock. Spanish America with its sierras of silver was the asylum and paradise of idlers, and descendants of the men who looted the treasures of Mexico and Peru had succeeded to the spoil of the missions. The settlers sent in by the government to till the soil were little better, being, in the main, "superannuated troopers and retired office-holders." The *pueblos* were places of refuge for invalided soldiers and runaway sailors, "sinks of profligacy and riot," avoided by the better sort of Spaniards, who preferred the neighborhood of the *presidios*, notably Santa Barbara. "What a splendid country, whether we consider its internal resources or its commercial capabilities, to be thrown away upon its present possessors — on men who do not avail themselves of their natural advantages to a much higher degree than the savages whom they have displaced, and who are likely to become less and less energetic from generation to generation and from year to year."

The *rancheros*, who succeeded to the lands and property of the *padres*, lived on their estates in ease and abundance. Their cattle throve on the nutritious *alfileria* [114] and wild oats, and needed no shelter nor winter feed. Unless the pastures failed with a dry season, the herd doubled every year, over and above the annual slaughter. Horses ran wild and multiplied so rapidly that they were occasionally driven across the hills into the San Joaquin Valley. The breed, according to de Mofras, had not degenerated and was well adapted to cattle-tending. They were as tall as the English race horse and had the speed and endurance of the Arabian. Good riding horses were accustomed to gallop from twelve to fifteen hours a day without food or rest, but they had no acquired gaits. Their owners were content to lasso them and break them to the saddle, turning them loose again when they were no longer needed. California horses were highly esteemed in New and Old Mexico, and on the frontiers of the United States; but the *rancheros* did not take the trouble to export them, leaving this profitable trade to the Indians and horse thieves of the Tulares. The redwood forests of the coast offered another promising export, but to fell the trees and deliver the timber at the sea-board exceeded the energy of the Californians. Gold had been discovered near San Fernando, [115] and it was prophesied that the mineral wealth of California would yet surpass the dreams of sixteenth-century fables; but the mountains remained unexplored.

The staple export of California was still hides and tallow.[116]   Hides served as the common currency of the country, and debts were paid in cattle. The *ranchero* got from $5 to $6 out of each animal killed; $2 for the hide and $3 to $4 for the tallow. Since one-fourth of the herd was killed each year, a man's income could be accurately reckoned from the number of cattle on his range. The consignment was sometimes paid for in silver, but more usually in goods, — calicoes, teas, wines, etc. Although his annual revenue amounted to several thousand dollars and the expenses of the business were almost nil, the *ranchero* was usually in debt to one or more of the hide factors. He bought so freely of the high-priced foreign commodities that he was not infrequently two or three years behind in his accounts. W. H. Davis, an experienced merchant of Yerba Buena, estimated the "drogher" trade for the twenty years of its continuance (1828–1848) at 1,068,000 hides exported and 62,500,000 pounds of tallow. The best years were those immediately following the secularization of the missions, when cattle were being slaughtered by the hundreds of thousands. The *rancheros* never equalled the *padres* in the number or quality of the hides furnished.

The merchants and the ship-owners who reaped large profits from the California trade were Americans and Englishmen and even Italians, but never Spaniards. For trade and manufactures the Californians had no gift, but all travellers agree that their skill in

riding, in lassoing and branding cattle, in bull and
bear baiting, in music and dancing, was marvellous.
Theirs was the pastoral age. They lived a free out-
of-door life, with plenty of food, few books, and little
learning, and were content to procure their clothing
and other supplies from the Yankee ships that carried
away the hides and tallow. No attempt was made
to provide by domestic industries the cloth and
leather goods that cost so dear, and even the salt used
by these luxurious gentlemen was brought from Boston. The wheat crop was rapidly diminishing, because slight attention was given to tillage. The
ground was merely scratched with a wooden plough,
and the grain was sowed broadcast and covered by
dragging a brush harrow over the field. The reapers
still used the picturesque but ineffectual sickle, and
when threshing time arrived, the straw was thrown
into a shallow pit and the grain trodden out by a band
of wild horses driven round and round by mounted
vaqueros. The yield had fallen to thirty-five and
forty bushels per acre. Some coarse flour was
ground by a domestic grist-mill hardly less primitive than the Indian *metate.* It consisted of two flat
stones, of which the nether one was stationary and
the upper was turned by a revolving lever propelled
by a donkey or long-suffering mule.[117.]

Not the least of the economic crimes of the Californians was the wasteful destruction of the Indian
population. There were in 1833 thirty thousand
mission Indians, docile and teachable, sufficiently
reconciled to the white occupation and admirably
adapted to field labor and the care of cattle. Secu-

larization deprived them of their lands and left them dependent on the *rancheros*. If Figueroa's policy had been carried into execution and the natives had been given farms of their own and encouraged to sell their surplus products as an incentive to tillage, a peasant population might have been developed and some of the old-time arts and manufactures maintained. The Indians who were so fortunate as to become domestic servants in the houses of well-to-do Spaniards were often contented and even happy. Those who succeeded in getting and holding land have handed down to their descendants considerable property and the traditions of industry and Christian morality. But the major part were huddled together in wretched villages where they died of neglect and starvation. There were perhaps thirty thousand *gentile* Indians in the interior, of a mental and physical calibre superior to the natives of the coast; but they distrusted and hated the whites and, far from rendering any service, preyed upon the outlying *ranchos*, stealing their horses and, not infrequently, kidnapping women. Commander Wilkes, who visited San Francisco Bay in 1841, observed that the mission Indians had relapsed into barbarism. Half of them had been killed off by the smallpox epidemic of 1838, and many of the remainder, disheartened by the struggle to maintain themselves in the midst of the white man's civilization, had joined the wild tribes of the interior and were leading their raids upon the *ranchos*. Sir George Simpson compared the reckless cruelty of the *rancheros* with the traditional Indian policy of the Hudson's Bay Company, much to the advantage of

VAQUEROS THROWING THE LASSO.

the latter. By a wise combination of firmness and justice, the Canadians had conserved the native races and utilized their skill as hunters. The Russians on Bodega Bay had been equally successful, for the Indians fled from the thraldom of the missions and the cruel mercies of the Valléjos to find food and fair wages at Fort Ross.

Seventy-five years of Spanish occupation had failed to develop the latent resources of California. The *hijos del pais* were content to subsist off the spontaneous products of their fertile soil and genial climate, taking no pains to improve upon nature, even allowing the orchards and vineyards and wheat fields cultivated by the *padres* to dwindle and perish from neglect.

PART II

EXPLORATION AND THE FUR TRADE

CHAPTER I

THE NORTHWEST COAST

SECTION I

Russian Explorers

FAR into the eighteenth century, the viceroys of New Spain maintained their monopoly of the South Sea, the depredations of certain English pirates to the contrary notwithstanding; but the region north of the trade route between Mexico and the Philippines was beyond their ken. The first voyage of discovery into the north Pacific was undertaken at the behest of that far-sighted autocrat, Peter the Great. Speculations of European geographers concerning lands to the east of Japan had come to his ears, and he proposed that the Russians, who had recently come into possession of Kamchatka, should be first in the field. From his death-bed (1725) he issued a decree ordering that Vitus Behring, a Dane in his employ, should cross Siberia to the shores of the unknown sea, build there two ships and go in search of the fabled passage to the Atlantic and the still more fabulous mid-Pacific continent which the Portuguese maps named Gamaland. Otter hunters of the Kamchatka coast had seen driftwood floating in from unknown forests, the bloated bodies of whales struck by harpoons of unknown workmanship, and wooden canoes whose

193

makers did not belong to Asia; but the fog banks of that stormy sea and the hurricanes that drove down from the north had discouraged pursuit of these suggestive clews. Behring's first expedition consumed three years in crossing the seven thousand miles between St. Petersburg and Petropaulovski. The route ran by way of Irkutsk — the fur mart frequented by the traders of eastern Asia and merchants from Pekin — and Yakutsk — a frontier post on the Lena — to Okhotsk, Russia's only port on Pacific waters. Here boats were improvised to convey men and equipment to the rugged peninsula that divides the Sea of Okhotsk from the ocean. At Avacha Bay two sloops were built, spikes, ropes, and canvas having been brought from Russia for the purpose, and on July 9, 1728, the enterprise was launched. Sailing northward, Behring touched at an island lying about sixty-four degrees north latitude which he named St. Lawrence and, pressing on to the Arctic Circle, discovered that the coast bore continually to the northwest. He was forced to conclude that there was no new continent in that direction and no passage through to the Atlantic that would be practicable for merchantmen. Another voyage to the southeast was undertaken, but proved fruitless because of storms and adverse winds.

The following spring, Behring returned to St. Petersburg for new supplies, and early in 1733 he set out for Kamchatka equipped for a second expedition. This time the simple sea captain was accompanied by scientists who had conceived learned theories about the sea-to-sea passage and possessed maps of the continent they intended to discover, and instructions from St. Petersburg ordained that nothing was to be undertaken without their approval. So handicapped, the journey across Siberia occupied seven years, and the two new ships, *St. Peter* and *St. Paul*, did not set sail from Petropaulovski till June, 1741. The scientists decreed that Gamaland lay to the southeast, and Behring, who had small faith in the new continent, steered southeast to the forty-sixth parallel, then, one theory being exploded, north to the Alaskan coast. There, at the sixtieth parallel, they came face to face with a lofty mountain range and named one glittering cone, soaring white above the huge mass of rock and snow, St. Elias. The scientists were eager to explore; but provisions were running low, the crew was stricken with scurvy, and the commander himself was under the depressing influence of that dread disease. Pausing only to fill the water casks, Behring ordered immediate return to Kamchatka. As they coasted along the labyrinth of islets and rock reefs now known as the Aleutian Islands, in hourly danger of shipwreck, the bravest were panic-smitten, and when at last the *St. Peter* was driven under the lea of a cliff-girt island and into a quiet harbor, the crew were for going ashore. They had lost all reckoning and could not know that Avacha Bay was but two hundred miles to the west, and here, in spite of Behring's protests, it was determined to winter. The chance for life on this wind-swept refuge was better than he had hoped. There was fresh water in abundance, and the rocks swarmed with animals unknown to contemporary naturalists, — sea-cows, sea-lions, sea-otter, and seal. The first furnished nourishing food, and the skins of the smaller beasts enabled the men to protect themselves against the Arctic cold. There on the barren islet since called by his name, died Behring, the bravest and most unlucky of explorers, together with half his crew. The remnant of the castaways survived the winter, built a crazy boat out of the wreckage of the *St. Peter*, and found their way back to Kamchatka in the following spring. Chirikoff, commander of the *St. Paul*, had reached Petropaulovski in the autumn preceding. He had zigzagged over much the same course as Behring, having touched the coast of the mainland at the fifty-seventh parallel, and discovered Mt. Edgecombe and Norfolk Sound. Thus after long years of hardship and a reckless expenditure of money and human life, the ukase of the great Czar resulted in the addition of a vast subarctic waste to the Russian Empire.

Behring's men, returning to Petropaulovski in August, 1742, brought with them furs of the sea-otter, which they had used for coats and bedding, and found for them a ready market at $200 a pelt. The "sea-beaver" had been taken on the shores of Japan and Kamchatka, but it did not breed there; the catch was rapidly decreasing, and the fur was a luxury to the wealthy classes. Now that its winter haunts and breeding grounds were discovered, and the ease with which the animal might be caught in the kelp beds off the Aleutian Islands, the otter herds of the north Pacific became no less important to Russia than were the gold mines of Mexico and

Peru to Spain. The crown renounced its monopoly of the fur trade, and the opportunity was thrown open to all Russia's subjects, with the single reservation that one-tenth the skins taken must be surrendered to the customs officers. Thenceforth the fur trade was the shortest road to fortune for the adventurers of that wild and lawless frontier. Russian officers and sailors, Siberian exiles, Cossacks, Tartars, Kamchatkans, ventured their all in the otter hunt. Expenses and profits were divided among the crew, share and share alike, though some merchant usually furnished the supplies and goods for the Indian trade, stipulating for half the returns in payment. Ships were built in mad haste at Okhotsk, — the "sawed vessels," wrought of green timber brought down from the mountains, bound together with reindeer thongs, and caulked with clay and tallow. The cost of boat and outfit might be $30,000; but since the season's catch would sell for from $50,000 to $100,000, the venture was one in which men were willing to risk life and limb, and they made slight inquiry into the hazards. Scurvy, starvation, shipwreck, massacre, awaited half the adventurers, yet among the rude and reckless population of eastern Asia, there were always men to fill the places of the lost. Within five years after the discovery, there were seventy-seven of these profit-sharing companies engaged in catching sea-otter on the storm-beaten reefs of the Aleutian Islands. Thereafter the government had no need to finance exploring expeditions to the Pacific, for the frail craft of the fur traders penetrated every sound and inlet.

The hunt was carried on with utter disregard of everything but immediate profit. Driven in by wind and tide, the helpless animals were clubbed to death in shallow water or, if found in the open sea, the herd was surrounded by a cordon of boats, and the otter were speared as they came to the surface to breathe. The aid of the Aleuts was enlisted by the lure of iron bars or cheap trinkets of civilization, and since they went to the hunt by hundreds and thousands under the oversight of a handful of white men, their good faith was secured by hostages — women and children left in care of the ship's guard. The trust was often abused, for the whites were lawless and brutal men with small fear of retribution from God or the Czar. If the hunt was unsuccessful, or if a Russian met with death, the hostages were not infrequently murdered. Resistance on the part of the men was sternly dealt with, and whole villages were not infrequently visited with fire and sword. At last the desperate Aleuts made a concerted effort to destroy the invader. In the summer of 1761, three crews touching on the island of Unalaska were massacred or harried to death among the rocks and caves of the mountainous interior. The Russian government sent a punitive expedition which reduced the natives to subjection, and for the first time an effort was made to regulate the traffic. No ship might sail to the islands without a license, and the Indians must be treated with justice. But such regulations were useless since they could not be enforced. The labor of the natives continued to be mercilessly exploited, and they were forced to undergo hardships and to run risks that meant rapid extermination. In 1792, for example, the hunting parties were overtaken by storm, and out of seven hundred *bidarkas* [1] and fourteen hundred Aleuts, only thirty *bidarkas* and sixty men returned. Von Langsdorff, the physician of Krusenstern's ship, described conditions as he saw them in 1804, as worse than slavery. "In the countries that I have seen, where negro slaves are employed in the labour, great care is taken to feed them well, and keep them in health, since they must be purchased at a high price ; but the case is otherwise here. The poor, vanquished, and enslaved Aleutians are ill-fed, ill-clothed, and perpetually thrown into situations where their lives are in danger ; they are deprived of all their property, and are commonly governed by Promüschleniks, who are for the most part criminals from Siberia : under all these circumstances the depopulation must advance rapidly. Scarcely any of the native Aleutians are to be seen, excepting superannuated old men, with women and children : the men capable of working are sent continually on hunting parties for sea-otters, and are thus separated from their families for months together." [2] On the farm at Kodiak, the wretched natives were obliged to draw the plough in lieu of oxen.

Even less mercy was shown to the furred prey. Indiscriminate slaughter of male and female, young and old, depleted one fishing ground after another so that new and remoter regions must be found. The headquarters were always moving farther east and south, from Behring Island to Unalaska, from Unalaska to Kodiak, and from Kodiak to Sitka;

but the devastation went on unchecked, while the Chinese market was flooded with furs, and prices fell to a ruinous level. Finally, in the last decade of the eighteenth century, two masterful spirits, Sheli-koff and Baranof, undertook to combine the chief rivals into one great company and so to regulate the catch. With the aid of Chamberlain de Resanoff, a nobleman with influence at court, a charter was secured for the Russian-American Company (1799), giving the incorporators monopoly of the trade in the Pacific above fifty-five degrees north latitude, the limit of Russian exploration. The year following, a trading post was built on Norfolk Sound — called Sitka from the native tribe — and Baranof was appointed governor with powers over his motley force extending to life and death. A supply ship, the *Neva*, was despatched round the Horn in 1804 under the command of Krusenstern, with Count de Resanoff on board in the capacity of plenipotentiary. The post had been destroyed in 1802, and the reënforcement arrived just in time to avert a second massacre of the garrison. The Kolosh Indians of the Alaskan coast were a finer race, physically and mentally, than the Aleuts and not so easily reduced to the white man's service. They hated the enslaved islanders hardly less than they feared the Russians, and they determined to rid their land of both. Fortunately for Baranof's scheme, their well-devised ambush was betrayed and their palisaded fort destroyed by the guns of the *Neva*. A Russian fortification was immediately built on the ruins of the village and christened New Archangel.

Finding supplies short at Sitka and the agricultural resources of the region dubious, de Resanoff determined to have resort to the Spanish missions made known to Baranof by the Boston fur traders, O'Cain and Winship. He sailed to San Francisco Bay and succeeded in purchasing from San José a quantity of provisions, but his attempt to negotiate a regular exchange of products was thwarted by the exclusive commercial policy of Spain. Von Langsdorff thought that the profits from such a trade could never be great, since the manufactured goods required in California must be brought from Europe, and he therefore proposed that a Russian settlement be established at some point on this coast, where soil and climate were suited to the raising of cattle and where sea-otters might be taken sufficient to meet all the expenses involved and pay a handsome profit beside.[3] Six years later, Baranof carried out the California project by the establishment of a trading post at Bodega Bay, a deep cove to the north of Point Reyes. There a palisaded fort was built (1813), timber being cut from the heavy forests of the surrounding hills. Russian soldiers, Finnish artisans, and Kodiak hunters were imported for the service of the post, and a considerable number of domesticated Indians were induced by the prospect of money wages and fair treatment to work the land in the vicinity.

The harvest of furs in this unexploited region was a rich one. Von Langsdorff had noted that seal was abundant and that "the valuable sea-otter was swimming in numbers about the bay, nearly unheeded." [4]   The Russians were able to spear from seven to eight hundred otters per week in the creeks and inlets of San Francisco Bay, while at the hunting station on the Farallones, eighty thousand skins were secured in one season. Foreigners were prohibited by Spanish law from taking sea-otter within thirty leagues of the coast, but this obstacle was overcome by a friendly arrangement with the *commandante*. For a time the shiploads of grain, jerked beef, and tallow sent to the northern posts were purchased from the missions, payment being made in silver or in European goods; but before many years had passed, a farm and stock ranch were installed on the San Sebastian River (where Santa Rosa now lies) which furnished food in abundance for all the Russian settlements. In 1820 a larger post, known to the Spaniards as Fort Ross, was built about twenty miles up the coast. A strong palisade, eighteen feet high, enclosed the soldiers' quarters, two octangular block houses frowned upon intruders, and four brass howitzers stood guard at the gate. Fort Ross was far more formidable than any Spanish *presidio* and was regarded by the Californians as a real menace. The device of establishing two missions to the north of San Francisco Bay was adopted. San Rafael was founded on San Pablo Bay (1817) and San Francisco Solano in the fertile Sonoma Valley (1823).

For the next twenty years, the operations of the Russian-American Fur Company extended from Santa Barbara and the Farallones to Unalaska and the Commander Islands, a wild and stormy stretch

FORT ROSS IN 1828.

of coast, four thousand miles in extent. Thirty
fortified posts guarded its property, and twelve
vessels were engaged in transporting furs and supplies. Russians were excluded from Chinese ports,
so the furs collected at the various stations were
conveyed to Okhotsk, whence they were carried overland by dog sledge and camel train to Irkutsk,
where the Chinese merchants loaded the precious
bales on camel trains for Pekin. The tea and silks
and muslins for which the furs were exchanged were
loaded on pack animals and sent to Nishni-Novgorod,
Moscow, and St. Petersburg. Sitka, the centre of
this trade, was the principal port on the northwest
coast. Eight hundred white families were established there, and the dark-skinned servitors numbered thousands. Its beautiful church was furnished
with gifts from the stockholders and others of the
Russian nobility. In its shipyard, sea-going vessels
were built, while its bell-foundry cast chimes for
the missions of California and Mexico. The settlement at Bodega was hardly less imposing. Lieutenant Slacum of the United States navy visited
the post in 1839 and found it well maintained.
Four hundred men were in the employ of the company, — sixty Russians, eighty Kodiaks, and two hundred and sixty native Indians. There were fifteen
hundred head of cattle, eight hundred horses, five
hundred sheep, and three hundred hogs on the
ranch in charge of Indian herdsmen, and the yield
of the wheat fields tended by these unprotesting
laborers was seventy-two hundred bushels. Two
ships came annually from Sitka for the grain, tallow,

and dried beef without which the northern settlements could not have been fed; but the harvest of furs was exhausted. The otter herds of California had been exploited in the same reckless fashion that had reduced the northern fisheries. The catch had fallen off to one hundred skins per year, and, since the fur was inferior to that taken in Arctic waters and not worth carrying to China, the skins were sent to the City of Mexico and sold for from $60 to $70 each. There was no longer any profit in the otter hunt. Land otter were to be had, and beaver and deer, but this involved trapping expeditions into the interior, and the pelts would bring no more than $2, $3, and $4 apiece. By 1840 the Russian-American Fur Company was ready to withdraw from California, and offered its property for sale to the highest bidder.

Section II

Spanish Explorers

It was Bucareli, the able viceroy of Charles III, who renewed the endeavor to discover the Straits of Anian and so to forestall Russian aggression on the northwest coast. In 1773 he despatched an exploring expedition under Perez with instructions not to turn back till the sixtieth parallel had been attained. The prevailing northwest winds, so favorable to the Siberian trade, rendered approach from the south difficult. Baffled by head winds, Perez turned back at 54° 40′; but not before he had discovered a sheltered C-shaped bay which he called

SPANISH EXPLORATION ALONG THE COAST OF CALIFORNIA.

San Lorenzo (Nootka Sound) where the natives were eager to trade excellent otter skins for the veriest trifles. The following year two vessels under Bruno de Haceta and Bodega y Quadra were despatched in the hope of larger results. Haceta rounded Cape Mendocino and, landing, took possession in the name of his Catholic Majesty; but he failed to find de Fuca's strait. On the return voyage, he approached the coast in latitude 46° 10', and anchored in a roadstead where a strong offshore current rendered his ship unmanageable. "These currents and eddies of the water caused me to believe that the place is the mouth of some great river, or of some passage to another sea. Had I not been certain of the latitude of this bay, I might easily have believed it to be the passage discovered by Juan de Fuca, in 1592, which is placed on the charts between the 47th and the 48th degrees." [5] Haceta's crew was prostrated with scurvy, so that he had not force enough to lower and lift the anchor or to man a long-boat, and he was obliged to forego farther investigation; but his description of the muddy tide, the bar, and the two headlands corresponds so exactly to the geography of the region that there can be no reasonable doubt that he had hit upon the mouth of the Columbia. On Spanish maps of the day, the entrance is indicated as Haceta's Inlet, and the hypothetical river is called San Roc.

Meantime Bodega y Quadra in the companion vessel had reached Mt. Edgecombe (1775) and the land-locked harbor already known to the Russians as Sitka. In a subsequent voyage (1779) this same intrepid mariner reached the sixty-first degree, sighted Mt. St. Elias, and learned from the Indians of the Russian trading posts, but encountered no foe. Unhappily for Spanish prestige, Bucareli's successors failed to follow up these clews. The northern coasts were bleak and stormy, and seal fishing, though remunerative, had small attraction for men of southern blood. In the endeavor to conceal these discoveries lest they profit her enemies, the government of Spain unwittingly consigned the really remarkable achievements of her explorers to oblivion.[6]

SECTION III

English Explorers

Far different was the response accorded to the achievements of British explorers. In the year following Haceta's voyage, the Royal Geographical Society sent Captain James Cook, already famous for his exploration of the South Sea, to rediscover Drake's Bay in the hope of substantiating Britain's shadowy claim to New Albion, and thence to push north until he came upon the open route to the Atlantic that Drake had sought in vain.[7] Sailing from London in midsummer of 1776, his two stout ships, the *Resolution* and the *Discovery*, forged across the Atlantic and round the Horn and over the Pacific and so hit upon the group of tropic islands named by Cook for Lord Sandwich.

Recruiting their supplies of food and water at this siren's haven of wave-tossed mariners, they sailed eastward to California. At 40° 33', the latitude of

Drake's landfall, they descried the line of cliffs called by the Spaniards Cabo Mendocino; but the ships were driven out to sea by a hurricane of hail and snow. Land was sighted again eight degrees farther north (Cape Flattery), but again they were driven off by perverse winds. The exasperated explorer recorded his conviction that no such opening as Juan de Fuca's strait had ever existed. Pressing on to the north, Cook was soon rewarded by a discovery not in his instructions, but destined to be far more profitable to English merchants than the much-sought sea-to-sea channel could have been. Becalmed off a mountain-girt coast, the vessels came to anchor in Perez' C-shaped harbor (named by Cook King George's Sound), and there a commercial El Dorado was disclosed. Hundreds of shapely wooden canoes came out to visit the ships, whose painted occupants were eager to barter their otter skin clothing for the merest trifles (a sixpenny knife would buy a skin worth $100), and a stock of furs was laid in that later sold in China for $10,000. Here the *Resolution* and the *Discovery* were repaired and supplies of wood and water taken on. Toward the end of April, 1777, the expedition was again moving north. Skirting the chain of islands that guarded the secret he hoped to penetrate, Cook gazed astonished upon snow-capped mountains that loomed higher and higher as they approached the Arctic Circle. The Fairweather Range and Mt. St. Elias seemed to bar the way to the eastward, but still the dauntless explorer pushed on. The estuary called by geographers Cook's

Inlet gave promise of penetrating the continent, but it proved to be an *impasse,* and Turnagain Arm marks the abandonment of this clew. The stanch British ships threaded the Aleutian Islands, rounded Cape Prince of Wales, sighted East Cape, and so north to Icy Cape where Cook finally abandoned his quest. It was hazardous to battle farther against deadly cold in pursuit of a geographers' dream. The exploration of the Arctic Ocean having been abandoned, Cook returned to the "Paradise of the Pacific" in January, 1779, and there the great explorer met his death at the hands of the natives. The chivalrous Englishman gave the name of Behring to the strait discovered by the Russian explorer fifty years before.

Cook's geographical discoveries along our northwest coast were of minor importance since he failed to find De Fuca's strait or Haceta's river, but his report of the wealth of furs to be had from the Indians set on foot a movement that was destined to have vast consequences. The nearest and most profitable market was the Orient, but here the East India Company held an undisputed monopoly which Englishmen might evade only by sailing under a foreign flag. The first ship sent out from London (Captain James Hanna, 1780) carried Portuguese colors, and her success was such as to encourage farther ventures. In 1785, the King George's Sound Company was chartered for the Nootka trade and sent out two vessels under Captains Portland and Dixon, who explored the islands to the north and secured a load of furs but, being denied access to

Chinese ports, reaped no great profit. The East India Company sent out a ship in 1781 and again in 1788, under Captain Robert Meares. On his second voyage, Captain Meares sailed into the strait between Vancouver Island and the Olympic Range and gave the long-sought channel the name of its traditional discoverer. Hoping to find Haceta's river, Meares neared the coast again at latitude 46° 10', but he was discouraged from entering the promising inlet by a line of huge breakers that stretched from headland to headland. He concluded that San Roc was a myth,[8] and contented himself with naming the promontory Cape Disappointment and the baffling roadstead of tempestuous water, Deception Bay.

Jealous of these new interlopers, the Spanish viceroy sent out a vessel (1788) under orders to collect a cargo of furs and carry them to Canton; but this official enterprise was not a success, for the sale of peltry did not cover the costs of the expedition. The next year Martinez and de Haro were commissioned to explore the northern coasts and to determine on sites suited for Spanish colonies. They found the Russians strongly intrenched on the northern islands, and a protest against these encroachments was addressed to St. Petersburg, but with no effect. When they arrived at Perez's landlocked harbor, the Spanish envoys found even more formidable competitors in control. Two vessels flying the Portuguese flag, but financed by British capital, and two American sloops, the *Columbia* and the *Lady Washington*, lay at anchor in the sheltered bay, and two English ships, sent out from Macao by Meares and equipped with materials to build a trading post at Nootka Sound, were soon added to the array of foreign traders. Meares' enterprise was overt trespass, and Martinez arrested the British officers and confiscated their cargoes, pending a final settlement of the questions at issue. An international embroglio was averted by the Nootka Convention (1790), wherein the right of Englishmen and Spaniards to navigate the Pacific, fish in Arctic waters, and trade with the Coast Indians was fully recognized; but neither power was to found colonies north of Spain's northernmost settlement nor to claim sovereign rights. Vancouver met Bodega y Quadra, the Spanish commissioner, at Nootka Sound in the summer of 1792, but they failed to reach an agreement as to the property rights in question. All difficulties were finally adjudicated in the treaty of 1794.

At this time there were eight American vessels [9] engaged in the fur trade on the northwest coast, but since they appeared to have no settlement in view, there was no interference. The right of citizens of the United States to trade in these waters was recognized in the treaty negotiated with Spain in 1795, and Nootka became a neutral port.

SECTION IV

The Americans

Ledyard's *Journal of Cook's Last Voyage* was printed at Hartford, Connecticut, in 1783.[10] It found eager readers. The War of the Revolution at an end and independence achieved, American merchants were under no obligation to respect the East India Company's monopoly and might avail themselves of the profitable trade between China and the northwest coast. A group of Boston merchants, Charles Bulfinch at their head, formed a partnership, with a capital of $50,000, and sent out two vessels round the Horn to this far-away wilderness. The *Columbia*, a full-rigged two-decker of two hundred and twelve tons, was commanded by Captain John Kendrick, a retired naval officer. The *Lady Washington*, a sloop of ninety tons, had a much younger man, Robert Gray, for captain. The commanders had no experience of Pacific waters, but Woodruff, first mate of the *Columbia*, had been to Alaska with Cook.

The ships sailed from Boston the first of October, 1787, in abundant time to make the Straits of Magellan during the Antarctic summer; but Kendrick timidly delayed at Cape Verde until the stormy season set in, and the vessels had a rough experience rounding the Horn. In the Pacific, new dangers awaited them. The jealousy of the Spanish government was evidenced in the orders given to the *commandante* at San Francisco to stop the American vessels, should they enter the harbor, and to arrest the officers and crew. Kendrick did put into Juan Fernandez for repairs and fresh provisions. The governor of the islands was afterward severely reprimanded by the viceroy of Chili for rendering aid to the invader of the South Seas. Meantime Gray pushed ahead toward the goal of their enterprise. He first sighted the coast of North America at Cape Mendocino,

August 2, 1788. Twelve days' run up the cliff-girt shore brought him to Tillamook Bay, where the scurvy-infected crew was given a few days' respite, and fresh food was laid in. A treacherous onslaught from the Indians gave to this inlet the ominous name of Murderers' Bay. The sloop reached Nootka Sound on September 17, 1788, well-nigh a year after her departure from Boston, only to find that British traders had got in ahead. Two English ships under Captain Meares and Douglas were anchored in the harbor and already well loaded with furs, while a third vessel, the *Northwest America*,[11] was rising from the stocks. The Yankees were received with much courtesy by the Englishmen, and there was great show of hospitality; but they were regarded as interlopers, none the less, and Captain Meares resorted to all the tricks of the trade in the endeavor to dishearten his unwelcome rival. Skins were scarce, he said, and their quality much overrated; the Indians moreover were unfriendly and treacherous. Gray assisted in the launching of the *Northwest America* and furnished some much needed supplies for the China voyage; but he indicated quite clearly his determination of sticking to his task. Toward the end of October, the British vessels sailed for Hongkong, and the Americans were left to their own devices. The *Columbia* had arrived at last, battered by hurricanes and ravaged by scurvy, and the two vessels spent the winter of 1788–1789, cruising from one Indian village to another in the purchase of furs. The Americans became thoroughly familiar with the islands from the

Strait of Juan de Fuca to Dixon Entrance and the Portland Canal. The natives knew nothing of the market values of Europe and Asia, and astonishing bargains could be driven ; *e.g.* two hundred otter skins, worth $8000, were bought for a rusty iron chisel. Having accumulated a large stock of furs, the captains sailed for China (July 30, 1789), there to exchange this cargo for tea, a commodity even more salable in New England. Kendrick returned to Nootka Sound in the *Lady Washington*, while the *Columbia* began the homeward voyage across the Indian Ocean and around the Cape of Good Hope. On August 11, 1790, she dropped down Boston Harbor, and was received with great rejoicing. Governor Hancock gave a public reception to the commander of the first American vessel to circumnavigate the globe.

The voyage of fifty thousand miles, though a glorious achievement, was financially unprofitable, and several of the partners withdrew their capital ; but Bulfinch was not discouraged. Under Gray's command the gains would not be eaten up in needless delays, and if he could succeed in getting to Hongkong before the English, he could forestall a glut of the market. The *Columbia* was again fitted out, and within six weeks of her arrival in Boston set sail for the northwest coast. Only eight months were consumed in the outward voyage, and Gray arrived at Nootka (June 5, 1791), bent on prosecuting a vigorous campaign. Having experienced some rough treatment at the hands of Meares, the Nootkans had grown suspicious, and they now gathered courage to attack the white man's floating house. A strong body of warriors boarded the *Lady Washington* and got possession of the powder magazine, and but for Kendrick's quickness and resolution, ship and crew would have been blown to atoms. It was deemed wise therefore to build a log fort for the protection of men and furs. At Clayoquot (called Hancock Point by Gray) a little to the south of Nootka, barracks were erected, and a stout palisade, furnished with loopholes and surmounted by two cannon, frowned defiance upon all comers. They built this same winter (1791–1792) a sloop, the *Adventure*, out of timber cut from the best spruce forests in the world.

Gray and Kendrick were destined to be not mere fur traders but discoverers as well. Cruising the channels back of Nootka, Kendrick found his way into the archipelago, later named Puget Sound, and sailed through de Fuca's strait back to Nootka again, proving the traders' headquarters to be placed on an island. What we know as Vancouver Island was called Washington Island by the fur traders, in honor of the brave little vessel in which Kendrick made this cruise. Gray, meantime, was sailing south along the coast in search of new tribes less sophisticated in the price of furs. Near the forty-sixth parallel he sighted Cape Disappointment and directly after encountered a current so strong as to carry his vessel out to sea. For nine days he battled with wind and tide, and not till May 11 did he discover the channel through the breakers. Once over the bar, there opened up before his delighted eyes a large river of fresh water flowing swiftly between forested shores.[12] He sailed up the channel some thirty miles, trading with the natives who followed in canoes, and then, convinced that this was the long-sought river, named it, after the first ship that had ploughed its current, the *Columbia*. Being a loyal son of Massachusetts, Gray renamed the north headland Cape Hancock and the south, Adams Point. On May 20, the *Columbia* recrossed the bar and returned to Nootka for the summer's trade. There Gray showed to the Spanish commander a sketch of the bay and the river channel above. In October he sailed for Canton, where his season's catch was sold to good advantage. In July of 1793, Gray and his good ship were once more in Boston Harbor, but no ovation was given him. Few men understood the significance of his discovery, and the government was in no position to follow up the claim thus established. The discoverer of the River of the West died, poor and unknown, some time between 1806 and 1809, years in which the value of his achievement should have been recognized.

In this same year, a British squadron was sent to the northwest coast to enforce the terms of the Nootka Convention. Captain George Vancouver, the commander, who had some knowledge of the Pacific since he served as midshipman on Cook's third voyage, was instructed to "acquire information as to the nature of any water passage which might serve as a channel of communication between that side of America and the territories on the Atlantic

side occupied by British subjects," *e.g.* "the supposed strait of Juan de Fuca." Arriving off Cape
Disappointment (April 27, 1792) Vancouver noted
the current of "river-colored water"; but having
Meares' experience in mind and convinced that no
battleship should venture into that stretch of boil-
ing breakers, he concluded that the discoloration
was caused by some small streams falling into the
bay, and so withdrew. "Not considering this opening worthy of more attention, I continued our pursuit to the N. W. being desirous to embrace the
advantages of the now prevailing breeze and pleasant
weather, so favorable to our examination of the
coast." [13] Next day the British commander hailed
the *Columbia,* and learned from Captain Gray that
he had been "off the mouth of a river in the latitude
of 46° 10', where the outlet, or reflux, was so strong
as to prevent his entering for nine days." [14] "This,"
concludes Vancouver, "was, probably, the opening
passed by us on the forenoon of the 27th; and was,
apparently, inaccessible not from the current, but
from the breakers that extended across it." The
Discovery and the *Chatham* pursued their northward
course, while Gray turned south to have another
try at that difficult passage. His persistence was
rewarded as we have seen.

Vancouver devoted the summer of 1792 to the
exploration of the network of sounds and passages
already disclosed by the operations of the fur traders.
He was bent on proving that the northwest passage
was a myth, and this he did with English thoroughness. His officers traced the coast in all its involu-

tions with such detail and exactness that their charts may still be used. They saw and named Mt. Baker, as it soared, a white cone without visible base, far above the wooded shores of the Gulf of Georgia, and they exhausted the roll of the ship's officers in the designation of the various geographical features noted. At Point Possession, Vancouver landed his crews and with due ceremony claimed the country from New Albion to the Strait of Juan de Fuca for Great Britain (June 4, 1792). Not till he reached Nootka Sound did he learn that the *Columbia* had crossed that tumultuous line of breakers at 46° 10′ and sailed up a great river, and not till mid-October did he undertake to verify Gray's chart of the discovery. On October 21, Vancouver was again off Cape Disappointment and again the ominous line of breakers deterred him from risking an entrance with the *Discovery*. The smaller ship *Chatham* actually rounded the bar and managed an anchorage in the inner harbor; but Vancouver sailed away to the safe port of San Francisco, leaving Lieutenant Broughton to complete the survey. The commander justified his withdrawal with characteristic caution. "My former opinion of this port being inaccessible to vessels of our burthen was now fully confirmed, with this exception, that in very fine weather, with moderate winds, and a smooth sea, vessels not exceeding four hundred tons might, so far as we were enabled to judge, gain admittance." [15] When the *Chatham* rejoined the *Discovery* in San Francisco Bay a month later, Vancouver reluctantly accepted the fact that Broughton had proven the despised river navigable for at least one hundred miles above its *debouchement*. The persistent lieutenant had made his way up the river in a launch, only turning back when his week's supply of provisions was exhausted. He saw and named Mts. Hood, St. Helen, and Rainier, and reached the wooded knoll called Point Vancouver. Here the Indians indicated in sign language that farther up the river was a fall of water that would prevent the boats from passing. Even Broughton thought the river unpromising, and so, estimating its possibilities as a sea to sea channel, it doubtless was. He contented himself with taking possession of the adjacent territory in the name of His Britannic Majesty, "having every reason to believe that the subjects of no other civilized nation or state had ever entered this river before." [1] It was Broughton's theory that Gray had not penetrated to fresh water; but he considerately named the outer harbor Gray's Bay, and accepted the name given the river by the Yankee skipper.

When Broughton returned to the *Chatham,* he found an American schooner rid ng at anchor within the capes, the *Jenny* from Bristol, Rhode Island, and he gratefully followed her lead to the open sea. The adventurous little craft was the first of a long series of Yankee vessels whose safe entry and exit over the dreaded bar was to belie Vancouver's extraordinary caution. For twenty years thereafter New England merchants enjoyed the lion's share of the fur trade between the northwest coast and China. Nootka Sound and the Columbia River were visited by some forty American vessels annually, and so preëminent was Massachusetts in this commerce that all white men came to be known among the Indians as "Bostons."

From 1796 to 1814, the maritime energies of England, Spain, and France being absorbed in the Napoleonic wars, Yankee whalers and fur traders enjoyed the lion's share of Pacific commerce. Vessels were fitted out in New York or Boston or New Bedford with goods suited for the Indian market. Setting out in August or September, they rounded the Horn during the Antarctic summer and, stopping at the Sandwich Islands for fresh supplies of food and water, arrived off the Columbia in the following spring. The summer was spent in collecting furs. If the coasting trip was successful, the vessel put off before the autumn rains set in, stopped again at the Sandwich Islands to make good any deficiencies in her cargo by a supply of sandalwood, and so on across the Pacific to China. The valuable commodities secured from the Coast Indians and the Hawaiians for scraps of old iron and tawdry finery were disposed of in the Canton market for many times their purchase price. Bales of tea and silks and muslins were there taken aboard, and the sea-worn ship set out for home with a cargo that might net one thousand per cent on the original costs. The commerce had its heavy risks. Many a brave ship was wrecked in Magellan Straits or on some coral reef in the South Seas. The Coast Indians coveted the white man's goods and had little fear of reprisals. More than one vessel was looted and her crew massacred as she lay at anchor surrounded by native canoes. The fate of the ship *Boston* (1803) of whose crew only two men survived, has been graphically told by her armorer, John R. Jewitt.[17] Notwithstanding such disasters, Yankee skippers pursued the trade with zeal and success, rejoicing in its wild hazards; but the business was soon demoralized by unscrupulous competition. Rival traders vied with one another in offering whiskey and firearms, and the savages grew bold and quarrelsome. The price of the furs advanced on the fishing grounds and declined in China till the margin of profit disappeared. Two brothers, Captain Nathan and Jonathan Winship, contracted with the Russian-American Fur Company (1804) to take sea-otter on the coast north of the Spanish settlements. Fifty *bidarkas* and one hundred Aleuts were furnished them and the furs were to be turned over at Sitka at half the Canton price. These same enterprising Yankees projected a base of operations on the Columbia. Their post at Oak Point and the plantation immediately about was carried away by a summer flood, but the notion was entirely practical.

The northwest coast was a no-man's land where might made right and where the first comer was free to exploit Indian tribes and fur-bearing animals at will. Spain, Russia, Great Britain, and the United States had established defensible claims to the fur country, but no power cared to go to war in behalf of so remote a possession.

CHAPTER II

THE OVERLAND SEARCH FOR THE WESTERN SEA

SECTION I

French Explorers

THE fur traders of Montreal were no less zealous than the Jesuit missionaries for the exploration of the region drained by the St. Lawrence and the conciliation of the aborigines. While the Jesuits were establishing mission stations at Sault Ste. Marie, Michillimackinac and St. Xaviers, the traders were driving a brisk traffic with the friendly Hurons and Algonquins who brought canoes full of furs down the Ottawa and the St. Lawrence every spring. But they were not long satisfied merely to purchase the peltry brought to Montreal. It was evident that there were more numerous tribes and richer beaver grounds in the unknown regions beyond the Great Lakes, whence the trading Indians got their furs. Indeed, the Algonquins had learned from the Sioux of a "forked river" to the west, in a country barren of trees, which led the way to limitless hunting grounds, and their tales of this remoter source of wealth lured to new adventure. Two young men of Three Rivers, Pierre Radisson and Jean Groseiller, determined (1659) to return with the Algonquins to their winter quarters and learn for themselves what lay beyond. From Michillimackinac, already the fur mart of the Great Lakes, the adventurous young townsmen paddled up Jean Nicollet's river, the Fox, and down the "Ouisconsing" till they came to the east branch of the great "forked river," and then, passing through the land of the Iowas to the west fork, they made their way up the Missouri to the Mandan villages. They had found the land where no trees grew and whence mountains could be descried toward the setting sun; but their guides would venture no farther west, and, supplies being exhausted, the gallant explorers turned their faces eastward and found their way back across the plains to the head of Lake Superior. Thence they readily returned by way of the lakes and the Ottawa to Montreal. This great adventure was barren of result, because in his endeavor to develop the vast territory he had discovered, Radisson quarrelled with the French governor, gave umbrage to the all-powerful Jesuits, and excited the hostility of rival traders who reaped the fruit of his labors. His *Journal,* suppressed by the authorities, was lost in the archives of Paris and never brought to light until it was printed by the Prince Society of Boston in 1885. It is probable, however, that his account of the Mississippi and Missouri rivers and the region beyond the Great Lakes had much to do with the undertakings of Marquette, Joliet, and La Salle.

The farther the French explorers penetrated the unknown, the farther the mystery opened out before them. Rumors of a river beyond the mountains, that flowed to a sea whose waters were bitter to the taste, were gathered from the Mandans and brought back to Montreal, where they excited much interest. There was good reason to suppose that an overland route across America might be known to the Indians. In 1731, two years before Behring set out on his great adventure, Sieur Varennes de la Verenderye undertook to find a route from the Great Lakes to the Western Sea. His expedition was fitted out by the fur merchants of Montreal, and Algonquin canoes conducted the party to the head of Lake Superior, where the Crees guided them to the Lake of the Woods and Lake Winnipeg. There Verenderye built a fort for the winter's sojourn, and endeavored to establish friendly relations with the neighboring tribes. The Assiniboins were finally induced to guide the party to the Mandans who knew a people who had seen the westward flowing rivers. Up the Souris River and across the buffalo plains that divide the Assiniboin from the Missouri was a weary march and one that taxed the endurance of the Frenchmen to the utmost. Arrived at last on the Missouri, it proved that the Mandans could tell little more of the Western Sea than the Algonquins and the Hurons knew; but the chief was induced to receive a French flag and the country was claimed as an appanage of the French crown (December 3, 1738). Then the man who had carried the French colors to the heart of the Continent was summoned to Montreal to make good his failure to recoup in furs the expenses of the expedition, and his sons were left to carry on the quest. Following the lead of the Little Missouri, they reached the Big Horn Mountains and were able to journey thence, in company with a war party of Crows, to the foothills of the Rockies (January 1, 1743). There the continental divide loomed before them, a seemingly impassable barrier, the Crows abandoned the war-path, and the explorers had no choice but to return. Though they failed to find a practicable route to the Pacific, the Verenderyes had discovered the beaver dams of the Saskatchewan Valley, and their apparently bootless wanderings opened up the commercial empire from which a wealth of beaver and other peltry was collected and shipped to Montreal. The fur trade was the one profitable industry of the new world dominion that France ceded to Great Britain in the treaty of 1763.

Section II

English Explorers

The first Englishman to attempt the exploration of the Far West was a certain Jonathan Carver, captain of a company of provincial troops in the French and Indians wars. The importance of exploring Britain's new territory was impressed on the mind of this young soldier, and he undertook (1766–1768), apparently on his own responsibility, a tour of investigation by way of Niagara, the Great Lakes and the Fox and Wisconsin river portages to the Mississippi, up the Mississippi to the Falls of St. Anthony, and on to the St. Francis, the farthest point reached by Father Hennepin. He made this voyage in an open canoe with but two servants, a French Canadian and a Mohawk Indian. It was a picturesque and significant enterprise. His dugout canoe, with the calumet of peace fixed in the bow and the Union Jack floating at the stern, traversed waters hitherto unknown to Englishmen and hardly yet penetrated by the French fur traders. Returning to the falls, he ascended the St. Pierre (the Minnesota) two hundred miles to the village of the "Naudoweses of the Plains" — a tribe affiliated with the Assiniboins — where he spent seven months learning their language and collecting information as to what lay beyond. With coals drawn from the embers of the camp fire, the Indians made maps on sheets of birch bark. They said that the St. Pierre took its rise in a plateau bordered on the west by the "Shining Mountains." From its source, the distance was not great to the "Messorie," while from the head of the Missouri one might cross the mountains to the River of the West, the "Oregan," which ran down to the salt sea. It was an alluring prospect but one not to be ventured with so slight an outfit. Carver returned to England and succeeded in interesting several London capitalists in his daring scheme. He contemplated no less an enterprise than the crossing of the Continent, somewhere between the forty-third and forty-sixth parallels, and the building of a trading post on Pacific waters. It was conceived that a commercial route giving direct access by sea to China and the East Indies would be eventually profitable. Meanwhile it was most fitting that Englishmen should follow up Drake's discoveries on the west coast by such actual occupation as should guarantee British possession of the intervening territory. From such a post, moreover, the search

The Falls of St. Anthony as Carver saw Them.

for the northwest passage might be prosecuted with better hope of success than through Hudson's Bay. Government sanction for the expedition was secured by one Richard Whitworth, M.P., of Staffordshire, a gentleman of influence and public spirit. The party — Whitworth, Carver, and Colonel Rogers of Michillimackinac, with fifty or sixty men — was to have set out in 1774; but, unfortunately for British interests on the Pacific, the rupture with the colonies and the seven years' War of Independence delayed the enterprise and ultimately gave control of the upper Mississippi to the United States.

Carver was bitterly disappointed; but he found some consolation in writing an account of his travels and describing the marvellous resources of the region he had broached, in the hope that some more fortunate adventurer might realize his dream of an English commonwealth on the Pacific coast. From his Indian informants, Carver inferred that the four great rivers of the Continent, the Missisippi, the St. Lawrence, the Bourbon (Red River of the North), and the Oregan, all rose in this central plateau — indeed within thirty miles of each other, though the head waters of the Oregan might be "rather farther west."[1] The commercial significance of so vast a transportation system he deemed of prime importance to the future development of the region. The mineral wealth of the subsidiary territory was no less auspicious. At the head of Lake Superior was "abundance of virgin copper" which an English company had been successfully working when the outbreak of hostilities interrupted all business ventures. The

ore was to be shipped direct to Quebec, and thence
abroad.[2] The Winnebagoes told Carver of the mule

CARVER'S MAP OF WESTERN NORTH AMERICA, 1778.

caravans by which the Spaniards conveyed silver
from their mines on the Rio Colorado to their settlements farther south. These Indians, who had apparently been driven north by the Spaniards, said
that in Mexico the trappings of the horses and their
very shoes were of silver. The Pacific Coast Indians, who had also been expatriated by the Spanish
conquest, "have gold so plenty among them that
they make their most common utensils of it." [3] Car-

ver believed that the Shining Mountains "may be found to contain more riches in their bowels than those of Hindoostan and Malabar." The immediate wealth of the Mississippi region, represented in the fur trade, seemed very great. At Prairie du Chien, an Indian village of some three hundred families, an annual fair or mart was held in the month of May, to which came traders from the St. Lawrence and from the lower Mississippi. The place was neutral ground by Indian usage, and the chiefs of the neighboring tribes were wont to discuss whether to dispose of the season's hunt here or to take the packs on to Michillimackinac or to New Orleans.

Alexander Mackenzie, a partner in the North West Company and factor at Fort Chippewyan on Lake Athabasca, next took up the quest for the Western Sea. The duties of his remote post were not so exacting but that he had leisure to dream of the future possibilities of the region that lay beyond. From the west came the Peace River, whose sources no man knew, while to the north ran the Great Slave, flowing none knew whither. Either might lead to the Pacific and prove to be the route to a new fur country. Moreover, the British government had offered a prize of £4000 to the discoverer of the Northwest Passage. This, at least, Mackenzie determined to win. In the summer of 1789 (June 2 to July 14) his canoe, manned by Indians of the post, voyaged down river and lake to the Arctic Sea. The partners at Montreal received the announcement of this exploit with no enthusiasm, since they saw small chance of profit in the discovery, but they consented that the

daring young factor should try his luck on Peace
River. After the trading season closed in the spring
of 1793, Mackenzie's party set out in two well-stocked
canoes. As they approached the mountains, navigation grew difficult, and the river was beset with
cascades and cañons whose precipitous walls shut out
the day. The men grew frightened and mutinous, but
Mackenzie forced them on by threats and promises,
himself setting the example of hardihood, and at last
succeeded in attaining the summit of the continental
divide. On the western slope they came upon a river
(the Frazer) flowing directly south, and this they
followed in the belief that it would guide them to the
Pacific. Fortunately some Indians were encountered
who warned them against the dangers of this turbulent
stream and assured them that a march of eleven days
directly west would bring them to salt water. On
July 22, 1793, the exhausted party reached an arm of
the Pacific near Cape Menzies, where the leader in-
scribed his name and the date and the words "from
Canada by land" on a great rock on which the men
had taken refuge from the hostile natives. Mackenzie
returned immediately to his duties at Fort Chippewyan, and not till nine years later did the English
government offer the tribute of knighthood to the
man who had twice crossed the Continent and determined the boundaries of British America.

Section III

American Explorers

John Ledyard. — It was doubtless Carver's enterprise that Jefferson had in mind when he wrote to George Rogers Clark in 1783, "I find they have subscribed a very large sum of money in England for exploring the country from the Mississippi to California. they pretend it is only to promote knolege. I am afraid they have thoughts of colonizing into that quarter. some of us have been talking here in a feeble way of making the attempt to search that country. but I doubt whether we have enough of that kind of spirit to raise the money. How would you like to lead such a party? tho I am afraid our prospect is not worth asking the question." [4]   That the hope of extending American influence to the Pacific had taken firm hold on the potential mind of Jefferson became evident during his sojourn in Paris (1786–1787) where he discussed a similar project with a visionary Connecticut Yankee, John Ledyard. Ledyard was born with the *wanderlust* in his blood. Despaired of by his family because he would not study law, disapproved by the faculty of Dartmouth College because he preferred live facts to books, at twenty-five years of age he took his life in his own hands and got a berth as common sailor on a schooner bound for England. Reaching London just as Cook was enlisting men for his third voyage round the world, the Yankee boy had the good luck to secure appointment as corporal of marines. What he saw of Nootka Sound and the Russian trading post on Unalaska implanted a firm determination to secure some share in the fur trade for his own compatriots. "If it was necessary that a European should discover the existence of the continent, in the name of *Amor Patriae* let a native explore its resources and boundaries. It is my wish to be the man." Returning to the United States, Ledyard wrote an account of Cook's last voyage, by way of attracting attention to the rich possibilities of the northwest coast, and he actually succeeded in inducing so canny a business man as Robert Morris of Philadelphia to propose the fitting out of a trading vessel; but the merchants of Boston and New York distrusted the dreamer.

Concluding that America was not ripe for such an enterprise as he had conceived, Ledyard turned to France for financial backing and, arriving in Paris in 1784, he found there two American sympathizers, Paul Jones and Thomas Jefferson. The former was ready to take part in a trading venture, provided the French government would furnish aid. This, however, was not forthcoming. The latter saw a chance to realize a daring dream. Jefferson tells the story of his relations with Ledyard in his life of Captain Lewis (printed as introduction to Biddle's *Lewis and Clark*): "I proposed to him to go by land to Kamschatka, cross in some of the Russian vessels to Nootka Sound, fall down into the latitude of the Missouri, and penetrate in and through that to the United States." This was a simple programme on paper, but practically impos-

sible, since Ledyard had no capital, the permit that
Jefferson had hoped to secure through the French
embassy was refused, the Russian hunters did not then
go so far south as Nootka Sound, and the latitude
of the upper Missouri was quite unknown. However, neither of these devoted optimists was wont
to be daunted by cold facts. Ledyard went to Stock-
holm and, unable to secure a sledge, tramped the
whole distance to St. Petersburg (*via* Lapland, Fin-
land, and Tornea), twelve hundred miles around the
Gulf of Bothnia. There a passport was grudgingly
vouchsafed (June 1, 1787) and Ledyard joined an
emissary of the Empress Catherine—Dr. William
Brown—for the journey to Barnaul midway of his six-
thousand-mile journey. Thence the indomitable
Yankee travelled with the Cossack mail carriers
across Siberia to Irkutsk and thence to Yakutsk.
Here he encountered an old acquaintance of Cook's
company, one Billings, sent by the Russian government to chart the islands of the North Pacific. The
realization of his hopes seemed at hand, and Ledyard
was readily induced by the rival explorer to accompany him back to Irkutsk. There Cossack police,
sent express by the empress, arrested the American
and carried him post haste five thousand miles back
across Siberia and Russia and deposited him in Po-
land, west of the frontier. The importunities of the
Russian fur traders, determined to maintain their
monopoly of the Aleutian Islands, had raised an impassable barrier between Ledyard and his goal. It
was a crushing blow. Broken in health and utterly
disheartened, the dreamer, bereft of his hope, re-

turned to London. "I give up," said he to his English friends. "I give up,"[5] he wrote to Jefferson. His reputation for courage and resource was such as to secure for him the leadership of the expedition that was being sent out by the African Association to discover the source of the Nile; but his life was spent. He died (1788) at Cairo on the way out.

Undiscouraged by this tragic failure, Jefferson ventured a new project. In 1792, he induced the American Philosophical Society, of which he was then vice-president, to undertake the financing of an expedition that "should ascend the Missouri River, cross the Stony Mountains, and descend down the nearest river to the Pacific," for the purpose of finding a feasible trade route. André Michaux, the botanist and explorer, was selected to head the enterprise; but unluckily the French consul, Genet, had need of Michaux, and he was despatched to Louisville to confer with George Rogers Clark as to the prospect for detaching the aggrieved Kentuckians from their allegiance to the United States. Thus Jefferson's second scheme came to nought. Meantime another member of Washington's Cabinet, Attorney General Knox, was moving in the same direction. He instructed General Harmar, then in command on the Ohio, to send a party up the Missouri to its source. Captain John Armstrong was selected for this hazardous duty. Alone, in a dug-out canoe, he set out to paddle up the alluring river (1790). He had proceeded some distance when he encountered fur traders descending, who told him that the Indians

were on the war-path and that no white man would
be allowed to pass. Rightly deeming that discretion was the better part of valor, Armstrong returned
to St. Louis.

The authorities of this frontier post of the Spanish
dominions had been by no means negligent of the
great possibilities of the mysterious river that poured
its muddy tide into the Mississippi within their jurisdiction. Zenon Trudeau, the ambitious governor of
Spanish Illinois, had organized the "Commercial
Company of the River Missouri" for the purpose of
developing the fur trade, and he hoped to find a route
to the South Sea. Three expeditions were sent up
the Missouri. The first (1794) was led by J. B.
Trudeau, the schoolmaster of St. Louis, but he was
attacked and robbed by the Sioux and got no farther
than the Pawnee villages. The second effort under
Lecuyer was no more successful; but the third
under James Mackay, a Scotchman from Montreal
who had become a Spanish subject, had better fortune. Mackay founded three trading posts between
the Platte and the Niobrara, and John Evans, a
Welshman of the party, succeeded in reaching the
Mandan villages. The result in furs was so slight,
however, that the Commercial Company decided to
abandon the enterprise, and the expedition was recalled. Evans died soon after, crazed by drink and
exposure, but Mackay was adequately rewarded by
the far-seeing Carondelet, who assigned him a land
grant of 55,000 *arpents* on the north bank of the
Missouri and the position of *commandante* at St.
André.[6]

Lewis and Clark. — As president, Jefferson had unforeseen opportunity to promote the exploration he had so long had at heart. The acquisition of Louisiana gave the United States control of the Missouri River and direct access to the Shining Mountains, beyond which lay the Oregan of Carver's hopes. On January 18, 1803, three months before the signing of the purchase treaty, Jefferson sent a confidential message to Congress recommending the appropriation of $2500 to meet the expenses of an expedition up the Missouri to its source and beyond to the Western Ocean. The object assigned for this extraordinary government enterprise was the extension of "the external commerce of the United States" and the promotion of our trade with the Indian tribes, who were then furnishing "great supplies of furs and peltry to the trade of another nation, carried on in a high latitude through an infinite number of portages and lakes shut up by ice through a long season." [7] The president did not conceal his hope that the furs hitherto monopolized by the British traders might be diverted to St. Louis. Down-stream transportation by rivers open for navigation the year round offered advantages which must ultimately prevail.

Meriwether Lewis, Jefferson's private secretary, was appointed to command the expedition. This remarkable man was then barely thirty years of age. Born in Albermarle County, Virginia, under the shadow of the Blue Ridge, he had inherited the best traits of a race of patriots and pioneers. His father and uncle had served in the Revolutionary War, the latter on the Cherokee frontier. From boyhood he had been accustomed to the life of the hunter and woodsman, and he had seen military service in the Northwest Territory, having fought under Mad Anthony Wayne. That his imagination was captivated by the possibilities of the vast realm beyond the Mississippi is evidenced in the fact that he had applied for this adventurous post when it was offered to Michaux. Lewis lacked the technical training in botany and astronomy required for such scientific observations as were proposed, and with a view to making good this lack, he went to Philadelphia, where the *savants* of the Philosophical Society gave him all the assistance in their power. While in this city, he superintended the manufacture of the arms for his party in the arsenal at Lancaster. With Captain Lewis in this arduous enterprise was associated his friend and companion in arms, William Clark of Louisville, Kentucky, a younger brother of George Rogers Clark and an experienced backwoodsman. Besides distinguishing himself at the battle of Fallen Timbers, Clark had shown marked ability in conducting large trains of pack horses through a difficult country, and had given evidence of tact and good judgment in the negotiations carried on with the Spanish posts beyond the Mississippi.

The news of the ratification of the treaty of purchase, signed May 2, 1803, reached the United States early in July. On the fifth of that month, Captain Lewis left Washington for Pittsburgh. There he learned to his delight that William Clark had consented to serve as his aid and would join the party at Louisville. He proceeded down the Ohio, stopping at the various garrisons to find his men. Fourteen soldiers were enlisted and two French boatmen. Clark brought with him nine Kentuckians and his body servant York, a faithful friend who proved useful in more ways than one.[8] Thirty picked men were secured, Kentuckians for the most part, men of courage, resource, and endurance. All were carefully tested as to physical fitness, and some hundred volunteers were rejected as unequal to the strain likely to be imposed. All were young men and single. One, George Shannon, was a mere boy of seventeen when he met Captain Lewis, caught the fever of adventure, and ran away from home to join the party. He proved by no means the least dependable man of the force. The pecuniary inducements held out by the recruiting officers were army pay and the soldier's portion of public lands with which a needy government was wont to meet its obligations.

The party arrived at Cahokia in the autumn of 1803, too late to ascend the Missouri before ice formed. It was therefore determined to go into winter quarters on a little stream emptying into the Mississippi opposite the Missouri, the Dubois or Wood River. Here in United States territory, as Jefferson shrewdly opined, the soldiers' pay and winter rations might be charged to the War Department. A far more important consideration, and one that must have appealed to the commanders, was separation from the dissipating influences of the trading post across the river.

The delay was necessitated not only by the lateness of the season, but by the fact that the purchase had not been ratified in Upper Louisiana, and the Spanish officials were still in authority; but it proved a most fortunate postponement. The winter was spent in drilling the men and inculcating a *corps d'esprit* that proved an all-important factor in their ultimate success. This body of "robust, healthy, hardy young men" accustomed to the freedom — not to say license — of the frontier, were led with a tact and firmness that evoked their steadfast loyalty. Plenty of muscular exercise was provided by the emergencies of camp life. Men like Gass, who had some skill as carpenters, sawed planks and raised the cabins; John Shields, the blacksmith of the party, manufactured the nails and rough tools; other men were sent out to hunt; others still made sugar from the maple trees, pioneer fashion. Target practice made an important part of every day's programme, and guard duty was rigidly maintained. The little company was divided into three squads of eight men each, and each squad was under the command of a sergeant elected by the group. Ordway, Floyd, and Pryor were the men thus honored. Captain Lewis insisted that as ready obedience be rendered to the sergeant in command as to himself or to Captain Clark. The camp regulations were at first galling to these backwoodsmen. No one was to absent himself from camp without express permission, and no whiskey was to be served from the contractor's store except the legal ration of a half gill per man each day. The winter's discipline brought the little force to the highest point of efficiency. Each man was like tempered steel, a tool wrought for its task.

The equipment was provided no less carefully than the men, and the meagre appropriation of $2500 was expended with the strictest economy. Lewis estimated that there would be required for "mathematical instruments, $217; arms and accoutrements extraordinary, $81; camp equipage, $255; medecin & packing, $55; means of transportation, $430; Indian presents, $696; provisions extraordinary, $224; materials for making up the various articles into portable packs, $55; for the pay of hunters guides & Interpreters, $300; in silver coin to defray the expences of the party from Nashville to the last white settlement on the Missisourie, $100." [9]

There remained barely $87 for the contingencies that might arise in the course of a journey of four thousand miles by an unknown route to a destination far beyond the limits of the United States authority. Never was so momentous an enterprise so thriftily furnished! Strict attention was given to the prevention of waste, and provisions were of the simplest description. "Parchmeal," cornmeal, hulled corn, flour, biscuit, pork, coffee, beans, peas, and lard were laid in at St. Louis. These, with seven barrels of salt and the sugar made at Wood River camp, did not admit of much luxury.[10]

The ceremony of the formal transfer of Upper Louisiana to the United States (March 10, 1804), Lewis attended as the official representative of the American government. It was a strangely symbolic occasion. The change of allegiance from Spain to France had not yet taken place, and so the mingled Spanish and French population of Laclede's village watched the Spanish flag lowered to give place to the French, and that in turn to give way to the Stars and Stripes. Contending emotions of chagrin and hope must have swayed the aliens present. The traders probably approved the change, but the *habitants* who had left their farms in the Illinois Country to escape English rule could not see the American flag floating over St. Louis without dismay.

At St. Louis boats were secured for the transportation of the party to the Mandan villages, the farthest known point on the Missouri. A keel boat carrying a large square sail and twenty-two oars, and two pirogues, one of six and one of seventy oars, were deemed sufficient. The keel boat was fifty-five feet long and drew three feet of water. A ten-foot deck at the bow served as a hold for the luggage, while the stern boasted a cabin and forecastle. A swivel gun was mounted amidships. For propelling power the main reliance was the wind, which served admirably in smooth stretches of water; but when the current was narrow and tortuous the navigators had recourse to the *cordelle*, a taut rope attached to the mast with which the boat was towed up-stream by a line of men walking along the bank. When the *cordelle* was impracticable, they were obliged to pole or row, forcing the craft over shallows and rapids by means of these more laborious devices. Seven bales and one box contained the supplies, clothing, implements, ammunition and medicine, while there were fourteen bales and one box of articles to be used in traffic with the Indians. The goods were carefully distributed among the several packages so that the loss of any

one would be less felt. The powder, a necessity of
life in the wilderness, was packed in leaden canisters
of such size that there was just enough powder in
each package to fire the bullets that could be made of
the lead. The canisters were tightly sealed so as to
be water-proof. Sixteen more men, soldiers and
voyageurs, were engaged at St. Louis to accompany
the party as far as the Mandans, bringing the total
force up to forty-five. Two horses were provided to
be led along the bank as an assistance in bringing in
game.

On Monday, May 14, 1804, the little flotilla set
out on the long voyage up the Missouri. Captain
Clark was in command, Lewis being detained in
St. Louis, and he proceeded but a short way up the
river, meaning to test the balance of his lading.
Three times the keel boat ran upon sunken driftwood, and it became clear that the luggage must be
shifted to the stern, so that the boat might surmount these obstacles. At St. Charles, Captain
Lewis overtook the party, bringing with him some
interested visitors, several officers of the United
States army, A. Chouteau, C. Gratiot, and "many
other respectable inhabitants of St. Louis." The
people of St. Charles were no less desirous of doing
honor to the explorers. Clark describes them as
"pore, polite and harmonious"; but poverty did not
prevent their giving a ball, which proved somewhat
too exhilarating to the men. In spite of the notice
posted on May 16: "The commanding officer is fully
assured that every man of his Detachment will have
a true respect for their own dignity, and not make it

necessary for him to leave St. Charles for a more retired situation," Captain Clark was "compelled to punish for misconduct" next day. A court-martial was organized to hear and determine the evidence adduced against Warner, Hall, and Collins "for being absent last night without leave, behaving in an unbecoming manner at the ball last night, and speaking in language tending to bring into disrespect the orders of the commanding officer." The sentence, fifty lashes for Collins and twenty-five for the other two, must have seemed severe to these young blades from Kentucky; but the lesson was not heeded. On June 20 the two last were again court-martialled, Collins "charged with getting drunk this morning out of whiskey put under his charge as a sentinel and for suffering Hall to draw whiskey out of the said barrel intended for the party." This time Collins received a hundred lashes and Hall fifty. A few days later Willard was tried for lying down and going to sleep at his post. He pleaded "guilty of lying down but not guilty of going to sleep." He was, however, found guilty on both counts and sentenced to one hundred lashes, twenty-five to be administered in the evening of four successive days. Two more cases of discipline occurred early in the voyage. For some mutinous words uttered in a bad humor, John Newman was sentenced to receive seventy-five lashes and to be disbanded. An even more serious defection was that of Moses B. Reed, who deserted (August 4) in company with two of the *voyageurs*. Being recovered, he was sentenced to "run the gauntlet four times

through the party, and that each man with nine
switches should punish him, and for him not to be
considered in future as one of the party." This was
the last case of discipline. The company had been
thoroughly sifted, and thereafter every man served
with the steadfast devotion that befitted their high
mission. The *Journals* contain frequent allusions
to the loyalty and courage of the men. The general
health of the party and the absence of serious illness
was due in large measure to the thorough training
they had undergone. But one man was lost during
the exposure and unexpected vicissitudes of fourteen
months in the wilderness.[11]

In accordance with Jefferson's instructions, Lewis
made such observations of the fauna and flora, the
soil and mineral wealth, as might be managed from
the vicinity of the river. Missouri looked to him a
land of promise. The bottoms were well wooded with
walnut, hickory, ash, oak, and cottonwood. Thickets
of wild plum, crab-apple, grape-vine, and honey-
suckle adorned the banks, and there were great
plantations of mulberry trees. Back from the river
lay fertile prairies covered with native grass, growing like timothy but flowered like a hop vine. The
French hunters reported lead deposits on the lower
Missouri, but Lewis was unable to verify their statements. On the upper river, pit-coal was in frequent
evidence, horizontal strata from one to five feet in
depth of "carbonated wood" showing in the river
bluffs. At some points, pumice-stone and a kind of
lava indicated that these surface deposits had been
on fire. On the voyage through the plains there

was no lack of subsistence. It was the "constant practice" to send the hunters off into the wooded bottoms where game abounded. Deer and wild turkeys were always to be had on the lower Missouri, plenty of elk were found near the Kansas, while in the Dakotas vast herds of buffalo appeared. Meat that was not needed for immediate consumption was "jerked" against a day of scarcity. Buffalo humps, elk steaks, venison, beaver tails, wild pigeons, turkeys, geese, and fish in great variety afforded a luxurious menu, so that the salt pork remained untouched among the stores. Yet one man came near starving to death in this land of plenty, for the want of ammunition. George Shannon, who was sent to look for missing horses (August 22), had pushed on ahead of the party, thinking to overtake them. He was discovered on September 11, well-nigh famished. "He had been 12 days without any thing to eate but Grapes & one Rabit, which he Killed by shooting a piece of hard Stick in place of a ball." [12] Another kind of game, even more abundant but less appreciated, was a winged creature recorded by Captain Clark as "musquiters" or "musquetors" or "misquetors" indiscriminately; but they were always "verry bad" or "verry troublesome" and rendered the night camps along the Missouri veritable torture.

At this season of high water, the river offered no serious difficulties even to large boats, but the man at the bow had always to keep a sharp lookout. A muddy current, five hundred yards wide, swirling and eddying among the islands and sand bars, and beset with sunken timber, afforded many a chance for shipwreck. A sudden squall from the prairie often rendered the sails unmanageable and threatened the capsizing of a boat and heavy loss of supplies, if not of life. The shifting channel baffled all experience, for the bottom rose and fell as the treacherous flood carried the sand from place to place. One night when the boats were beached on a sand bar in the middle of the river, the watch suddenly called out that the ground was sinking. The bar was being undermined so rapidly that the men barely got the boats off before their camping ground disappeared. The bluffs frequently caved under force of the current, and tons of gravel, sand, and silt sank beneath the tide. It was therefore unsafe to steer the boat too near the shore or to anchor for the night under a bank.

Notwithstanding these difficulties, the Missouri was already the fur traders' highway. The mighty river with its great tributaries, the Osage, the Kansas, the Platte, the Niobrara, etc., penetrated to the very heart of the beaver country. Our travellers frequently came upon fortified trading posts, some of them abandoned long since and some apparently in use the year previous. Trappers and *voyageurs* were floating down the tortuous channel in *batteaux* and dugout canoes, heavily laden with peltry, furs, and buffalo hides, the fruit of their season's traffic among the Otoes, the Pawnees, the Kansas, or the Sioux. One such party had been twelve months in the Omaha country. Their catch was worth $900, but they were "out of provisions and out of powder" and heartily glad of the hospitality proffered by the captains. Pierre Durion, a Frenchman who had lived twenty years among the Sioux, was encountered coming down the river to St. Louis, and he was easily persuaded to return with the exploring expedition.

On the lower Missouri there was serious danger of a brush with the Kansas, — "dissolute, lawless banditti," as Lewis terms them. Fortunately for the expedition, the " Kaws " were off on a buffalo hunt at this season. In general the Indian tribes were quite friendly to the whites because they brought goods in exchange for their furs, but they were frequently at war among themselves. The nomad tribes, the "Kites" of the western mountains who had acquired horses from the Spaniards, and the Sioux of the northern plains who had secured guns from the British, were the scourge of the agricultural villages of the Osages, Otoes, Cheyennes, Aricaras, and Mandans. An important part of Lewis' mission was to establish peaceful relations between the Indian tribes and the newly established government. He therefore was at great pains to convene representative assemblies of the Indians and to impress upon their chiefs the power and friendly intentions of the United States and the importance of arbitrating their intertribal differences.

On October 21, the explorers reached Heart River, the Mandans' land (Bismarck, N.D.). Here on the bluffs overhanging the east bank were the ruins of nine villages surrounded by earthworks, but abandoned since the smallpox epidemic of 1782.

The surviving Mandans had their dwellings and corn-fields a few miles farther up the river, and here (47° 21′ 27″) the captains determined to establish their winter quarters. The weather had turned very cold, snow was falling, and the men were beginning to suffer from rheumatism. A council was held with the Mandans, peace was negotiated between that nation and the Ricaras, and a friendly understanding was established so that a regular supply of food might be obtained. Captain Clark, who had been looking up and down the river for a suitable camping ground, reported a good position about three miles below the villages, where there was plenty of timber and a spring of good water. There on a point of low ground (Elm Point, heavily timbered to-day), sheltered by bluffs from the dreaded northeast storms, the cabins were built of heavy cottonwood, elm, and ash, stone for the chimneys being brought in the pirogues. The men were divided into squads, some to fell timber, others to burn charcoal and shell corn, others still to hunt the deer and buffalo and lay in a good stock of meat. The northern winter was approaching fast, there was a hard frost every night, and the geese were flying south. By the middle of November, ice began to float down the river. Then the keel boat was unpacked, and its contents deposited in the storehouse. The huts were completed by the twentieth of the month, and not a whit too soon. By the end of November, there was a foot of snow on the ground, and the river was frozen over so that it could be crossed without risk.

A Mandan Village, Bull-boats in the Foreground.

Fort Mandan was sixteen hundred miles from the mouth of the Missouri, and the expedition, being well on its way, could afford some relaxation. A Dakota winter, moreover, was a foe before which the Indians retreated to their lodges, and its severity was quite beyond the experience of these Kentuckians. By the middle of December the thermometer fell to forty-five degrees below zero, and several men were suffering from frozen hands and feet, snow-blindness, and pleurisy. The fort was snug enough and capable of prolonged defence against savage foes. Larocque, a North West Company trader who visited the Mandans that winter, thus describes it: It was "constructed in a triangular form, ranges of houses making two sides, and a range of amazing long pickets, the front. The whole is made so strong as to be almost cannon ball proof. The two ranges of houses do not join one another, but are joined by a piece of fortification made in the form of a demicircle that can defend two sides of the Fort, on the top of which they keep sentry all night; . . . A sentinel is likewise kept all day walking in the Fort." [13] To guard against annoyance from the Mandans, the gates were locked at sunset, and no Indian was allowed to remain in the fort over night except by express permission.

The storehouse was well stocked with venison and buffalo, and the Indians brought plenty of corn which they had cached for winter use in pits near their lodges. One by one the chiefs visited the fort, each attended by a squaw laden with corn or fresh meat. The women would sometimes present for the white man's delectation the favorite Mandan dish, — "a kittle of boiled Cimnins [pumpkins], beens, corn and choke cherries with the stones, which was palitable." [14]   Such donations were scrupulously rewarded in trinkets or tobacco. The par of exchange was very unequal, if cost of production be the measure of value. For example, a fillet of deerskin two inches in width was regarded by these people, who knew nothing of the tanner's art, as equivalent to a fine horse. Even so, the supply of Indian goods might have been exhausted, but for the labors of John Shields, the blacksmith, whose forge was regarded as "great medicine." To him were brought tomahawks and kettles to be mended, and he wrought battle-axes and knives after a pattern of his own that gave great satisfaction to the Mandan braves who coveted the white man's weapons.

"Had these Whites come amongst us," said the chiefs, "with charitable views they would have loaded their 'Great Boat' with necessaries. It is true they have ammunition, but they prefer throwing it away idly than sparing a shot of it to a poor Mandan." The Indians admired the air-gun, as it could discharge forty shots out of one load, but they dreaded the magic of the owners. "Had I these white warriors in the upper plains," said the Gros Ventres chief, "my young men on horseback would soon do for them, as they would do for so many 'wolves,' for," continued he, "there are only two sensible men among them, the worker of iron and the mender of guns." [15]

At the Mandan villages were found several

French Canadians, *voyageurs* and trappers, who had taken native wives and settled down at this remote trading place. Their knowledge of Indian languages and customs, together with the friendly status accorded them, rendered them indispensable as guides and interpreters, although they often proved tricky and unreliable. Lewis at first engaged Jessaume, a crafty fellow, who had lived fifteen years in the region; but he was later dismissed as untrustworthy. Chaboneau, who had lived among the Minnetarees and had married a Shoshone woman, was finally secured. Personally, he was not a great acquisition; but it was thought that his squaw, Sacajawea, might render valuable service when the expedition should reach the land of her people, the Snake Indians of the Rocky Mountains. From the Indians and trappers, the captains obtained much information concerning the country as far as the Rocky Mountains. Beyond the great divide no man of them had ventured.

Not only Mandan chiefs and French *voyageurs*, but British fur traders, were hospitably entertained at the captains' chimney corner. Fort Mandan was not more than one hundred and fifty miles from the North West Company's post on the Assiniboin, and during the winter three or four trading parties arrived, bringing tobacco, beads, guns, and blankets, to be exchanged for furs and horses. McCracken of the North West Company was on his return trip to the Assiniboin factory (November 1), and to him Captain Lewis intrusted the passport given him by the British Minister at Washington as an indication of the peaceful character of the expedition. On December 16, Mr. Hugh Haney brought back a return message, a polite note from Mr. Charles Chaboillez, one of the partners, offering to render any assistance in his power.[16] Since the Americans were not come to trade, there was no occasion for rivalry, and the most friendly relations were maintained. Mackenzie (Charles) writes as follows of this winter at Mandan: "Mr. Larocque and I having nothing very particular claiming attention, we lived contentedly and became intimate with the gentlemen of the American expedition, who on all occasions seemed happy to see us, and always treated us with civility and kindness. It is true, Captain Lewis could not make himself agreeable to us. He could speak fluently and learnedly on all subjects, but his inveterate disposition against the British stained, at least in our eyes, all his eloquence. Captain Clark was equally well informed, but his conversation was always pleasant, for he seemed to dislike giving offence unnecessarily." [17] The facts seem to be that Lewis, charged with the diplomatic responsibilities of the enterprise and hearing that Larocque had attempted to distribute British flags and medals among the Indians, told him firmly that this would not be permitted on United States territory.   Larocque having denied any such intention, he was permitted to use one of Lewis' interpreters in the prosecution of his business, on the express understanding that he would not discuss any subject but that of his traffic and would sell no liquor to the Indians.   This same

Larocque was eager to accompany the party on their journey up the Missouri, but Lewis thought it best to decline his proposal.

Other indications of national rivalry contributed to justify Lewis' caution. The interpreter, Chaboneau, visited the lodges of the Minnetarees, some ninety miles to the north of Mandan, and brought back word that "the Clerk of the Hudson Bay Co. with the Me ne tar res has been Speaking Some fiew expresss[ns] unfavourable towards us, and that it is Said the NW Co: intends building a fort at the Mene-tar-rès." [18]   When Fort Mandan was visited by the Minnetaree chiefs (January 15) they were received with special attention, and their friendship was secured. The hostile influence of the traders was particularly evident in the case of the Yankton Sioux, who had been armed against the Chippeways by Mr. Cameron, an independent trader, from his factory on the St. Peters. They had declared their intention of destroying Lewis' party as "bad medicines," but they dared nothing more than the theft of some horses taken down river by a hunting party. The explorers were destined to experience a farther instance of the deleterious effect of the fur trade on the Indians in the hostility of the Assiniboins, the hereditary foes of the Mandans and Minnetarees. Their neighborhood to the British factories meant that they were well supplied with liquor and firearms, which they doled out to the more distant tribes at their pleasure. Lewis refused to furnish the Mandans with firearms, advising them to keep the peace and await the time when American traders would bring them supplies of every kind. Here, as on other barbarous frontiers, refugees from justice found asylum and added their defiance of law and order to the Indians' instinctive distrust of the whites.

By the middle of February the winter had moderated, and the party began to make preparations for the voyage up the Missouri. Spring came none too soon, for the stock of meat laid in during November and December was exhausted, and it was difficult to procure more. The hunters went sixty miles in pursuit of game, but the deer and elk and buffalo they brought back were so lean as to be poor nourishment. On February 18 the men were reduced for the first time to a vegetable diet, — the corn and dried squashes brought in by the squaws. The pirogues were soon chopped and pried out of the ice, and dragged to the shore with a windlass and elkskin ropes. The barge proved unwieldy for these devices, and it was decided, moreover, that she was too large for the upper Missouri. Canoes enough to take her place were built by a gang of men sent out to a cottonwood grove under direction of Sergeant Gass. By the first of March the river began to break up, and swans, ducks and wild geese were seen flying toward the northeast. The boats and pirogues were ready on the twenty-first. On the twenty-ninth the river, which had been rising for several days, broke through the ice, and the water came down in floods. The men were set to getting out the stores and Indian goods that they might dry in the sun, and the supplies were packed in eight duplicate divisions "so as to preserve a portion of each in case of accident."

From Fort Mandan, Lewis sent to President Jefferson a letter reporting the journey up to date, together with a map of the region still to be traversed, based on "testimony of a number of Indians who have visited that country, and who have been separately and carefully examined on that subject, and we therefore think it entitled to some degree of confidence." [19] On the same day that the expedition set out up the Missouri, the barge started back to St. Louis, with seven soldiers, two Frenchmen, and Mr. Gravelines as pilot. Lewis' letter, together with the journals kept by himself and Captain Clark, were communicated to Congress (February, 1805), and furnished the first authentic information to reach Washington concerning the party. Plans for the future were more or less hypothetical, but the captains anticipated little difficulty in reaching the Great Falls of the Missouri. There the pirogues were to be abandoned, and the voyage pursued in skin canoes to the head of navigable water. Beyond this "any calculation with respect to our daily progress can be little more than mere conjecture." It was hoped that the journey overland from the sources of the Missouri to the Columbia might be greatly facilitated by horses to be purchased of the Indians for the transportation of luggage.

On the seventh of April, 1805, the little flotilla, two pirogues and six dugout canoes, set out on its great adventure. Lewis wrote to Jefferson, "At this moment, every individual of the party are in

good health, and excellent sperits; zealously attached to the enterprise, and anxious to proceed;
not a whisper of discontent or murmur is to be
heard among them; but all in unison, act with the
most perfect harmoney. with such men I have
every thing to hope, and but little to fear." [20]   All
superfluities were dispensed with. Firearms and
ammunition, carpenter's and blacksmith's tools, the
iron frame of a boat which Lewis had brought from
Harper's Ferry and expected to put together for the
voyage beyond the falls, and such of the provisions
as had been saved — some parched meal, portable
soup, pork, and flour — made up the luggage.

Navigation of the upper Missouri proved to be
comparatively easy. The water was shallow and
muddy, and sand bars were frequent; but the
caving banks and treacherous driftwood that beset
the lower river had well-nigh disappeared. Sails
could be used for long stretches, and the *cordelle*
was readily worked from the low banks. The only
serious difficulties were the occasional strong head
winds and the sudden squalls that threatened an
unwary steersman with capsize. The ever present
mosquitoes besieged the night camps, and dust
storms arising in the waterless plains blinded the
eyes; but, with these exceptions, the voyage was a
pleasure excursion. Traces of Indians were seen,
abandoned lodges and empty whiskey casks, indicating the recent presence of Assiniboins. The
captains were on their guard, but by great good
fortune they had no encounter with this "vicious,
illy disposed nation."

The Little Missouri was passed on April 12, and here two Frenchmen, who had accompanied the party up the river, stopped, thinking the prospect for beaver excellent. They were the first white men to trap in this region. A few miles above they passed a stream (Indian River) which they called Chaboneau's Creek because this man had once camped there. It marked the limit of his knowledge of the Missouri. Lapage, one of the *voyageurs*, had penetrated a little farther; but beyond Mussel Shell Creek, the great waterway was unexplored. On April 26, the beautiful river, known to the French as the Rochejaune, was reached. The Indians had assured them that this tributary took its rise in the mountains, near the source of the Platte and Missouri rivers. Lewis suggests in his journal that the plateau on the right bank of the Missouri, two miles above the mouth of the Yellowstone, would be a good point for a government trading post. Building stone was at hand and fresh, sweet water, and the two rivers gave access to rich fur country. "The beaver of this part of the Missouri are larger, fatter, more abundant and better clad with fur than those of any other part of the country that I have yet seen; I have remarked also that their fur is much darker." [21] The first considerable river flowing in from the north or left bank was called the Milk, because of "the peculiar whiteness of its water, which precisely resembles tea with a considerable mixture of milk." [22] Exploration proved that this great river drained a beautiful valley, with wide, fertile bottom lands of rich loam. It was surmised that the source might be near the Saskatchewan and that the Milk might afford communication with British waters. On May 9, they passed "a most extraordinary river," which they decided to call the Bigdry; "It is as wide as the Missouri is at this place or half a mile wide and not containing a single drop of runing water; some small standing pools being all the water that could be perceived," [23] although there were indications that in the rainy season the river bed was filled with a mad torrent. Here, too, the ravages of the beaver were evident. "In [one] place particularly they had cut all the timber down for three acres in front and on nearly one back from the river and had removed a considerable proportion of it, the timber grew very thick and some of it was as large as a man's body." [24]

As the explorers entered the foot-hills, the temperature fell, and ice appeared along the river's edge; pines and cedar trees began to supplant the cottonwood, and the air was astonishingly dry and pure. As the stream grew more rapid, "riffles and rocky points" rendered navigation difficult. The current was too strong for oars and too deep for the pole, and the canoes had to be dragged along by the *cordelle*. The men were frequently obliged to jump into the water to stave the boats off the rocks, and the strain on their endurance was great. "The men are compelled to be in the water even to their arm-pits, and the water is yet very could, and so frequent are those point[s] that they are one fourth of their time in the water, added to this the

Beaver on the Upper Missouri, showing the Brush Cutting.

banks and bluffs along which they are obliged to pass are so slippery and the mud so tenacious that they are unable to wear their mockersons, and in that situation draging the heavy burthen of a canoe and walking acasionally for several hundred yards over the sharp fragments of rocks which tumble from the clifts and garnish the borders of the river." [25]

On May 25, Captain Lewis ascended some hills near Windsor Creek, Elk Rapids, and descried the snowy peaks of the "Rock Mountains." The sources of the Missouri must be near at hand as well as that pass over the great divide which would lead to westward-flowing rivers, and Lewis was keenly aware that the difficulties of his journey had begun. On June 3, they came upon a river flowing in from the north, as large as the Missouri and so similar in general character that the captains were at a loss to determine which was the real Missouri. "To mistake the stream at this period of the season, two months of the traveling season having now elapsed, and to ascend such stream to the rocky Mountain or perhaps much further before we could inform ourselves whether it did approach the Columbia or not, and then be obliged to return and take the other stream would not only loose us the whole of this season but would probably so dishearten the party that it might defeat the expedition altogether." [26]

The men, notably the *voyageurs*, held that the northern fork, a shallow, muddy stream, was the course to follow; but the captains were inclined to think that the south branch, being clearer and more rapid, came more directly from the mountains. Reconnoitering parties were therefore sent out up the two rivers and into the hills in the hope of getting some definite clew. The first day's effort bringing no decisive result, the two captains set out, Lewis up the north fork and Clark along the south, two days' journey. The result confirmed them in their first opinion. Lewis followed his river fifty-nine miles and, observing that the mountain range was trending to the northwest, concluded that the stream must drain the vast intervening valley and could lead to no divide. He named it Maria's River for a cousin back in Virginia. Clark, on the other hand, after working his way with great difficulty forty-five miles up a narrow valley with precipitous sides, was fully convinced that the south branch had its source in the snow-clad mountains to the southwest. Meantime the men, relying on the views of Cruzatte, the most experienced of the boatmen, held to their contrary opinion. There was one sure criterion. The Mandans had been positive that on the Missouri, a little to the south of the setting sun, there was a great waterfall not to be confused with any rapids. Lewis therefore determined to push up the south fork until he should reach the falls or encounter the mountain barrier so dreaded by the men. He set out on June 11, taking with him four men. Captain Clark, meantime, employed the others in dressing elkskins for the light canoes and in caching the pirogue and all the luggage that could be spared, together with some provisions, tools, and powder, to await the return journey. After three days' march, Captain Lewis' heart was gladdened by the roar of a distant waterfall, and from a point of high land he saw "the spray arrise above the plain like a collumn of smoke which would frequently dispear again in an instant caused I presume by the wind which blew pretty hard from the S.W." [27] Seven miles' rough walking brought him to the Great Falls of the Missouri. Shields was despatched down the river to direct Captain Clark to bring the party to this point, while Lewis, seating himself on a rock under the centre of the falls, surrendered himself to enjoyment of "this truly magnificent and sublimely grand object which has from the commencement of time been concealed from the view of civilized man." [28] The mighty rush of water was more to him than a natural wonder; it was the vindication of his foresight, the assurance that he was on the right trail to the mountain pass that should lead him to the Columbia.

The eighteen-mile portage round the Great Falls occupied a fortnight and seriously taxed the endurance of the men. A rude wagon was constructed for transporting the canoes and heavier luggage, sawed sections of cottonwood trees serving for wheels. Never was a more awkward cart trundled over a rougher road by human muscle. The improvised vehicle broke down again and again, and finally the load had to be transferred to the men's shoulders. Lewis spent the two weeks in making a full and exact description of Giant Spring, the Falls, and the ten miles of cataract above and below.

His word picture, together with Captain Clark's map, make up an account of the region that is still standard, notwithstanding the changes wrought by the Great Northern Railroad, the smelters, and the town of fifteen thousand inhabitants that render Great Falls a centre of prosperous industry.

Elk and buffalo were still abundant, and the hunters were engaged in bringing in game, jerking the meat for the mountain journey and tanning the skins for the covering of the iron boat frame. This was now set up and the hides carefully fitted on. Elk-skins were preferred because stronger and more durable than buffalo, and less liable to shrink. Having no tar to calk the seams, they used a composition of charcoal, beeswax, and buffalo tallow; but this unfortunately cracked off when the boat was placed in the water, and "the Experiment" that had cost so much time and labor was regretfully abandoned. The beeswax and tallow composition held to the untanned buffalo hides, and the captains were forced to the conclusion that these would have served the purpose better; but it was too late to make the change. The buffalo were fast retreating to the plains, the season was advancing, and the party must be over the divide before winter set in. Resort was had to the cottonwood, and two additional dugouts were manufactured. The men, meantime, had repaired their clothing and made new moccasins with double soles, calculated to resist the spines of the prickly pear.

It had been the original intention to send back a canoe from the Falls with journals, etc., to inform

the President of the safety of the party; but that was
now thought unwise. "Not having seen the Snake
Indians or knowing in fact whether to calculate on
their friendship or hostility we have conceived our
party sufficiently small and therefore have concluded
not to dispatch a canoe with a part of our men to St.
Louis as we had intended early in the spring." [29]   The
decision was a wise one, but the failure of the expected
report occasioned Jefferson much anxiety.

On July 15 the canoes were launched in the upper Missouri, and the mountain journey was begun.
The river wound through a narrow valley, well
wooded and radiant with bloom. Sunflowers, wild
cucumbers, and lambs-quarter covered the banks,
while the levels were beset by the prickly pear, "one of
the greatest beauties as well as the greatest incon-
veniences of the plains." Navigation grew laborious
as the velocity of the current increased, and the
men walked, to lighten the canoes. Parallel to the
river ran an Indian road, evidently much used, and
this it was hoped would guide them to the encamp-
ments of the Snake or Shoshone Indians. From
these people Lewis expected to get horses and information as to the most practicable route; hence it
was of the utmost importance neither to miss them
nor to encounter their hostility. Horse tracks in the
road, willow huts recently abandoned, and signal
fires lighted to warn stragglers of the neighborhood
of their inveterate foes, the Minnetarees, indicated
that the Shoshones were not only near, but were on
their guard. To prove that his people were white
men and friends, Lewis directed that pieces of cloth,

linen, and paper be left along the trail. Captain Clark followed the road with three of the men, while the canoes were poled and towed through the picturesque cañon, then first seen by white men and appropriately named the Gates of the Rocky Mountains. Arrived at White Earth Creek, Sacajawea recognized the clay banks where her people were accustomed to come for the paint with which they tattooed the bodies of their braves, and she said that the Three Forks of the Missouri was at no great distance. This was the point of rendezvous where the canoes were to await the walking party. Lewis camped for several days at a spot where Sacajawea said she had been captured five years before, and explored the three rivers, which they named after the leading statesmen of that day, Jefferson, Madison, and Gallatin; but although three Indian trails converged here, they failed to find the Shoshones.

On the thirtieth of July, Lewis took the road, leaving Clark, who was well-nigh exhausted, to bring on the canoe party. Travelling was laborious and slow by both canoe and trail. Beaver were extraordinarily abundant, damming the streams and diverting the water in a way that was sometimes inconvenient. The river was so tortuous that they had to travel twelve miles to make four, and they were in constant danger of capsize. Horses had become a necessity. Pushing on up the Jefferson, they passed streams which they named Philosophy, Wisdom, and Philanthropy, after the "cardinal virtues of that justly selibrated character" (names long since degraded to Willow Creek, Big Hole River, and

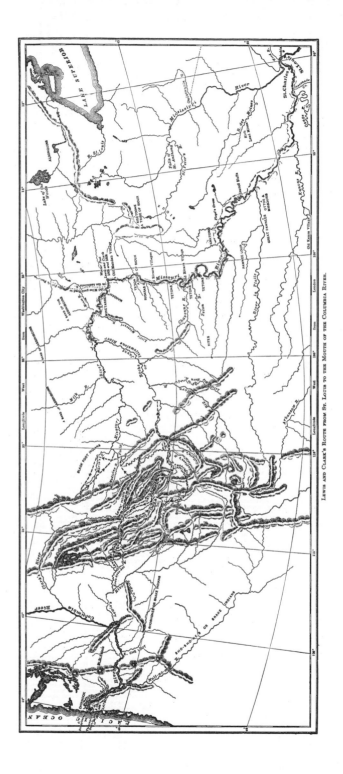

LEWIS AND CLARK'S ROUTE FROM ST. LOUIS TO THE MOUTH OF THE COLUMBIA RIVER.

Stinking Water). Lewis, determined to find the Indians at any cost, pressed on by forced marches to the Two Forks of the Jefferson (Beaverhead River). After a careful reconnoissance, he decided to take the south branch (Trail Creek), and followed it to its source in Lemhi Pass. Crossing the divide, they found a stream flowing to the west, "a creek of the Columbia" (Lemhi Creek or Lewis River). Here the jubilant pioneers camped for the night (August 12) and, building a fire of dry willow brush, cooked their last piece of pork. They were three thousand miles from the mouth of the Missouri and out of provisions, but happy with the prospect of success.

The next morning "very early," Lewis and his companions followed the Indian road down the valley of the Lemhi, hoping to come upon an Indian camp. They were soon rewarded by the sight of two women, a man, and some dogs, but the people ran away in terror. To disarm their suspicions and to get speech of them required all the diplomacy of which Lewis was master. Some women were finally persuaded, by presents of beads and vermilion paint, to lead the white men to their camp. Cameahwait, their chief, was induced to smoke the pipe of peace, and a United States flag was presented to him as an emblem of alliance. The hungry travellers were then feasted on cakes made of dried berries, the only food in the lodge, and the important business of securing horses and guides was undertaken.

Cameahwait feared that the strangers might be in league with his dreaded foes, the Minnetarees; but Lewis assured him that they were an advance guard of a large party of white men who had crossed the mountains to find the road by which to bring the Shoshones arms and merchandise in trade, that the rest of the party were now waiting on the Jefferson River, and that he could prove the truth of this statement by accompanying them back to the Forks. To this proposal the chief assented, and set out next day accompanied by eight warriors. The success of the negotiations now depended on the prompt arrival of the main party. Lewis reached the Forks on the sixteenth to find no trace of Clark. Cameahwait's suspicions were allayed with difficulty, while Drewyer was despatched down the river to hasten the coming of the canoes. Captain Clark's party came in sight next day, and the fears of the Shoshones were set at rest, once for all, by the appearance of Sacajawea. In true fairy tale fashion, Cameahwait recognized her as his long-lost sister, and she was welcomed to the tribe with every token of joy and affection. Henceforth the Shoshones were ready to serve the white men to the extent of their ability.

The chief wealth of the Shoshones was in their horses. Cameahwait's tribe possessed some seven hundred, as well as a few mules which were prized even more highly. Both horses and mules were secured by trade with the Spaniards, from whose settlements they were ten days distant *via* the Yellowstone route.[30] Cameahwait complained bitterly that the Spaniards would sell no guns, and that they were defenceless against the Minnetarees, who were supplied by the British factors and therefore invincible.   The Shoshones were no less war-like by nature.   "If we had guns, instead of hiding ourselves in the mountains and living like bears on roots and berries, we would then go down and live in the buffalo country in spite of our enemies, whom we never fear when we meet them on equal terms."

Lemhi Pass is comparatively easy of access, but it leads to some of the most difficult territory in the Rocky Mountains.   Cameahwait drew on the ground a map of the mountain chains and rivers that lay between his country and that of the Chopunnish (Nez Perces), and said they had told him that the streams he knew flowed into a river that "ran a great way toward the seting sun and finally lost itself in a great lake of water which was illy taisted, and where the white men lived." [31]   The Indians reported the mountain streams so dangerous for canoes and so difficult of navigation that it was evident the luggage must be transferred to pack horses.   Thirty-two animals were purchased at a cost of one hundred dollars in trinkets, and pack saddles were put together out of oar handles and rawhide.   An old man who knew more of the region than any other Shoshone was engaged as guide, and on August 30 the expedition set out in quest of the Pacific.   The two weeks' sojourn had given the men time to recruit their strength and to repair their moc-casins and deerskin clothing.   Little food had been accumulated, for deer and mountain goats, the only game in the mountains, were scarce and shy.   The Indians had nothing to eat but salmon, berries, and roots, dried for winter use, and were about to migrate to the buffalo ranges on the upper Missouri. There was plenty of trout and mullet in the creeks, but to supply so large a party with so small a fish required more time than the approach of winter allowed, and they were forced to depend on the pork, flour, and parched corn brought out from St. Louis. The Indians having assured them that the route directly west, along the Salmon and Snake rivers, was too rough to be practicable for horses, the party followed the guide, "over the worst road that ever was travelled," back across the divide directly north by the Nez Perces Pass to a branch of the Bitter Root River which they called Clark's in honor of the second in command. On September 3 the first snow fell, a plain warning that delay was dangerous. Yet they were obliged to halt two days at Traveller's Rest Creek (Lou Lou Fork) in order to rest, mend their moccasins and collect food, their scant store of provisions being almost exhausted. The utmost efforts of the four hunters could not feed the company, however, and they were forced to have recourse to the colts, three of which had followed the horses.

Lolo Pass led them from the Bitter Root Valley to the Kooskooskee, the south fork of the Clearwater River. They were now on the Columbia watershed, but travel was increasingly difficult. The mountains overhung the river, and the road, often covered with snow, was only "a narrow, rockey path generally on the side of [a] steep precipice, from which in many places if e[i]ther man or horse were precipitated they would inevitably be dashed in pieces." Horses and men were suffering for lack of food. The record for September 18 reads: "We took a small quantity of portable soup, and retired to rest much fatiegued. several of the men are unwell of the disentary."[32] Captain Clark pushed ahead in the quest of game and arrived on September 20 at an encampment of Nez Perces. The Shoshone guide could not speak their language, but by signs he made them understand the friendly intentions of the white men and their famished state. The Indians offered what food they had, some jerked buffalo meat, dried salmon, berries, and roots, "all of which we eate hartily."[33] Clark succeeded in buying some of this food to send back to Lewis and his men, who had exhausted their provisions and were reduced to crow's flesh. The unaccustomed luxury of sufficient food made them all ill. Even the captains were thrown out of commission for a few hours; but they cheerfully dosed one another and the men with Rush's pills, and were soon fit for travel. Twisted Hair, the Chopunnish chief, drew a map of the river on a white elkskin with a charred coal. According to this, they were still two days' journey from the point where the Kooskooskee emptied into the Snake River and seven days' from the great river that flowed from the northwest; thence it was five days by boat to the falls where the whites came to trade. The junction of the Kooskooskee and Snake rivers was reached on the twenty-seventh, and there all the able-bodied men set to work building the canoes that were to transport them to the sea. The horses were branded and left in charge of

Twisted Hair, while the saddles and part of the ammunition were cached for the return journey. The Columbia itself was not reached till October 16. The down-stream voyage in the canoes was luxurious after the four months of strenuous mountain travel, and relaxation came none too soon, for nearly all the men were ill. The only serious difficulty still to be encountered was scarcity of food and fuel. Dogs, purchased of the Flathead Indians, made more wholesome eating than dried fish and roots, but the lack of fire-wood often occasioned real suffering. Fortunately the salmon season was at hand, and the Indians from far and near had come to lay in their winter food. Their lodges and fish-flakes were frequently seen along the shore, and plenty of fresh salmon was to be had for a song. In spite of rapids and sand bars, the canoes made from thirty to forty miles a day. On October 19 they came in view of a snow-clad peak to the west which they rightly surmised to be the mountain named St. Helens by Vancouver. On the twenty-third they portaged round "the Great Falls," called *Timm* by the Indians in imitation of the rushing torrent.

Below the Great Falls, a new type of Indians, the Escheloots, were in possession. They dwelt in houses built of split timber, wove baskets of cedar roots, and wore well-made garments of skin. Their trade with the Skilloots of the lower river had supplied them with British muskets and kettles and the cast-off clothing of British sailors. One brave cut a ridiculous figure in a pea-jacket and a round hat beneath which he wore his hair in a queue. The dangerous passage of the Dalles was made in the canoes, to the astonishment of the natives, to whom the expertness and daring of Cruzatte were a marvel. On the first of November they portaged round the Great Shoot or Cascades and launched their boats in tide-water at last. The banks of the lower Columbia and the slopes of the mountains were well wooded with pine, spruce, white oak, cottonwood, and alder, and there was no longer any scarcity of fuel. Game and wild fowl were abundant. Canvasback duck and red char were the delicacies with which these way-worn travellers were regaled on their voyage down the river. Indian villages were frequent, and the trading canoes of the Skilloots were passing to and from the Great Shoot. The mountain tribes had been timid, but hospitable and honest. The Skilloots proved to be altogether too familiar with white men, and their overtures were even annoying. "We soon found them to be very assuming and disagreeable companions." They stole whatever they could lay their hands on, even the pipe which they were smoking in token of amity. Association with the traders had demoralized the Coast Indians, and it was necessary to impress them with the necessity of keeping their distance.

The Cascade Range once passed, the dry air of the mountains gave way to fog and rain. On the seventh of November, the spirits of the party were greatly cheered by the sound of distant breakers, the tumultuous uproar made by the tide as it meets the outflowing current, — the terrible bore at the mouth of the Columbia. The much-desired Pacific gave them a most inhospitable welcome.   The canoes, not built for rough water, were tossed about like corks in the waves, and the little flotilla was obliged

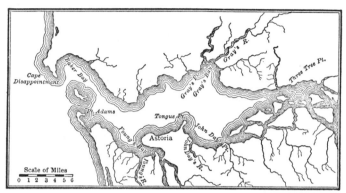

THE MOUTH OF THE COLUMBIA RIVER.

to put ashore at the first feasible landing.   A narrow beach with overhanging bluffs barely gave them room to draw themselves and their luggage free from the surf, and a south wind drove the driftwood over the water-logged canoes.   After spending the night in safeguarding their belongings, the men were glad to move.   A second camp, ten miles farther on, proved somewhat safer, though no less uncomfortable. A high west wind, continuous rain, and heavy surf held them storm-bound here from November 16 to 25.   Meantime, the two leaders were exploring both banks of the river for a point of high ground, accessible to wood, fresh water, and game, and suitable for a winter camp.   Not till the eighth of December was the location decided upon, but the excellence of the site justified the delay.   On a little river flowing into Meriwether's Bay (later Young's) about three hundred feet back from the Columbia and thirty feet above the level of the high tides, in a grove of lofty pines, they determined to erect their fort. Here were built seven cabins and a storehouse, and a strong palisade surrounding all. A secondary camp was established on the near-by coast, where a detachment of men was employed in the manufacture of salt. They moved from the leaky tents into the huts on the twenty-fourth, and Christmas Day was celebrated by a very light-hearted company.

Fort Clatsop seemed to be as well built and as well provided with the necessities of life as Fort Mandan; but the contrast between a camp in the dry cold of North Dakota and one at sea level, under the sway of the Japanese Current, soon became evident. The journals record rain, rain, rain, day after day. In the five months spent at the mouth of the Columbia, there were but twelve days free from rain. The effect upon the health of the party soon became apparent. Working and sleeping in soaked leather clothing, a week at a time, the men sickened and grew discouraged. The salt makers gave out first, but they succeeded in putting by twelve gallons of salt for the return journey before the works were abandoned. The Clatsop Indians of the coast were a demoralized set. Smallpox had ravaged their villages in 1775 and 1800, and familiarity with the whites had broken down their native virtues. They were amazingly shrewd at a bargain, and were ready to sell anything, from wappatoo to women, to the highest bidder. In spite of their friendly bearing, the commander, assured that their fidelity was not to be depended on, ordered the men to be always on their guard against treachery. The Indians were never allowed within the fort in large numbers, and they were regularly excluded at night. The men were kept busy indoors dressing elkskins and fashioning the clothing that was to serve for the return journey, and Gass records that they made three hundred and thirty-eight pairs of "mockasons," for their own use and to trade with the Indians. The captains employed the long winter months in making careful studies of the race traits and customs of the Indians, and in compiling minute descriptions of the fauna and flora of the region; but to the men, the depressing weather and comparative inactivity were more trying than the hardships of that forced march across the mountains. They suffered much from rheumatism and general debility, and, though they were systematically dosed with Rush's and Scott's pills, saltpetre, sage tea, and laudanum, they did not readily recover tone. So many had not been ill at one time since leaving Woods River. Toward the end of February, the hunters reported that elk were retreating to the mountains some nine or ten miles to the eastward, a distance to which it was practically impossible to follow them through the dense forest and bring the meat back to camp. This was most unwelcome news, "for poor and inferior as the flesh of this animal is, it is our principal dependence for subsistence." The flagging strength of the men required better food than the dried salmon and wappatoo roots,

which was all the Indians had to sell.   The record for
February 26 reads: "We have three days' provisions only in store, and that ·of the most inferior
dryed elk, a little tainted.   A comfortable prospect
for good living!"   On March 5 there was no more
elk meat, fresh or dried, and but two days' supply
of other food.   The captains began to discuss the
advisability of breaking camp and moving slowly
up the river, procuring subsistence by the way.

Just this emergency had not been foreseen.   Jefferson had provided Lewis with letters of credit that
might be drawn against the president of the United
States in any part of the world; but they were of no
avail to entice elk from the mountains and could not
be converted into food and clothing and goods for the
Indian barter until the arrival of the trading vessels,
and these did not usually put into the Columbia
before April.   The government should have sent a
supply ship to meet the expedition at the mouth of
the Columbia, but such a measure might have
entailed international complications.   By the end
of March the situation had become intolerable, and
they only awaited suitable weather to set out for
the mountains.   Lewis' journal states (March 20),
"We have accomplished every object which induced
our remaining at this place except that of meeting
with the traders who visit the entrance of this river.
. . .   It would have been very fortunate for us
had some of those traders arrived previous to our
departure from hence, as we should then have had
it in our power to obtain an addition to our stock
of merchandize which would have made our home-

276 EXPLORERS AND COLONIZERS

ward bound journey much more comfortable." [34]
Their stock in trade was indeed lamentably reduced.
All the small articles, says Lewis, "might have been
tied up in two handkerchiefs." There were, beside,
half a dozen blue and scarlet robes, Captain Clark's
artillery coat and hat, five robes made of the United
States flag, and some ribbons. Little enough to pay
their way back to St. Louis!

With great difficulty they secured two of the
Indian canoes, which, with the three pirogues,
served to accommodate the party. The price paid
for one of these beautiful boats, equal in value to a
wife in Clatsop estimation, was Captain Lewis'
uniform laced coat and half a carotte of tobacco.
"I think," says the despoiled owner, "the U'States
are indebted to me another Uniform coat, for that of
which I have disposed on this occasion was but little
woarn." [35] A rostrum of the party was posted at the
fort with a brief statement of the objects and achievements of the expedition and a sketch of the connection
between the upper branches of the Missouri and the
Columbia rivers and of the route by which they proposed to return. Several copies of the statement were
left with the Indians, in the expectation that one might
fall into the hands of some trader and so find its way
back to the United States. Two at least of the French
voyageurs elected to remain with the Clatsops. Philip
Degré and Louis Rivet took to themselves Indian
wives and built cabins on French Prairie, an open
meadow on the Willamette River.

If Lewis' party had been able to hold out a fortnight longer, they would have been relieved. Jewitt's

INDIAN TEPEES ON THE COLUMBIA RIVER.

INDIAN CANOES ON THE COLUMBIA RIVER.

Narrative records that the *Lydia* of Boston, the ship by which he was rescued, put into the Columbia in April, 1806. "When about ten miles up the river at a small Indian village, we learned from the inhabitants that Captains Lewis and Clark from the United States of America had been there about a fortnight before, on their journey overland, and had left several medals which they showed us." Captain Hill carried away one of the written statements; but since he was bound for Canton, his news did not reach the United States until January, 1807. Oddly enough, on the very day (March 14, Old Style) that the captains broke camp, de Resanoff's ship, the *Neva*, attempted to run into the Columbia, but was prevented by the sudden shifting of the wind from northwest to southeast. Von Langsdorff entered Gray's Bay in a *bidarka* and saw the smoke of the Indian villages, but had no communication with the inhabitants.

All arrangements being complete and the weather partially clearing, the canoes started up the Columbia on March 25. The Multnomah (Willamette), unnoticed hitherto, was explored by Captain Clark for a few miles to the falls and a map of this river secured from an aged Indian. From the point where the city of Portland now stands, Clark descried four snow-covered peaks — Jefferson, Hood, St. Helens, and Adams. Mt. Rainier he does not seem to have distinguished from St. Helens, with which it lies almost in line. "At this place I think the width of the river may be stated at 500 yards and sufficiently deep for a Man of war or ship of any burthen." [36]   In spite of the pilfering propensities of the Falls Indians, the luggage was safely portaged round the Cascades, but one of the pirogues was lost. At the Dalles, the current proved too strong for navigation. The boats were therefore exchanged for horses enough to carry the luggage, and the journey pursued by land. The dry, pure air of the plains proved very invigorating, and the invalids rapidly recovered. The party was most hospitably received by the Wallah-wallahs, and here additional horses and a dozen dogs were purchased for crossing the mountains. Captain Clark was able to defray the expenses of the journey by his medical services to the natives. Broken arms and sore eyes and skin diseases were the ailments treated by this empirical physician.

On Chopunnish (Touchet) River they came upon Twisted Hair and found, to their relief, that the horses left with him were in good condition. Sixty-five animals, the pack-saddles, and the ammunition were recovered without difficulty from this honorable chief, and a stock of dogs and Indian bread was accumulated. The party had come to consider dogs' flesh very good eating, more nutritious than elk or salmon. In the mountains the situation was far more difficult. The Indians themselves had exhausted their winter supply of provisions, and could offer little more than dried roots, a diet that made the men ill. Recourse was again had to horse-flesh, and the colts proved not bad provender, yet the march up the Kooskooskee was seriously hampered by lack of food. The hunters went so far afield as to be in frequent danger of being lost, yet brought in nothing but pheasants and a sand-hill crane. All hope of laying in dried meat for the journey across the mountains had to be abandoned, and the stock in trade was divided among the men, that each might purchase roots at his own discretion.

The snow lay deep, but the Indian guides kept the road so skilfully that wherever the ground appeared, the track was clearly discerned. The caches were found in good condition, and the supplies of powder, salt, and medicine fortunately reënforced. At Traveller's Rest Creek, beyond the Bitter Root Range, the party divided. Captain Lewis, with nine men, undertook to cross the divide by the usual Indian trail over Lolo Pass to Medicine River and the Great Falls, for the purpose of exploring Maria's River and ascertaining whether it might not afford a practicable trade route to the Saskatchewan. The remaining men and Chaboneau's family went with Captain Clark by way of the Big Hole or Gibbons Pass to the Wisdom River, and thence down the Jefferson and up the Gallatin to the Yellowstone and the Missouri. A better plan to render the return trip serviceable to fuller knowledge of the region could hardly have been devised. The two parties were to reunite at the mouth of the Yellowstone.

Once on the buffalo ranges east of the mountains, all danger of starvation was at an end. Clark undertook to shorten his road by striking directly across from Clark's (Salmon River) to the head of Wisdom River, the practicability of the route being indicated by buffalo paths and Indian trails. The other party, meantime, had no difficulty in reaching the Great Falls, whence Lewis set out to explore the Maria's. Gass and Ordway, with six men, he sent to White Bear Island to build canoes, with instructions to start down the Missouri in case he himself did not return by the first of September. Lewis, with Drewyer and the two Fields, set out on horseback directly north. They had got to Battle River, within one hundred and fifty miles of the British trading post (as far as where the town of Cut Bank now stands) when they fell in with the dreaded Minnetarees of Fort de Prairie, and were forced to turn back. These treacherous miscreants attempted to steal the guns and horses, and in the scuffle that ensued, in spite of Lewis' endeavor to avoid bloodshed, two of the Indians were killed. To avoid meeting the larger band, as well as to warn Ordway's party of the neighborhood of hostile Indians, the four men mounted their horses and rode at a desperate pace to the mouth of Maria's River, one hundred and twenty-five miles to the southeast. There they arrived in safety on July 28, a full week before they were expected; but the canoes were fortunately ready, and the whole force embarked immediately and thus avoided farther difficulty. They overtook Clark's contingent on August 12 at the junction of the Missouri with the Yellowstone, and here two hunters — Dickson and Hancock of the Illinois country — joined the party, intending to accompany them as far as the Mandans.

The voyage to St. Louis was uneventful. The canoes made from eighty-five to one hundred miles a day, and the mosquitoes were the only serious foes encountered. At the Mandan villages they purchased a supply of corn and dried squash with beaver skins taken on the Yellowstone for this purpose. There they left Chaboneau and the faithful Sacajawea and picked up a deputation of Indian chiefs — Minnetarees and Mandans — who were to visit Washington. Several trading parties were pushing up the river, eager to profit from the new fur regions revealed by the explorers. John Colter, one of Lewis' men, obtained permission to return with them as guide to the Yellowstone country. Early in September, the party reached the first white settlements and noticed that there had been a marked increase during their two years' absence. The sight of cows grazing on the bank caused the men to raise a shout of joy. At La Charette, they fired a salute and, landing, were received with all courtesy by the inhabitants. "Every person, both French and americans seem to express great pleasure at our return, and acknowledged themselves much astonished in seeing us return. they informed us that we were supposed to have been lost long since, and were entirely given out by every person " [37] except the president. The night of the twenty-first was spent at St. Charles; the twenty-second, with a cantonment of United States troops on Coldwater Creek. On the morning of the twenty-third, the expedition "decended to the Mississippi and down that river to St. Louis at which place we arrived about 12 o'Clock. we suffered the party to fire off their pieces as a Salute to the Town. we were met by all the village and received a harty welcome from it's inhabitants, &c." [38] The two captains immediately ordered civilized garments, that they might be equipped for polite society. On the twenty-fifth they paid some formal calls and attended a dinner and a ball given in their honor. The final record for September 26 states, "We commenced wrighting"; apparently the journals were now elaborated from the rough notes taken *en route*.

Lewis' first concern was to secure adequate compensation for the men who had so faithfully followed his lead. They were rewarded by a generous grant of bounty lands in addition to their arrears of pay; but the journals state that most of the men disposed of their claims within ten days. They preferred hunting to farm life. Clark was appointed superintendent of Indian affairs, a most suitable position and one which he ably filled for many years. In one capacity or another he administered justice in Louisiana Territory until 1824. His wide knowledge of the Indian tribes, their languages and customs, and his reputation for decision and courage, gave him great influence everywhere on the frontier. His word was law with the Indians, from the Mississippi to the Pacific, while his fearless integrity made him the terror of evil-doers, both red and white. Lewis' later career was not so fortunate. He was immediately appointed governor of Louisiana Territory, a post for which his experience at Washington as well as his knowledge of the Missouri country rendered him eminently fit. Summoned to Washington in 1809, he was journeying thither on horseback along the Natchez Trace, when he met with a violent death at Grinder's Stand, a rough frontier inn in the Chickasaw country. Jefferson accepted the statement of Grinder's wife that her distinguished guest shot himself in the night, and he cited a tendency to fits of depression as adequate explanation of the act. But nothing short of mental aberration could account for suicide on the part of a man who was returning home to an aged mother and many friends, and who had every reason to expect an appreciative reception both from his friend and patron Jefferson and from the government officials; who had, moreover, still to perform a highly important task — the editing of those journals that were to give to the world the full results of the most successful expedition yet achieved by an American explorer. Quite another story was currently believed by the settlers along the Natchez trail. Grinder's reputation for rascality was such that they made no doubt he had killed Lewis for the money he carried.

Pike; Expedition to the Sources of the Mississippi

No less significant for the future of the fur trade was the expedition to the head waters of the Mississippi carried through by Lieutenant Z. M. Pike under the auspices of the War Department, — August 9, 1805, to April 30, 1806. The voyage up the Father of Waters was by no means so difficult as the ascent of the Missouri. A keel boat was used to Prairie du Chien and there exchanged for a flat-bottomed bateau[39] which transported the party to the Falls of St. Anthony, and thence a light barge, more practicable for the portages, was used as far as Little Falls. Here the bulk of the party was left in winter camp, while Pike and two men pushed on with canoes and sledges over the seven hundred miles between this point and Cass Lake. He found the North West Company in full possession of the beaver grounds of Minnesota. They had trading posts at Sauk Rapids, Sandy Lake, and Leach Lake, whence they transported the furs by easy carries to Lake Superior and Montreal.

PIKE'S MISSISSIPPI EXPEDITION, 1805-6.

Their Indian trade extended as far south as Prairie du Chien, while their bateaux descended the Mississippi to St. Louis and New Orleans. On the river St. Peters, Murdoch Cameron was prosecuting an independent business.

It was an important part of Pike's mission to assert the authority of the United States in this border country and to enforce the regulations in respect to the fur trade. The law of 1786 required that every trader should obtain a license from the territorial authorities, and imposed heavy penalties for the sale of liquor to the Indians. Jay's treaty (1794) permitted British subjects to trade within American territory so long as they conformed to the law, but their influence over the Indians was thought to be dangerous. It was to keep these British agents in check and to convince the aborigines of the good-will and resources of the United States that Congress had indorsed the policy of maintaining government trading posts at strategic points along the Canadian frontier — such as Fort Wayne, Detroit, and Chicago — where goods were sold at cost and furs received at fair and even liberal prices. Pike recommended that such factories be established at the mouth of the Ouisconsing, at the Falls of St. Anthony, on the St. Peters, and on the St. Louis River at the head of Lake Superior, in the belief that the trade *via* the Mississippi, the Red River of the North, and the Great Lakes might thus be brought under control. The representative of the United States government made it his business to see that the laws were enforced. Finding that Murdoch Cameron "had taken liquor and sold it to the Indians on the river St. Peters, and that his partner below had been equally imprudent, I pledged myself to prosecute them according to law; for they have been the occasion of great confusion and of much injury to the other traders." [40] When

La Jeunesse was detected in the same underhand practice, this energetic disciplinarian sent him the restrictions in writing and demanded his license. The accused could show only a tax certificate indicating that he had paid the required fee on the goods sold in Indiana territory.

With the representatives of the North West Company, our young lieutenant was no less firm. This ambitious association had pushed its commerce from Athabasca to the head of Lake Superior and across the St. Louis River portage to the rich beaver country about the sources of the Mississippi. While maintaining the most cordial relations with the factors, Pike insisted that they should respect the authority of the United States and abstain from distributing British medals among the Indians and disseminating among them ideas hostile to the rightful government. At Sandy Lake, the famished explorers were received by Mr. Grant (agent for Mr. Dickson of Sauk Rapids) in his very comfortable quarters and treated to a sumptuous repast of bread, tea, and fresh venison; but the British flag was floating over the fort, and Pike could not forbear a protest. "I felt indignant, and cannot say what my feelings would have excited me to do, had he not informed me that it belonged to the Indians. This was not much more agreeable to me." [41] At Leech Lake, Hugh McGillis, of the North West Company, was no less hospitable. The wayworn traveller "had a good dish of coffee, biscuit, butter, and cheese for supper," and was entertained for the fortnight (February 1–12) of his stay; but no considerations of courtesy could deter Pike from asserting the sovereign rights of his government. "Mr. McGillis asked if I had any objections to his hoisting their [British] flag in compliment to ours. I made none, as I had not yet explained to him my ideas." [42]   A few days later (February 10), however, the record reads: "Hoisted the American flag in the fort. The English yacht [jack] still flying at the top of the flagstaff, I directed the Indians and my riflemen to shoot at it. They soon broke the iron pin to which it was fastened, and brought it to the ground." [43]   Against this exhibition of frontier diplomacy, McGillis had nothing to say.   During his sojourn at Leech Lake, Lieutenant Pike drew up a careful statement in writing of the limitations under which a foreign trader might operate within the boundaries of the United States, and McGillis accepted the justice of his rulings.   Pike stipulated that British traders coming into United States territory were amenable to the jurisdiction of our government. They must obtain licenses of our agents, pay duties at the frontier on goods imported from Europe (this would have amounted to $13,000 in 1806), abstain from giving or selling liquor to Indians, from distributing British flags and medals to the natives, and from flying the British flag over forts. These measures were calculated to put the Americans on a par with the British traders and to check the southward extension of the North West Company's operations.[44]   On the downstream voyage, the expedition frequently encountered traders from St. Louis coming up the river in barges, bateaux and dugout canoes, eager to avail themselves of the new opportunities opened up by the explorers.

Pike's expedition had no lasting influence however. Congress and the men of the East were preoccupied in the contest with Great Britain that culminated in the War of 1812. The fur trade of the Mississippi continued to be exploited by the North West Company, which maintained posts at Mackinac, Fond du Lac, and Prairie du Chien. The Union Jack floated at the latter post until 1815.

CHAPTER III

THE FUR TRADE

Section I

Government Control vs. Laissez-faire

Spanish Policy. — During the Spanish occupation of Louisiana Territory the fur trade was prosecuted, although under heavy handicaps, along the Missouri, Osage, and Kansas rivers. The firm of Maxent, Laclede & *Cie.*, chartered by the French intendant in 1762, continued to carry on business from St. Louis throughout the Spanish régime. Other lesser houses were granted licenses to trade in restricted areas, on terms varying with the state of the market.[1] Permits were put up at auction and knocked down to the highest bidder. The small trader, who had usually offered more than the normal yield of his district, was forced to make good his obligations to the governor and to the merchants of New Orleans by extortionate dealings with the Indians from whom the furs were purchased. Goods were sold them at exorbitant prices, liquor and firearms were offered as the most enticing bait, and the unbusinesslike redman was tricked into the trader's debt by the credit system. Supplies for the winter's hunt were furnished with the stipulation that the advance be repaid in skins the following spring. The unsophisticated Indians regarded these advances as tribute given for permission to pass through their territories unharmed. They brought the trader such furs as they could spare, to induce him to return with another cargo of goods, but they did not understand the necessity of balancing accounts. Any attempt to force a fulfilment of obligations was met by reprisals. Having the advantage of superior numbers, the braves attacked the trading posts, plundering and maltreating the unlucky occupants. They had little fear of destroying the trade that brought them the much coveted fire-water and blankets; for one trader ruined, a new man was sure to appear, with wares even more alluring. The Missouri tribes were wont to say: "The white men are like dogs, the more you beat them and plunder them, the more goods they will bring you, and the cheaper they will sell them." [2] Occasionally, when their outrages passed all bounds, when some man of importance was killed or some frontier settlement attacked, the governor would sally forth on a punitive expedition; but the slow-moving Spanish force was no match for the cunning of the natives. The only effect was to deepen their contempt for the white man's authority. The war, notwithstanding, was reported to Madrid with due solemnity, and the expenses charged to the king's treasury at several times the actual cost. Under a government so demoralized by "graft," no business could flourish. Manuel Lisa, who had enjoyed the monopoly of trade on the Osage River under the Spanish administration, wrote General Clark (1817) of his satisfaction in the change of masters : "I have suffered enough in person and property, under a different government, to know how to appreciate the one under which I now live." [3]

The Spanish governors could not even protect their licensees against foreign interlopers. British traders from Montreal despatched their bateaux down the Mississippi and up the St. Peters and Desmoines rivers, quite undisturbed by the cumbrous galleys sent to intercept them; and rich cargoes of furs, collected at their trading mart, Prairie du Chien, passed up the Wisconsin and Illinois portages every spring.

British Fur Traders

The policy of the British government had always been to foster this pioneer industry without regard to public revenue. The Hudson's Bay Company, through its century-old monopoly of trade on all waters emptying into its ice-guarded sea, had waxed stronger than the colonial government and enjoyed sovereign powers within its vast territory. Exempt from the fear of competition, its policy had been to send no more furs to European markets than the condition of trade might warrant and to husband the resources of Prince Rupert's Land for future generations of merchant adventurers. Factories were built at convenient points where navigable rivers emptied into the bay, and the Indians were taught to bring their season's catch to these depots, to which the goods for trade were brought direct from London. By this system the heavy costs of river transportation were met by the redmen, and the whites were spared the labor and the risks of voyages into the interior. Under the guns of the forts, moreover, the factor had the Indians completely in control. Intoxicating liquors and firearms were withheld, and the demoralization of the natives prevented. Since the fur-laden canoes could make their way down to the factory only in the months when the rivers were free from ice, the beaver meadows and deer parks were left undisturbed during the breeding season, a circumstance that meant much for the conservation of the industry. The dams and the young were free from molestation till the winter's hunt, so that the propagation of each season made good the season's kill, and the skins were taken only when the fur was in prime condition. The Hudson's Bay Company had authority to expel from its territory all unlicensed traders and persons who were deemed prejudicial to peace. Its control of the market enabled it to carry out a policy of fixed prices and standard goods; its employees — factors, clerks, and *engagés* — were well paid and well fed. They were assured of continuous service and of provision against sickness and old age. The British government stipulated that an employee who had faithfully fulfilled his contracted term must be reëngaged or returned to his home. He might not be abandoned in the wilderness. The result was to attach to the Company's service a body of devoted men who had no other ambition than to deserve well of the great business organization to which they belonged.

Toward the end of the eighteenth century the placid monopoly of the Hudson's Bay Company was rudely broken. The treaty of Paris opened the rich possibilities of the St. Lawrence River and the Great

Lakes to the Scotch merchants of Montreal. These
upstarts sent their trading parties along the routes
discovered by the French and reaped a rich harvest.
Restrained by no licenses, regulations, or traditions,
they intercepted the Indians on their way to the
Hudson's Bay Company factories, offered them
higher prices or more attractive goods — liquor and
firearms if need be — and succeeded in wheedling
away the stock of furs intended for the great
company. To secure their season's complement of
pelts, the agents of the Hudson's Bay Company
were obliged to adopt the methods of their competitors. *Coureurs de bois* were despatched up the
Albany and Nelson rivers and the lakes to which they
lead, where they came into conflict with the unlicensed traders from Montreal. Bloody encounters
followed. The rivals did not hesitate to rob and
even murder one another in the prosecution of their
business interests, and there was no authority strong
enough to prevent. The fur trade rapidly degenerated into a lawless ruffianism in which the most unscrupulous carried off the spoils, in which the Indians
were demoralized by the white man's worst vices,
and all profits were swallowed up in the costs of
armed defence.

At this melancholy juncture (1781) an epidemic of
smallpox decimated the tribes, carrying off whole
villages and putting a sudden stop to both hunt and
trade. The merchants of Montreal, on the verge of
ruin, determined to pool their interests. A combination was achieved in the years 1783–1805 which, under
the name of the North West Company of Merchants

of Canada, organized the western fur trade anew and on a scale that overshadowed the great company of the north. The partners of the North West Company were for the most part Highland Scotch, men of strenuous strain and far more forceful and enterprising than the officials of the Hudson's Bay Company. The business was organized on a profit-sharing basis that enlisted the best efforts of every man on the force, from chief factor to newly apprenticed clerk. The capital (£40,000 in 1788 and £125,000 in 1798) was furnished by the partners resident at Montreal. The personal contribution made by the wintering partners, whose headquarters were at the several posts, was regarded as a fair equivalent, so that to each one of the twenty to forty partners was accorded an equal share in the profits. Men entering the business must first serve a seven years' apprenticeship with a fixed salary; but they were sure of promotion more or less rapid in proportion to their skill and devotion, as evidenced in returns. The North West Company employed two thousand *voyageurs* at £40 per year and an equal number of free trappers and *coureurs de bois*, who were paid according to the number of skins brought in. The wages were high, but exorbitant charges for supplies brought most of the money back into the Company's coffers. Whiskey, for example, which cost $2 per gallon, was sold for $8 a quart, while the "Northwest currency" used throughout the fur country was reckoned at double the value of legal coin.

The Northwesters pursued the policy of carrying the trade to the Indian villages, but the trading parties were provided with recruiting stations in a series of fortified posts along the lakes and rivers from Fort William at the southern end of the Grand Portage between Superior and Winnipeg to the Rocky Mountain House on the upper Saskatchewan. Alexander Mackenzie even projected a transcontinental trade. With the prestige of his overland expedition fresh upon him, he went to London to promote the establishment of a Fishery and Fur Company that should exploit the fur trade of Nootka Sound and the Columbia River and the whaling grounds of the Arctic Sea. Trading goods and supplies were to be sent from Montreal, while the skins and oil were to be shipped to the East India Company's factories in the Orient.[4] It was a daring proposition, quite beyond the conception of contemporary Londoners; moreover, the Hudson's Bay Company had sufficient influence at Westminster to defeat the project.

For a generation to come the Northwest Company swayed the destinies of the stretch of wilderness between the Great Lakes and the Pacific coast. In the relentless pursuit of wealth, they explored the rivers, traversed the plains, and planted new posts, and thus established trade relations with the remotest tribes. Fort Assiniboin, Fort Athabasca, the Rocky Mountain House, Fort Kootenai on the upper Columbia, Spokane House at the junction of the Spokane River with the Cœur d'Alene, marked the westward reach of the Scotch trader.

These operations brought the Northwesters into conflict with the Hudson's Bay Company on the north and within the jurisdiction of the United States government on the south. The boundary of the British dominions was fixed at the forty-ninth parallel by the treaty of 1794, and it became necessary to ascertain the precise limits of their hunting grounds. In 1798 David Thompson, a self-taught surveyor and geographer, was sent to determine the relative location of the North West Company's posts. Thompson had served his apprenticeship with the Hudson's Bay Company; but when ordered by his superiors to forego discovery and devote his time to the pursuit of furs, he transferred to the North West Company where exploration was encouraged. He had already mapped the Saskatchewan and Assiniboin rivers and found his way up the Souris to the Mandan villages when intrusted with this larger commission. He now followed the Red River of the North to the headwaters of the Mississippi, and ascertained that Fort Pembina on Red River and the trading establishments on Sandy and Leech lakes lay south of the proposed boundary and well within American territory. However, since the privileges of British traders were expressly conceded in the treaty, the posts were not removed. In 1805 Thompson again visited the Mandan villages on the upper Missouri and bespoke the friendly offices of that then important tribe.

The faults of the Northwesters — and faults they had in plenty — arose from excess of zeal. The factors, being partners and profit sharers, worked under the keenest incentive. Wherever they had to meet competition, they resorted to underhand methods. They had no scruple about rum selling, and the prices for goods and furs were determined by the necessities of the situation. The *Journals* of Alexander Henry, the experienced factor of Fort Pembina, bear witness to the rapid deterioration of the natives under this reckless régime. The Assiniboins had no buffalo to hunt and were readily reduced to complete dependence upon the beaver trade. The annual journey to the factory being no longer required, they were able to trap through the summer, — the season when the fur was inferior. Thus the market was glutted with low-grade skins, while the animals were butchered, young and old, until the richest hunting grounds were exhausted.

The Hudson's Bay Company was forced to use similar methods or quit the field. Its traders were sent up the rivers to compete with the Northwesters, and posts were planted in the interior. The sale of liquor was permitted in the contested districts, and the Indians were cajoled or threatened by the rival traders until they lost their original respect for the British name. In defence of its prior claims to the Saskatchewan traffic, the North West Company did not scruple to use force, and posts were burned and traders murdered in that no-man's land under the shadow of the Rockies. The long warfare culminated in the struggle for possession of the Red River of the North. The Hudson's Bay Company undertook to found an agricultural colony in this fertile valley, the beaver being extinct, with a view to developing the latent resources of the territory. To this end a considerable grant of land (one hundred and sixteen thousand acres) south of Winnipeg was allowed by

Parliament to Lord Selkirk, a Scotch philanthropist who proposed emigration as a solution for the distressed peasants of the Highlands. A colony was sent out in 1812 with supplies and agricultural implements, and a promising beginning was made. But, unfortunately, the lands lay in the path of the North West Company. Its partisans attacked the settlement and scattered the colonists, burning and killing as if there were no law but their own interest. The home government was forced to interfere at last, and the only feasible solution, the consolidation of the two companies, was reached in 1821. The new Hudson's Bay Company was stronger than ever before, having undisputed monopoly of the fur trade throughout British America.

The American Policy

As early as 1796 Congress passed an act for the regulation of the Indian trade, restricting licenses to persons of good character and requiring heavy bonds for the observance of the law against the sale of liquor; but the law was never thoroughly enforced because the fur country was remote from official centres and evidence of infractions was difficult to obtain. Subsequent legislation considerably abated the rigor of the law. Fees and penalties were reduced, while the bond and the certificate of good character were altogether remitted. It was hoped that the maintenance of government factories at the several Indian posts where standard goods should be offered at reasonable prices and a fair rate paid for furs, would keep the private traders within bounds. One after another, government stores were opened, as new and remoter regions were reached by the fur trade, — at Arkansas Post and Natchitoches and on the Sulphur Fork of Red River, Belle Fontaine at the mouth of the Missouri, Fort Osage, Marais des Cygnes, and Desmoines in the interior. The government official, however, found great difficulty in competing with the independent traders, whether British or American. He was handicapped by the requirement that supplies must be bought and goods sold in the home market, where goods were higher in price and inferior in quality to those of foreign manufacture and where the supply of furs was in excess of the demand and prices correspondingly low. Advances on credit were not permitted because the practice was thought to be pernicious, but without these advances the Indian could not start on the season's hunt. The government factor, moreover, was usually stationed at a post distant from the beaver meadows, and the hunters were expected to bring their catch to him. This they were not likely to do while the Northwesters and *coureurs de bois*, Scotch, French, and American, followed the tribe to the hunting grounds and offered them blankets, whiskey, and firearms on credit for the season's take. The plan adopted by the United States government was admirable, but its non-enforcement left private traders pretty much to their own devices.

Section II

The Fur Traders of St. Louis

Louisiana Territory was rich in furs. The mountain rivers, not only those traversed by Lewis and Clark, but the sources of the Platte and the Arkansas and the numerous streams that spring from that core of the continent, the Wind River range, abounded in beaver meadows. The aborigines placed little value on the pelts and were glad to trade such as they had for whiskey, firearms and gewgaws; but they could rarely be induced to engage in systematic trapping expeditions. A Northwester familiar with the Assiniboins complained that the Indians of the Missouri would not take the trouble to hunt for beaver. "They often remarked to me that they would think it a pleasure to supply us with beavers if they could be secured the same as buffaloes by a chase on horseback, but they considered the operation of searching for them in the bowels of the earth, to satisfy the avarice of the Whites, not only troublesome, but very degrading. 'White people,' said they, 'do not know how to live, they leave their houses in small parties, they risk their lives on the great waters, among strange nations, who will take them for enemies. What is the use of beaver? Do they make gun powder of them? Do they preserve them from sickness? Do they serve them beyond the grave?'" [5] In default of native hunters, the fur traders were obliged to employ white trappers.

The Great Plains from the Missouri to the Rio

Grande made one immense buffalo range. The herds migrated with the season from north to south, seeking out the water courses which furnished them food and drink and the salt licks of the open prairie. With them moved the bands of Indian hunters, who depended upon the buffalo for existence. Gregg, the Santa Fé trader, describes the havoc wrought among the herds. "This animal furnishes almost the exclusive food of the prairie Indians, as well as covering for their wigwams and most of their clothing; also their bedding, ropes, bags for their meat, &c.; sinews for bow-strings, for sewing moccasins, leggins, and the like." "The continual and wanton slaughter of them by travellers and hunters, and the still greater havoc made among them by the Indians, not only for meat, but often for the skins and tongues alone (for which they find a ready market among their traders), are fast reducing their numbers, and must ultimately effect their total annihilation." [6]

Throughout the first half of the nineteenth century, the fur trade was the dominant industry of the Far West. The annual value of its operations at St. Louis rose from $200,000 to $300,000, and the returns netted the trader from fifteen to fifty per cent. Great fortunes were amassed in this business, until the animals upon which it thrived and the Indians who had served its ends vanished together from the vast regions exploited by its agents.

By its advantages of location, St. Louis was destined to be the primary market for the American fur trade. Lying at the confluence of the rivers

along whose reach lay the beaver haunts and
the buffalo plains, all water transportation centered
there. Thence, too, the Mississippi conveyed the
precious packs to the fur merchants at New Orleans
and by sea to the profitable markets of the east, or by
way of the Wisconsin and Fox rivers to Green Bay,
or *via* the Illinois and Chicago rivers to Lake Michigan, Detroit, Buffalo, and Montreal. Spring and
fall, the wharves "under the hill" were thronged
with craft bound to or from the Missouri: the keel
boat of the licensed trader, laden with Indian goods
for the out voyage; the Mackinaw or flat-bottom
scow, weighted to the water's edge with packs of
beaver and buffalo skins; the dugout canoe of the
free trapper, who had paddled in from some name-
less mountain or prairie stream with his season's
catch of furs, robes, tallow, and buffalo meat.

During the great days of this industry the number
of white men employed by the St. Louis traders grew
from five hundred to one thousand. They were
French or Spanish creoles, young *habitants* bent on
adventure, Canadian *voyageurs* who had drifted down
from the north, or American frontiersmen, — restless
spirits like Daniel Boone whom the restraints of civilization had driven into the new wilderness beyond
the Mississippi. Working as *engagés*, at a stipulated
wage and keep, or as free trappers, relying on a
competitive market to recompense them for the
season's outlay, they spent their hard-earned money
in drink and carousal,[7] and rarely realized more than
a bare subsistence from a life of extraordinary hardship. Frenchmen, whether from Canada or Loui-

siana, made up three-fourths of the *engagés* on the Missouri. Gay and volatile, readily assimilating with the Indians, illiterate, unenterprising, content with the scantiest fare, they were the "cheerful slaves of the fur trade." [8] The Americans, on the other hand, hailing from Kentucky or the Illinois country or even from far Virginia, were blood-kin to the Long Knives. Resourceful, intelligent, courageous, and self-reliant, scorning subservience and prone to desert under discipline, they were always dependable for self-determined service and usually preferred the position of free trapper to that of a hireling. From this class the ranks of the traders were recruited. A shrewd employer was governed by these race traits in the assignment of labor. The Canadians were the boatmen and the dressers of skins and performed the menial duties of the camp or post. At trapping or fighting or seeking out new fields of enterprise, they were less to be relied on. If Astor judged rightly that in river service one Canadian was worth three Americans, it was no less true that in the wilderness one American was worth three Canadians.

No sooner were the fur traders of St. Louis assured, by the observations of Lewis and Clark, of the rich resources of the upper Missouri than they made preparations to reap the golden harvest. The first considerable expedition was fitted out by Manuel Lisa, a man of Spanish antecedents, whose experience on the Osage had given him intimate knowledge of the Indian character and customs. In the spring of 1807 he left St. Louis in a keel boat laden with goods.

His first assistant was the same George Drouillard whom Lewis had found so valuable as hunter and interpreter. At the mouth of the Platte, they met a white man descending alone in a canoe. He proved to be none other than the intrepid John Colter, returning from a rather disastrous experience on the Yellowstone. Lisa induced him to join the party and venture his life a third time in the wilderness. A vivid account of Lisa's outfit is given in Brackenridge's *Journal*. Brackenridge was a young lawyer from Pittsburgh who had begged the privilege of accompanying Lisa's party in order to see for himself the possibilities of the Louisiana Purchase. He describes with enthusiasm the keel boat, the *voyageurs*, and the equipment. "Our barge was the best that ever ascended this river, and manned with twenty stout oars-men. Mr. Lisa, who had been a sea-captain, took much pains in rigging his boat with a good mast, and main and topsail; these being great helps in the navigation of this river. Our equipage is chiefly composed of young men, though several have already made a voyage to the upper Missouri, [a feat] of which they are exceedingly proud, and on that account claim a kind of precedence over the rest of the crew. We are in all, twenty-five men, and completely prepared for defence. There is, besides, a swivel on the bow of the boat, which, in case of attack, would make a formidable appearance; we have also two brass blunderbusses in the cabin, one over my birth, and the other over that of Mr. Lisa. These precautions were absolutely necessary from the hostility of the

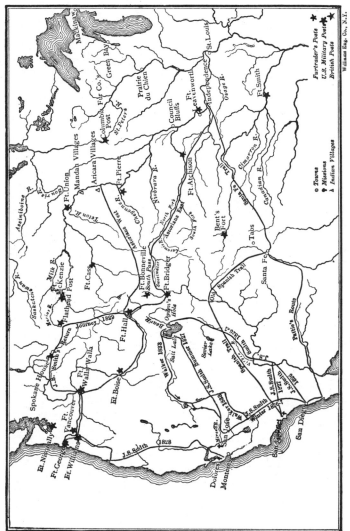

ROUTES OF THE FUR TRADERS.

Williams Eng. Co., N.Y.

Furtrader's Posts
U.S. Military Posts
British Posts

o Towns
Missions
Indian Villages

Sioux bands, who, of late had committed several murders and robberies on the whites, and manifested such a disposition that it was believed impossible for us to pass through their country. The greater part of the merchandise, which consisted of strouding, blankets, lead, tobacco, knifes, guns, beads, &c., was concealed in a false cabin, ingeniously contrived for the purpose; in this way presenting as little as possible to tempt the savages. But we hoped that as this was not the season for the wandering tribes to come on the river, the autumn being the usual time, we might pass by unnoticed." [9] Parties of traders were met coming down the river with the winter's catch of beaver and buffalo skins. They floated with the current on rafts made of "two canoes lashed together, and a platform raised upon them" [10] or in bull-boats such as the Indians used, a frame of willow boughs covered with buffalo skins, stretched tight and dried in the sun. They reported a prosperous season and the Indians peaceably disposed. Lisa was none the less wary, and his precautions were not taken in vain. He was soon apprised that the Sioux had learned that a number of traders were ascending the Missouri and in consequence remained on the river instead of going into the plains as usual and were determined to let no boats pass. The operations of the initial year were highly satisfactory, however, and Lisa returned to St. Louis in the following spring with a rich cargo of furs.

For many years thereafter, this daring pioneer of the fur trade made annual trips up the Missouri, carrying goods for the Indians and supplies for the trappers, wintering at one of his various posts, and returning in the spring with his fur-laden boats. His was the best known figure in the Missouri Territory, and to Indian and *voyageur* alike he was Uncle Lisa or, more familiarly, Uncle Manuel. With the facility of the Latin for bridging race barriers, he had married into the Omaha tribe and his policy was to treat the Indian as a human being. He thus explained his own success in fur trade: "First, I put into my operations great activity; I go a great distance, while some are considering whether they will start today or tomorrow. I impose upon myself great privations; ten months in a year I am buried in the forest, at a vast distance from my own house. I appear as the benefactor, and not as the pillager, of the Indians. I carried among them the seed of the large pompion, from which I have seen in their possession the fruit weighing one hundred and sixty pounds. Also the large bean, the potato, the turnip; and these vegetables now make a comfortable part of their subsistence, and this year [1817] I have promised to carry the plough. Besides, my blacksmiths work incessantly for them, charging nothing. I lend them traps, only demanding preference in their trade. My establishments are the refuge of the weak and of the old men no longer able to follow their lodges; and by these means I have acquired the confidence and friendship of these nations, and the consequent choice of their trade." [11]

The Missouri Fur Company, the first American firm to enter this field, had for incorporators Manuel Lisa, the Chouteaus — Pierre Sr. and Auguste Jr. —

William Clark, Benjamin Wilkinson, and Andrew
Henry; but the inspiring genius was Manuel Lisa.
Its capital amounted to $40,000, and its operations
were conducted on a scale hitherto unknown. In
1809, this company sent out a brigade of one hundred
and fifty men, with abundant supplies. Trading
stations were established among the Aricaras, Mandans, Minnetarees, and Crows, and a fortified post
was built at the Three Forks of the Missouri in
defiance of the hostile Blackfeet (1810). The
trappers found plenty of beaver, but they worked
at the risk of their lives. In three different on-
slaughts, twenty men were killed, among them
George Drouillard. Before the summer was over,
the main party returned to St. Louis, leaving Henry
with a small guard at the post. He was driven by
the Blackfeet across the divide to the north tributary of Snake River (called thereafter Henry's
Fork). There he built a log fort and secured forty
packs of beaver, but his little force well-nigh perished
of cold and hunger. In the following spring, Henry
made his way back to the Aricara Villages where he
met Lisa and reported his misfortunes. It was then
determined to abandon all the posts above the
Mandan Villages and a new Fort Lisa was built at
Council Bluffs.

Section III

Astoria

The Missouri Fur Company was made up of St.
Louis men. Their jealousy of outside influence was
evidenced in their refusal to sell stock to the New

York merchant, John Jacob Astor, who had bought out the Mackinaw Company and acquired complete ascendency in the Lake trade. This financial genius had discerned in the fur trade of Louisiana Territory a commercial opening of extraordinary promise, and he projected a scheme of operations that should eclipse the achievements of the Hudson's Bay Company. He made overtures to the North West Company as well as to the St. Louis house, but failing to secure coöperation, he entered the field as a remorseless competitor. The American Fur Company was chartered in 1808 as a holding corporation through which were to be managed Astor's several undertakings in this line. The depot of supplies for the Indian trade and the central accounting house were in New York; but the principal trading establishments were to be at Mackinaw, the old-time market of the Lake tribes, and St. Louis, the point of departure for the Missouri River traffic. Astor projected nothing less than a transcontinental and trans-Pacific trade route. Posts were to be located at strategic points along the trail blazed by Lewis and Clark, and a seaport at the mouth of the Columbia. Supplies and goods suited to the Indian trade were to be shipped from New York round the Horn and deposited at Astoria. An agreement was negotiated with Baranoff whereby Astor's ships were to carry supplies to the Russian posts, receiving in exchange the furs which American vessels could convey direct to Chinese ports. The shiploads of furs were there to be traded for tea and spices, silks and nankeens, goods that would bring a high profit in the New York market at the end of the return voyage.

For the prosecution of this brilliant enterprise, a subsidiary company was formed, the Pacific Fur Company. The capital of $400,000 was furnished by Mr. Astor, who assumed all financial risks. The personal risks were to be borne by the ten active members of the firm. These were for the most part experienced traders, drawn from the ranks of the North West Company and attached to the new association by the hope of profits, but Scotchmen and British subjects.[12] Astor's object in choosing so many Northwesters as partners was to secure men who knew the Rocky Mountains at first hand and who, being Canadians, would give less umbrage to Great Britain. Among his acquaintance in Montreal he easily found traders who were disaffected in the North West Company's service and ready to risk something in a new venture. They undertook to go out to the Columbia and prosecute the business to the best of their ability for half profits. Two expeditions were made ready, a vessel to carry men and supplies by sea and an overland party to ascertain the best sites for trading posts. In September, 1810, the *Tonquin*, Captain Jonathan Thorn, sailed from New York with thirty-three passengers, — four partners (Alexander McKay, Duncan McDougall, and David and Robert Stuart), five clerks, five mechanics, and fourteen Canadian *voyageurs*. Captain Thorn proved to be a martinet who succeeded in reducing the whole ship's company to the verge of mutiny by his petty tyrannies. A full hunting and trapping equipment, merchandise for the Indian trade, the frame of a coasting schooner, blacksmiths' and carpenters' tools, made up the bulk of the cargo. We owe to two of the clerks, Gabriel Franchère and Alexander Ross, our knowledge of the course of this six months' voyage. The *Tonquin* stopped at the Sandwich Islands for fresh supplies and a complement of Hawaiian sailors, who should prove useful in the coast cruises.

Arrived at the mouth of the Columbia, they were at a loss to find the channel. "The entrance of the river, which we plainly distinguished with the naked eye, appeared but a confused and agitated sea; the waves, impelled by a wind from the offing, broke upon the bar, and left no perceptible passage." [13] Captain Thorn sent a rowboat to seek out the entrance, but it was swamped in the tumult of waters. This disaster did not deter him from despatching another and another. Not till eight men were lost did the *Tonquin* finally hit upon the right channel and come to anchor within the bar (May 25, 1811). A month was spent in fixing upon a site for the fort and in discharging the tools and a portion of the supplies. Then (June 1) the impatient captain set out upon his trip up the coast in pursuit of furs. Alexander McKay, who had accompanied Mackenzie on his voyage to the Arctic Sea and was the ablest man in the party, went with him as supercargo. A week's voyage brought the *Tonquin* to Nootka Sound in advance of the English traders, and the Indians swarmed about the ship, offering their wares. In spite of the instructions of

Mr. Astor, the suggestions of his interpreter, and the earnest warnings of McKay, Thorn took none of the usual precautions to prevent an uncontrollable number of natives coming on board. So little comprehension had he of the nature of the tribe with whom he had to deal that he got into a controversy with the chief and struck him a blow in the face. Next morning the ship was surrounded by canoes filled with warriors, who thronged on board, offered bales of furs, and would take nothing but knives in exchange. Alarmed at last, Thorn ordered the crew to set sail; but all too late. With a hideous warwhoop, the Indians fell upon the captain and McKay and struck them down. The unarmed crew could make no defence, and all were killed but five men who fled to the cabin and, seizing firearms, succeeded in clearing the deck. But even so, their case was hopeless. They were too few to manage the vessel, and escape by the long boat would mean certain death either by capsize in the open sea or at the hands of the natives should they attempt to land. All that day the survivors remained below decks, and the Indians could only surmise their intentions, but on the morrow, when, tempted by the chance for plunder, the chief again boarded the *Tonquin*, an explosion of the powder magazine blew the ship to atoms and hurled captors and captives dead and dying into the waves.

To the party left at the mouth of the Columbia, the loss of the *Tonquin* was an irremediable disaster. The major part of their stock in trade had gone with her to the bottom, together with their best men and the most of the ammunition, and another supply ship could not reach the coast until the following spring. McDougall, the partner left in charge, was a man of "but ordinary capacity, with an irritable, peevish temper; the most unfit man in the world to head an expedition or command men." [14] The choice of a site for Fort Astoria had been hurriedly made, and it proved to be unfortunate. No adequate survey of the possibilities was undertaken, for Captain Thorn was in a hurry to land the outfit and be off for the northern trade. The ground was preëmpted by mammoth firs too large to be manageable for building purposes and difficult to remove, and their shade made the place gloomy and unwholesome. Two months' hard labor was spent in clearing an acre of land and putting up a temporary shelter. McDougall would have done well to shift to the site of the fort built by Lewis and Clark on Young's Bay. Its ruins were plain to be seen, "piles of rough, unhewn logs, overgrown with parasite creepers." [15] August and September were spent in building a weather-proof house, against the rainy season. It was sufficiently commodious, and contained a sitting-room, a dining-room, several sleeping rooms, and an apartment for the mechanics. The blacksmith's shop was close by. Meantime, provisions were running short. There were no sportsmen in the party, and the native hunters had retreated to the mountains. Thus the Astorians were reduced to smoked salmon and such elk and venison as one old Indian could bring in. The fish

FORT ASTORIA IN 1813.

diet proved unwholesome for all but the Hawaiians, and before the summer was over, half the force was on the sick list. No physician had been provided and few medicines, and the men complained bitterly of neglect. Ten of the more enterprising attempted desertion, but they were captured and brought back by the Indians, a misadventure that doubtless saved them from a worse fate. The framework of a coasting schooner, the *Dolly*, was put together, but she proved too small to risk the channel and so useless. Alexander Ross, a seasoned Northwester, grumbled over the trading stock as quite unsuitable. "Instead of guns, we got old metal pots and gridirons; instead of beads and trinkets, we got white cotton; and instead of blankets, molasses. In short, all the useless trash and unsalable trumpery which had been accumulating in his [Astor's] shops and stores for half a century past, were swept together to fill his Columbia ships. That these cargoes were insured need not be told; sink or swim, his profits were sure." [16]

It soon became evident that the North West Company did not intend to leave the Americans undisputed possession of the outlet of the river that afforded their best means of transportation to the west coast. Alexander Ross shall tell the story. "On the 15th of July, we were rather surprised at the unexpected arrival of a North West proprietor [partner] at Astoria, and still more so at the free and cordial reception given to an opponent. Mr. [David] Thompson, northwest-like, came dashing down the Columbia in a light canoe, manned with eight Iroquois

and an interpreter, chiefly men from the vicinity of
Montreal. McDougal received him like a brother;
nothing was too good for Mr. Thompson; he had
access everywhere; saw and examined everything;
and whatever he asked for he got, as if he had been
one of ourselves." [17] This reception seemed no
more than was due to so distinguished a representative of the rival house, especially as Thompson
announced that his was an exploring not a trading
expedition.[18] The others thought him "but little
better than a spy in the camp." [19] Franchère believed that the brilliant Northwester had intended to
take possession of the country in behalf of Great
Britain and that he was ill pleased to find the
Astorians installed at the mouth of the Columbia.
Mr. Thompson said that he had crossed the Continent during the preceding season, but that the
desertion of a portion of his men had compelled him
to winter at the base of the Rocky Mountains, at
the head waters of the Columbia. In the spring he
had built a canoe, the materials for which he had
brought with him across the mountains, and had
come down the river to this establishment. He
added that the wintering partners had resolved "to
abandon all their trading posts west of the mountains, not to enter into competition with us, provided
our company would engage not to encroach upon
their commerce on the east side: and to support
what he said, produced a letter to that effect, addressed by the wintering partners to the chief of
their house in Canada, the Hon. William M'Gil-
livray." [20]

The unsuspecting McDougal set about exploit-
ing the interior, his especial province. A trading
party, fitted out as well as the scanty supplies would
admit, was sent up Clark's River (the east branch
or main stream of the Columbia), and a trading
post was built at the junction of the Okanagan.
Here Ross spent the winter and succeeded in collecting fifteen hundred and fifty beaver skins from the
Indians. He estimated that his stock of furs,
worth £2250 in the Canton market, cost in merchandise only £35! David Stuart, who pushed farther north up the Okanagan, was no less successful.
The Flathead country was well stocked with buffalo; the Kootenais had plenty of beaver, deer, and
mountain sheep, and they knew so little of the value
of fur that twenty beaver skins worth £25 could
be bought for a gun worth twenty-seven shillings.
These tribes were peaceful, honest, clean, and chaste,
uncontaminated as yet by the white man. Astor's
representative agreed with McMillan, the factor at
the Spokane House, that no liquor should be sold
to the natives, lest they be degraded to the condition of the Chenooks of the lower Columbia.[21]

The overland expedition, meantime, had been in
desperate straits. The party embarked from Montreal on July 6, 1810, a full month before the *Tonquin*
had sailed from New York, and it was hoped that
the two companies would arrive at the mouth of the
Columbia at about the same time. Wilson Price
Hunt, who was intrusted with the command of this
venture, was from New Jersey, an excellent merchant and devoted to Astor's interests, but unfa-

miliar with the ways of the wilderness. The partners who were associated with him were experienced men and naturally jealous of his authority and critical of his decisions. Donald Mackenzie, an old Northwester, was "bold, robust, and peculiarly qualified to lead Canadian *voyageurs* through thick and thin." [22] Ramsay Crooks was a young Scotchman, who had been four years (1807–1811) on the Missouri prosecuting the fur trade from Council Bluffs. He was then a member of the Missouri Fur Company, but now cast in his lot with the Astorians. McLellan was an American whose life had been spent on the frontier. He was one of Wayne's runners and won distinction even among those valorous scouts for courage and resource. According to Ross, McLellan was "one of the first shots in America," "hardy, enterprizing and brave as a lion." [23] He had been associated with Crooks in the Missouri River trade and joined the expedition at Nadowa. Joseph Miller, who joined the party at St. Louis, was also familiar with the frontier and with the Indians. Having engaged at Montreal a sufficient number of *voyageurs* to manage their boat, Hunt and Mackenzie made their way by the Ottawa River to Mackinaw, the chief Astor post, and thence by Green Bay, the Fox and Wisconsin rivers to the Mississippi and St. Louis. Here the majority of the boatmen and hunters were collected. Mackenzie had urged that Canadians whom he knew and trusted be brought from Montreal, but to Hunt this seemed a needless expense. Moreover, he discounted the gay and volatile Frenchmen. He picked up a few *voyageurs*

at Mackinaw, to the infinite disgust of the Northwesters, who observed that the Canadians were
expert canoemen, while the Mackinas were expert
bottle men.

At St. Louis the difficulty of recruiting the force
was even greater. The men who lounged about
the wharves of this river port were "a medley
of French Creoles, old and worn-out Canadians,
Spanish renegades, with a mixture of Indians and
Indian half-breeds, enervated by indolence, debauch-
ery, and a warm climate." [24] True, some Americans
presented themselves, attracted by the prospect of
adventure in a new and untried field. Several
Yankees, "sleek and tall as pines of the forest," [25]
engaged as hunters and trappers, but they would
not put up with the meagre fare accorded the Canadians, and Hunt refused to make any improvement.
So these lordly backwoodsmen abandoned the expedition at Nadowa, their advance pay in their
pockets. One Kentuckian who stayed by the enterprise, John Day, proved a tower of strength. In
the autumn of 1810 the party went into camp at the
mouth of the Nadowa River, four hundred and fifty
miles up the Missouri, where the penny-wise-and-
pound-foolish Hunt, having wasted the summer recruiting his party, ordained they should spend the
winter to save the cost of a sojourn at St. Louis.
The best men deserted, Hunt was obliged to return
to St. Louis for substitutes, and the expedition did
not finally embark until March 12, 1811.

The preparations for the Astor expedition had
been watched with jealousy and suspicion by the

Missouri Fur Company, and it is probable that Hunt's difficulty in securing fit men had been augmented by the wiles of the opposition. No sooner had he set off than Lisa attempted, by a device not infrequent in the annals of the trade, to deprive him of his boatmen. A marshal was sent to St. Charles to arrest Pierre Dorion on the charge of an unpaid debt, but the man took to the woods and rejoined Hunt higher up the river. Balked of his prey, Lisa hurried his preparations for the spring trip to the Mandans, meaning to overtake and if possible forestall the Astorians. Hunt had three weeks' start, and was two hundred and forty miles up the river when his rival left St. Louis. He suspected that the wily Spaniard meant to defeat his enterprise by some despicable intrigue, and his fears were reënforced by a tale Crooks and McLellan had to tell of the way in which they had been betrayed into the hands of the Sioux. Consequently the cautious New Jerseyan made all possible speed. Lisa, meanwhile, was driving his patient *voyageurs* to desperate exertions. Brackenridge tells the story of this exciting chase. He overheard the poor fellows complaining: "It is impossible for us to persevere any longer in this unceasing toil, this over-strained exertion, which wears us down. We are not permitted a moment's repose; scarcely is time allowed us to eat or to smoke our pipes. We can stand it no longer, human nature cannot bear it; our bourgeois has no pity on us." [26] In such moments of depression, Lisa's courage flashed out like fire. He would seize the helm, pass round the grog, raise a song loved of the men, or make an encouraging speech, promising them rich reward at the end of this mad chase. In spite of head winds and almost continuous rain, he covered eleven hundred miles in two months, an average of eighteen miles a day, a feat unparalleled in keel-boat days on the Missouri.

Just beyond the Niobrara, the Astorians were overtaken, and none too soon, for the country was infested by bands of hostiles, who were only deterred from attack by this exceptional show of force. Hunt's suspicions were not allayed, however, and he and Lisa were on the point of fighting a duel over poor Dorion when Bradbury and Brackenridge intervened and patched up a peace. There is no evidence that the chief of the Missouri Company had any evil designs against the Astor party. The Columbia lay so far beyond his territory, actual or prospective, that he had no desire to compete.

Arriving at the Aricara villages, Hunt determined to strike directly west across the plains of the Little Missouri, hoping to find a route better furnished with game than that traversed by Lewis and Clark, and free from the murderous Blackfeet. For this enterprise, horses were indispensable, and here Lisa proved helpful and generous. He negotiated the purchases from the treacherous Aricaras, and brought animals of his own from the Mandans, taking Hunt's boats and superfluous luggage in exchange. A month was spent in effecting these purchases, but by the middle of July all was ready, and the party set out by the Grand River. They were sixty-four persons all told, Dorion's squaw and her two children being the only dependents. Seventy-six horses were loaded with the goods deemed necessary for the undertaking, and since the riding horses were not sufficient to accommodate all, the men had to take turns in walking.

The route chosen skirted the northern slopes of the Black Hills and the Bighorn Mountains, a maze of river and fell, through which Edward Rose, a renegade white man who had attached himself to the Crow Indians, served as guide. Leaving the Crow country and pushing up Wind River, the party rode along an Indian trail across the continental divide, and rounding the Three Tetons — a lofty landmark well known to Henry's men — they arrived at last (October 12) at his ill-starred fort on the north fork of the Snake River and there camped on westward-flowing water.[27]   Here the road-worn party clamored to be allowed to build boats and embark upon the river, and Hunt, knowing nothing of the character of the stream he had to deal with, foolishly complied. The horses were turned loose, and goods and men were packed into fifteen "crazy and frail" canoes. It proved an almost fatal mistake. For eight days they glided down with the current, congratulating themselves that their hardships were at an end, but on the ninth they were swept into a whirlpool, Caldron Linn,[28] where Crooks' boat capsized, and one of the *voyageurs* was lost. Then and not until then did Hunt bethink him to explore his "Mad river." The parties despatched down-stream returned after a few days to report that navigation was impossible. The river flowed between precipitous basalt walls

The Snake River Desert, American Falls in the Foreground.

over a bed so rocky and beset with rapids that no boat could live, even in the hands of the most expert boatman. A party sent back to Fort Henry to recover the horses returned without them. The situation seemed desperate and was in reality more ominous than they knew. Before them lay the Snake River Desert, one thousand miles of rock, ledge, and sage-brush, where game was scarce and water could be gotten from the river with difficulty. Winter was upon them, and there was no time to be lost. They cached all but the most necessary luggage and divided the men into four companies under the leadership of the four partners, thinking that by distributing their force they should be more likely to find whatever supplies the desert afforded. Hunt and Crooks took the left or south bank; McLellan took the right. "They counted on arriving very quickly at the Columbia; but they followed this Mad river for twenty days, finding nothing at all to eat, and suffering horribly from thirst. The rocks between which the river flows being so steep and abrupt as to prevent their descending to quench their thirst (so that even their dogs died of it), they suffered the torments of Tantalus, with this difference, that he had the water which he could not reach above his head, while our travellers had it beneath their feet. . . . To appease the cravings of hunger, they ate beaver skins roasted in the evening at the camp fire. They even were at last constrained to eat their moccasins." [29] Hunt and Crooks were so fortunate as to find a wretched Indian camp. The Shoshones fled at the sight of white faces, but left their horses behind them, and the starving Astorians shot them for food, leaving some trinkets in payment. Soon after Mackenzie and McLellan appeared on the opposite bank and made Hunt understand that their people were in desperate straits. Hunt had a canoe constructed of horse hide and managed to send them a little meat; but the attempt to bring the parties over was defeated by the capsizing of the fragile craft. Several of the Canadian boatmen, despairing of ever reaching civilization, abandoned the enterprise and found refuge with the Indians.

In this wilderness Mackenzie's party came upon a young American, Archibald Pelton of Connecticut, who had been crazed by its terrors. In his lucid intervals he told his story. He had come out with Henry, had escaped from the massacre at Three Forks, and had been wandering about for three years with no human company but that of the Snake Indians. The destitute wanderers gave him what help they could afford, and he was glad to join their forlorn hope. The north bank party, under Mackenzie, forged ahead, crossed the Blue Mountains by the Indian trail and, descending to the Walla Walla, reached at last a great river that they rightly deemed could be no other than the Columbia. Here they purchased boats of the natives and, making their way past the Dalles and the Cascades, finally arrived at Astoria on the tenth of January, 1812. Hunt and his people, handicapped by Dorion's wife and two boys, did not get through till February 15. In late April, as David Stuart's brigade was coming down

the river from the Okanagan post, they were hailed
near the mouth of the Umatilla by a shout in
English, — "Come on shore." They steered toward the sound and saw two white men "standing
like two specters." They proved to be Ramsay
Crooks and John Day, but "so changed and ema-
ciated were they, that our people for some time could
scarcely recognize them to be white men." [30]

Once reunited at the mouth of the Columbia, the
Astorians had little to congratulate themselves upon.
Food was still scarce, and there would have been
suffering but for the supply of fresh salmon brought
in by the natives. The Chinooks on the lower river
were well accustomed to trade, but the Falls Indians
and the "robber barons" at the Dalles were suspicious and hostile. An expedition sent up the river
to recover the goods cached on the Snake and to carry
despatches to New York was attacked at the long
narrows, "that noted resort of plunderers, where few
can pass without paying a heavy tax," [31] and forced
to turn back. The arrival of the supply ship *Beaver*
(May 12, 1812) cheered the hearts of the adventurers,
for she brought not only a valuable cargo, but a considerable reënforcement of men : John Clarke, a new
partner, half a dozen clerks (among whom was Ross
Cox, an inexperienced New Yorker), Canadian and
American *engagés*, and the usual complement of
Sandwich Islanders.

Hunt organized the season's campaign with zeal and
discretion. David Stuart returned to his Okanagan
post, John Clarke undertook to establish a trading
house on the Spokane in competition with the North

West Company's factory, Mackenzie was sent back to Snake River where he built a fort at its junction with the Boisé, while Robert Stuart started overland with despatches for Mr. Astor. With him went three Canadians and McLellan and Crooks, who had had enough of the wilderness 'and wished to return to St. Louis. Hunt, himself, set out on the *Beaver* to trade up the Alaskan coast (August 14, 1812), leaving McDougal in charge at Astoria. All these enterprises except the last were reasonably successful. Young Stuart led his party across the Blue Mountains to the Snake River, where he fell in with Joseph Miller and took him and his trapper in tow. Turning southeast from Caldron Linn, they came to Bear River, but instead of striking east where they might have found the South Pass and the Sweetwater, they apparently lost sense of direction and turned north till they were on Snake River again and then east through the Tetons, a hazardous and difficult journey, and finally came out upon the north fork of the Platte (October 30) into a "bleak and boundless plain," which, "destitute both of animals and firewood, appeared like an ocean of despair." [32] From this point, they might easily have reached St. Louis before snowfall; but they were entirely at sea as to their whereabouts and thought best to go into winter quarters in a sheltered valley where a herd of buffalo promised sufficient food. In the following spring they made their way down to the Missouri and reached St. Louis in April of 1813, after ten months of wandering.

Stuart's despatches gave Mr. Astor his first news of the safe arrival of the overland party and of the various trading ventures. He was highly pleased. "That will do," said he; "I have hit the nail on the head." [33] There was still, however, grave reason for anxiety as to the ultimate fate of Astoria. War with Great Britain had been declared on June 19, 1812, and the Atlantic ports were blockaded by the British navy. Moreover, English men-of-war were following our whaling ships into the Pacific and might get as far as Astoria. Influential as was Astor in Washington, the prospect of getting the government to send aid to the trading post seemed more than dubious. News of the war reached the Astorians from Montreal, but not till December, 1812, when two partners of the North West Company, J. G. McTavish and Joseph LaRoque, arrived at the Spokane House and communicated to the Americans there this startling intelligence. Mackenzie had come over from the Boisé to consult with Clarke as to the advisability of abandoning his station, and the war news clinched his decision that the position was untenable. He hastened back to collect his men and furs, and reached Astoria on January 15, 1813, having voyaged down the Columbia with the jubilant Northwesters, bringing with him the seven *voyageurs* who had abandoned Hunt on Snake River. He readily convinced McDougal that the part of wisdom consisted in abandoning a desperate undertaking and dissolving the partnership. The two canny Scots foresaw the probability that they could make comfortable terms with the North West Company. The defection of Crooks, McLellan, and Miller, and the absence of Hunt left the Montreal men in control. Franchère clearly indicates the prevailing state of mind. "When we learned this news, all of us at Astoria who were British subjects and Canadians, wished ourselves in Canada; but we could not entertain even the thought of transporting ourselves thither, at least immediately; we were separated from our country by an immense space, and the difficulties of the journey at this season were insuperable; besides, Mr. Astor's interests had to be consulted first. We held, therefore, a sort of council of war, to which the clerks of the factory were invited *pro formâ*, as they had no voice in the deliberations. Having maturely weighed our situation; after having seriously considered that being almost to a man British subjects, we were trading, notwithstanding, under the American flag; and foreseeing the improbability or rather, to cut the matter short, the impossibility that Mr. Astor could send us farther supplies or reënforcements while the war lasted, as most of the ports of the United States would inevitably be blockaded by the British,— we concluded to abandon the establishment in the ensuing spring, or, at latest, in the beginning of the summer. We did not communicate these resolutions to the men, lest they should in consequence abandon their labor; but we discontinued, from that moment, our trade with the natives, except for provisions; as well because we had no longer a large stock of goods on hand, as for the reason that we had already more furs than we could carry away overland." [34]

In April, McTavish and LaRocque arrived at Astoria with the announcement that they had come to await the arrival of their supply ship, the *Isaac Todd*, bearing letters of marque and accompanied by a frigate of the line under orders to seize the American factory. When Stuart and Clarke came down the river, a formal council was held, and the vote stood three to two for dissolving the partnership. Stuart and Clarke, the Americans, vigorously opposed this pusillanimous surrender of the results of two years' strenuous labor; but McDougal claimed Mr. Astor's proxy and cast the deciding vote. A manifesto was drawn up July 1, 1813, stating the reasons for terminating their contract with Mr. Astor. In the first place, supplies had run short, the *Beaver*, due November, 1812, had not returned from her trading trip, and the war would prevent another supply ship being sent round the Horn. Secondly, the trade at the interior posts had fallen short of expectations. Finally, the Pacific Fur Company could never expect to compete with the Northwesters, already intrenched in several well-equipped posts on the upper Columbia.

When Mr. Hunt finally returned to Astoria (August 20, 1813), more than a year after his departure in the *Beaver*, the fatal decision had been taken, and he could do nothing but comply. His own misadventures marked the culmination of the run of bad luck to which Astor's enterprise seemed fated. Trade with the Russians had proved remunerative but intolerably slow. The *Beaver* was injured in a gale off St. Paul, and the captain would not consent to brave the bore of the Columbia until his ship had been repaired. He sailed for the Sandwich Islands and thence to Canton, where, learning of the war, he remained in port till peace was declared, thus sacrificing the profits of the voyage. Hunt, meantime, was waiting at Lahaina for a ship in which to return to the Columbia. His first news of hostilities was brought by the *Albatross* (June 20, 1813) just a year after war had been declared. He promptly took passage on this vessel and reached Astoria (August 21) only to learn that the Northwesters had succeeded, by threats and promises, in inducing the Scotchmen to betray his interests. Finding protests useless, he returned to the Islands with the *Albatross*, hoping to secure a disengaged vessel in which to recover the Pacific Fur Company's property. There he learned that a supply ship, the *Lark*, had been sent out by Mr. Astor with instructions to remove men and goods to the Russian settlements until the outcome of the war should be apparent; but she unfortunately had gone to wreck on a coral reef with only the crew saved. Chartering another ship, the *Pedler*, the indefatigable Hunt again reached Astoria (February 28, 1814) only to find the British flag floating over the fort and the North West Company in possession. McDougal had accepted a proposition from Montreal for the purchase of the establishment for $80,500, a sum far below its actual value. The goods were reckoned at ten per cent of cost, plus transportation charges. Beaver skins were estimated at $2 and land otter at fifty cents apiece.[35] Hunt was "confounded" when he heard these terms and "censured in strong terms the precipitate (not to say dishonest) manner in which the sale had been effected."[36] His protests came too late, however, and he could do nothing but return to the United States with his loyal remnant.[37]

Franchère, Canadian though he was, thought such a financial sacrifice quite uncalled for. "From the account given in this chapter the reader will see with what facility the establishment of the Pacific Fur Company could have escaped capture by the British force. It was only necessary to get rid of the land party of the North West Company,— who were completely in our power,— then remove our effects up the river upon some small stream, and await the result. The sloop-of-war arrived, it is true; but as, in the case I suppose, she would have found nothing, she would have left, after setting fire to our deserted houses. None of their boats would have dared follow us, even if the Indians had betrayed to them our lurking-place. Those at the head of affairs had their own fortunes to seek, and thought it more for their interest, doubtless, to act as they did, but that will not clear them in the eyes of the world, and the charge of treason to Mr. Astor's interests will always be attached to their characters." [38]

McDougal accepted a partnership in the North West Company. McLennan, Ross, and Cox entered that service as clerks on advantageous terms, but Mackenzie, Stuart, Clarke, and the indignant Franchère returned with the spring brigade to Montreal. The free trappers, Americans for the most part, retreated to the Willamette Valley to hunt and fish and live at ease. They had become so wonted to the life of the wilderness that they were willing to settle there with their Indian wives. They refused to take service with the Canadian Company, but trapped on their own account.

That Astor's project was statesmanlike and entirely practicable, the later successes of the British company abundantly proved. There was no parsimony in the expenditure of money, and a sum of $400,000 was lavished on an enterprise that produced no financial returns. Neither was there economy of human energy. Three years of strenuous effort and sixty-five lives went into the establishing of this trading post on the Pacific.[39] In reviewing the mistakes that contributed to the failure of the undertaking, we recognize first of all that Astor's agents were not equal to the responsibilities imposed upon them. McKay was the only man of first-rate ability among them, and he was lost at the outset. No one of them, Captain Thorn, McDougal, Hunt, Mackenzie (not to mention the partners who deserted) had the resolute mastery of circumstance that compels success. Astor has been severely blamed for intrusting his enterprise so largely to Canadians and Northwesters. Had he foreseen war, he might have realized that their loyalty to Great Britain and to Montreal would prevail to the jeopardy of his business. Born a German peasant, and arriving in this country at the close of the Revolutionary War, he could hardly be expected to understand the qualities of the American. Moreover, the exaggerated jealousy of the Missouri Fur Company had deprived him of coöperation from St. Louis. He naturally turned to the fur traders of Montreal with whom he was already familiar. It was also to be expected of a New York merchant that he should regard the sea route as the most feasible means of communication with the Columbia. The existence of an

overland traverse practicable for pack animals and
much shorter than that traversed by Lewis and Clark
was demonstrated by Robert Stuart's party, in spite
of their unhappy wanderings. If they had marched
directly east from Bear River to the Sweetwater and
followed its lead, they would have covered the route
that later became the Oregon trail, and might have
accomplished the whole distance from Astoria to St.
Louis in six months. The voyage round the Horn
required nine months under favorable conditions,
and the chances of loss were far greater. Farther,
no business could be maintained against such disasters as the loss of the *Tonquin* and the *Lark* and the
profitless voyagings of the *Beaver*. Astor possessed
a great fortune and was the most daring entrepreneur
of that day, but even he found the odds too heavy.
The ultimate cause of failure arose from the inability
of the United States government to give aid to this
remotest venture of American commerce. Astor
besought President Madison to send a war vessel to
his distressed colony, but in vain. Public opinion
would not have justified so costly an expedition, even
if the ship could have been spared. Jefferson might
have taken the risks, but few other men in America
appreciated the far-reaching significance of Astor's
experiment.

The treaty of Ghent provided for the mutual restoration of all forts and private property seized during
the war. Astoria was not, however, mentioned or
thought of until Astor called the matter to the
attention of President Madison. Then (1818) J. P.
Prevost was despatched to the Columbia to take

possession. The United States flag was run up over the fort, but the property had been purchased by the North West Company and could not be recovered. The flag-raising ceremony having been successfully performed, the American emissary sailed away, and the British traders were left in undisturbed possession. The rights of the United States in the Oregon country were safeguarded, however, by the treaty of Joint Occupation concluded with Great Britain in this same year, according to which "any country claimed by either party on the North West Coast of America" together with all harbors, bays, rivers, etc., was to be "free and open" to the subjects of both powers for the term of ten years.

SECTION IV

Fort Vancouver

The career of the North West Company on the Columbia was not a brilliant one. According to Alexander Henry, who spent the winter of 1813–1814 at Fort George, the Northwesters were in quite as awkward a predicament as the Astorians had been. He found the atmosphere of the post demoralizing and the warm, damp climate depressing, while the trees that overshadowed the building, "very large, heavy and mostly unserviceable," made the place unwholesome. "Most of the men brought overland by the P. F. Co. are undisciplined, impertinent, ill-behaved vagabonds, devoid of that sense of subordination which our business requires."[40] The natives did not please him better. "Beavers are numerous, but the natives, who are also numerous, will not hunt them." They persisted in digging wappatoo, and "could not be persuaded of the benefit they would reap from working beaver." Indeed, the inconsiderate aborigines of the Willamette Valley showed a disposition to resent the intrusion of the hunters. "They said they did not wish white people to come up this river; that our guns had driven away the deer or made them so wild that they could no longer be killed with bows and arrows." After the departure of the *Racoon*, the British sloop of war, Henry felt considerable trepidation as to their chances of survival. "Left at the mercy of chance among hostile natives, with no goods to trade and scant provisions," an Indian uprising in behalf of the "Bostons" or the arrival of an American man-of-war would have quickly turned the tables and restored Oregon to the United States. The belated supply ship, the *Isaac Todd*, arrived toward the end of April, and trading parties were sent to the upper posts with plentiful stocks of English goods; but the business did not prosper. McDougal, who had been rewarded for his compliance with McTavish's plans by the office of chief factor of the Columbian district, was incapable of effective organization, and his timid counsels stood in the way of active prosecution of the trade. The freedom permitted in liquor-selling and credit advances demoralized the *engagés*, while the Indians were fast dying out under the influence of the white man's vices.

The North West Company had three hundred *engagés* west of the Rockies — a reckless, nondescript lot, Iroquois hunters, Hawaiian sailors, and renegade whites. They came into frequent conflict with the natives, whose notions of tribal property in land, timber, rivers, game, and fish the *parvenus* were not inclined to respect. The Dalles Indians were strong enough to extort tribute, but the Chenooks and Clatsops submitted meekly to the invasion, while the Chehallis on the Cowlitz and the Umpquas to the south were rendered hostile by wanton massacres. The only new post built was Fort Walla Walla (1818), which Donald Mackenzie deemed essential to the security of his trappers on Snake River. Alexander Ross, another Astorian, maintained his post on the Okanagan and carried his trading expeditions as far as the Yakima Valley, the resort of the Nez Perces.

With the merging of the interests of the North West and Hudson's Bay companies (1821), a new régime was established on the Columbia. John McLoughlin, a Canadian of Scotch and French parentage and formerly a partner in the North West Company, was appointed chief factor of the Columbia district in 1824, and under his strong and wise administration, an epoch of peace and prosperity was inaugurated. The principal factory was removed from Astoria, now called Fort George, to Bellevue Point, a wholesome elevation ninety miles up the river and nearly opposite the *debouchement* of the Willamette. The new post, Fort Vancouver, was equally accessible from the sea and a far less troublesome landing-place. Situated at the junction of three rivers, it commanded the canoe trade to north, south, east, and west. Fort George was thereafter maintained merely as a lookout station to furnish pilots to vessels coming up the river and to forward the intelligence of arrivals by sea to the chief factor. The Klackatucks who inhabited the north shore of the river from the Cowlitz to the Cascades were the best of the native hunters and brought in quantities of game and peltry. The soil was well suited to agriculture, and a neighboring stream furnished water-power for a sawmill. Here three thousand acres of fertile land were gradually brought under cultivation, and a sufficient quantity of grain was grown to supply the Columbia River force after 1828, and the interior posts after 1840. The hogs and goats brought from the Hawaiian Islands by the *Tonquin* had multiplied rapidly, and the four head of Spanish cattle imported on the *Isaac Todd* were carefully nourished. The chief factor allowed no cattle to be killed except one bull calf each year for rennet, and the only meat furnished to the force at Vancouver was elk and venison. This thrifty policy was rewarded by the accumulation of a fine herd. In 1828, there were 200 cattle, 50 horses, and 300 swine in the woods and pastures about the Fort, but not till 1838 was the embargo on slaughter removed. Three hundred people were employed on the farm and in the various industries of the establishment. Their dwellings, the barns, cowsheds, gristmill, threshing-mill, and workshops, the dairy and the salmon house, gave to the Fort the appearance of an agricultural village. The post itself was an imposing affair,—a stockaded enclosure, 250 by 150 yards square, surrounded the governor's house, the clerks' quarters, and the storehouses where the stock of furs, the supplies, and the goods for the season's trade were kept under lock and key. Flowers and vine-clad arbors, a flourishing vegetable garden and a promising orchard gave the post an air of comfort and refinement that made it seem a very paradise to the weary traveller from the mountains or from across the sea. The arrival of the supply ship from London was a great event, since it brought not only the all-important stock in trade, but news of the great world and, not infrequently, distinguished visitors from afar. The annual "brigade" from the interior came down the river in the month of June, a brave show of well-manned canoes, heavily laden with beaver packs and wilderness-worn hunters dressed in their gaudiest deerskins and eager for the sight of wives and children. The transcontinental "Express" made its annual journey up the Columbia to Fort Colville and over the "height of land" (Saskatchewan Pass) to the Saskatchewan, Lake Winnipeg, and York Factory, leaving Vancouver in March and returning the following autumn, with the regularity of an ocean liner. The mails for Canada and the United States were carried by this route as well as supplies for the interior posts.

Dr. McLoughlin's energetic personality was felt not only at Fort Vancouver, but throughout the vast fur region west of the Rockies. He reënforced the trading posts of Walla Walla and Okanagan, built a new and important depot, Fort Colville (1825), on the upper Columbia to supersede Spokane House as connecting link with New Caledonia, and planted pioneer establishments on the Flathead and Umpqua rivers and on Hood's Canal. Fort Boisé and Fort

Hall (1835) marked the easternmost reach of this commercial empire, but trading parties were despatched southward into the desert wastes of the Great Basin (1826) and along the Pacific Coast as far as the Sacramento Valley (1829). In 1835, the Columbia district could boast six trading posts on the sea (none, however, south of the forty-ninth parallel) and sixteen in the interior, while six armed vessels and one small steamer managed the coastwise trade. The season's accumulation of furs, whether gathered in the coast trade or collected in the interior, was brought to Fort Vancouver and stored to await the advent of the ship from London. The cargo of furs sent out annually brought from $500,000 to $1,000,000 in the London market. A year's supply of goods was always stored at the central depot to guard against the possible loss of this vessel. In accordance with an agreement effected with the Russian-American Fur Company in 1839, New Archangel was supplied with wheat flour (at $15 to $20 per barrel) and other provisions, in exchange for the seal, fox, and otter skins taken about the "Frozen Ocean." Pickled salmon and sawed lumber (at $60 to $100 per M.) were shipped to the Sandwich Islands in exchange for sugar and salt, and this trade was worth $60,000 a year.

The best traditions of the Hudson's Bay Company were observed at Fort Vancouver. Prices were fixed and reasonable, the quality of wares and supplies was as good as the English market afforded, strict justice was enforced for Indian and white man alike. No liquor was sold to the natives, and only a sparing measure was dealt out to the Company's servants, the treat being reserved for festive occasions, as Christmas and the return of the brigade. Such was the chief factor's reputation for fair dealing that he was known among the tribes far and near as the "Great White Chief," and the "White-headed Eagle." His influence with the redmen seemed unbounded. There were no Indian wars so long as Dr. McLoughlin was in command of Fort Vancouver, for his refusal to trade with a troublesome tribe was sufficient to bring the mutineers to terms. A school was maintained at the Fort for the benefit of the half-breed children of the officers and servants of the Company, and of the many orphan children of Indians who had been in the Company's employ. They were taught English (sometimes French), writing, arithmetic, and geography; and were subsequently either apprenticed to traders in Canada or kept in the Company's service. The expenses of a resident physician and a hospital were also met by the Company.

The resources of the vast region covered by the Columbia district were developed with zeal and efficiency, but with a concern for the preservation of the men and animals involved that was characteristic of the Hudson's Bay Company. The trappers were sent out under trained leaders and amply supplied with food and pack-animals. A trapping party is thus described by John Dunn, one of the clerks at Fort Vancouver. "The party generally consists of about fifty or sixty men — most of them the Company's servants, — others, free hunters. The servants have a stated salary, while the freemen receive so much per skin. Previous to leaving the Fort for their arduous adventure, they are allowed a small quantity of rum per man; and they generally enjoy a grand holiday and feast the night previous to starting. Each man has a certain number of horses, sufficient to carry his equipment. The free trappers generally provide their own animals. Both the Company's servants and the freemen frequently take their wives and families with them; the women are very useful on the expedition, in preparing meals and other necessaries for their husbands during their absence from the camp. In summer and winter, whether they have a sort of travelling camp or a fixed residence, they select the localities that most abound in fur-bearing animals.

"Though a party may be obliged, from a variety of circumstances, to winter in the plains, or in the recesses of the mountains, on the borders of lakes or rivers, some numbers of it return to the fort at *the fall*, with the produce of the season's hunt, and report progress; and return to the camp with a reinforcement of necessary supplies. Thus the Company are enabled to acquire a minute knowledge of the country and the natives; and extend their power and authority over both." [41]

One of the most notable of the Hudson's Bay Company servants was Peter Skeene Ogden, son of a Tory judge of Newark, New Jersey, who, bereft of home and property by the American Revolution, took refuge in Canada. Young Ogden entered the fur business as a clerk in the North West Company, but transferred to the Hudson's Bay Company with the consolidation and was soon after appointed chief trader to the Snake River country. His first party (1824) was made up of two gentlemen, two interpreters, seventy-one men and lads, eighty guns, three hundred and sixty-four beaver traps, three hundred and seventy-two horses, and was "the most formidable party that had ever set out for the Snakes." [42] Since the average catch per trap in this rich district was twenty-six beavers, the return anticipated from the hunt was fourteen thousand one hundred skins. For five successive winters, Ogden searched the new and difficult district between the Three Tetons and the Cascades, trapping every discoverable stream and returning each spring to the Nez Perces post with his take of peltry. The money return from these unexploited beaver meadows was gratifying, but a more permanent result was the contribution to geographic knowledge. Ogden followed the John Day River to the Blue Mountains and the Deschutes to its source in the Sierras. Harney and Malheur lakes in the wastes of eastern Oregon were familiar ground to this tireless hunter. Farther south, in the edge of the great desert, he came upon his "unknown river" later denominated the Humboldt, but which the fur traders more appropriately called the Ogden. Making his way across the Sierras, Ogden discovered the Klamath and Shasta rivers and confirmed for these as for snow-capped Mt. Shasta their wonted Indian names. The information he was able to give concerning this trackless waste of river and desert and mountain was used by the London map maker, Arrowsmith, as the basis for the maps prepared for the use of the Hudson's Bay Company. Thus did the fur trader, bent only on profit, supplement, even anticipate, the work of the explorer.

SECTION V

Rivalry of the American Companies

The war of 1812 had a demoralizing effect upon the fur trade of St. Louis. The foreign market being cut off, the price of furs fell to a ruinous point. At the same time, war duties raised the prices of foreign goods and their domestic substitutes far beyond the rate which British traders had to pay. Thus the profits of the business were wiped out while at the same time its risks greatly increased. Open hostilities were confined to the operations on the Atlantic and Gulf coasts and on the Great Lakes, but the animosities engendered bred trouble on the Upper Mississippi and the Missouri. Under the tutelage of the agents of the North West Company, the Sacs and Foxes of Illinois, the Iowas to the west of the Mississippi, the Sioux, the Mandans and the Aricaras along the Missouri, even those Bedouins of the Plains, the Crows and the Arapahoes, had learned to despise the Americans. The collapse of Astor's enterprise on the Columbia and the withdrawal of the Missouri Fur Company to the region below Council Bluffs confirmed the impression that the government at Washington was too remote or too feeble to protect its traders. American parties were attacked and robbed and the stolen furs forwarded to British posts. The fact that the marauding Indians were armed with British muskets lent color to the assertion, current at St. Louis, that trade rivalry had much to do with the hostility of the Indians. Fortunately for the river settlements, the diplomacy of "Uncle Manuel" and General Clark averted disastrous conflict, but, notwithstanding the treaties of peace negotiated with the leading chiefs (1815), traffic on the upper Missouri was unsafe. The several tribes still held that traders on the river owed them tribute and they ambushed such parties as seemed too weak to offer resistance. Their depredations grew so annoying that Congress was induced (1819) to send an expedition to overawe the insubordinate aborigines. Colonel Henry Atkinson with a regiment of United States troops was directed to proceed up the Missouri to the mouth of the Yellowstone and there erect a fort adequate to the protection of trade, while a party of scientists in charge of Major Stephen H. Long was to explore the region between the Missouri and the Rockies. The attempt was made to send the troops up the river in steamboats, although no experiment in steam navigation had yet been made on the Missouri. The undertaking was thwarted by the clumsy character of the boats provided, and the troops got no farther than Council Bluffs, where they were obliged to winter and where one hundred men died of scurvy. A march of three times the distance might have been made with half the loss in life and one-tenth the money expenditure. The project of going on to the Yellowstone was abandoned perforce, and the only persons benefited by the expedition were the contractors, who pocketed handsome profits. In the year following, Long's party went up the Platte River to the foothills of the Rockies, verified Pike's discoveries in that region, and returning by way of the Canadian River, proved that this misleading stream was not the Red River but a branch of the Arkansas.

The Aricara campaign was a military fiasco, which could have no other effect on the Indians than to render them even more contemptuous of the authority of the United States government. It is not surprising, therefore, that the trading party organized by William Ashley in the spring of 1823 was attacked and cut to pieces by the Aricaras and that another party of trappers and *voyageurs* operating for the Missouri Fur Company was destroyed by the Blackfeet on the Yellowstone. Colonel Leavenworth, in command of the military detachment at Council Bluffs, determined to forestall farther outrage by striking a stunning blow at the Aricara fortress. William H. Ashley and Joshua Pilcher, the able successors of Lisa at the head of the Missouri Fur Company's affairs, brought one hundred and twenty of their best men to his assistance, and four hundred Sioux warriors sided with the Americans. Such a force should have reduced the Aricaras to submission and guaranteed the security of the river road for years to come. Unfortunately Colonel Leavenworth was not accustomed to Indian diplomacy, and he made the mistake of suspending hostilities to consider offers of peace.

The treaty he negotiated was not worth the paper it was written on, and the perfidious Aricaras escaped punishment. Thereafter, in spite of the treaties negotiated by the second Yellowstone expedition (1825), the tribes of the upper Missouri regarded the traders as legitimate prey, frequenting the posts when they had furs to sell and robbing the trapping parties whenever they were strong enough to be sure of success.

The fur trade of the Far West, nevertheless, offered golden opportunities to whomsoever had courage and resources sufficient to overcome its inevitable hazards. In the years 1820 to 1830, the Missouri Fur Company [43] made determined efforts to get control of the upper Missouri. A new post, Fort Benton, was built at the mouth of the Big Horn, and a force of three hundred men was sent to this region, where the annual catch amounted to from $25,000 to $30,000. But the Company was finally ruined by the persistent hostility of the Blackfeet. These banditti of the plains ranged the high country from Judith Basin to the Three Forks, and they were determined not to surrender to the whites their rich beaver meadows. They fought the interlopers with British muskets and traded their booty of beaver skins at the North West Company's posts. Congress had been induced (1816) to take advantage of the silence of the peace of Ghent on this vexed subject by prohibiting foreigners from trading with the Indians within the boundaries of the United States. This exclusive legislation was largely due to the influence of John Jacob Astor, who was thus able to turn the tables on the North West Company, to purchase the posts that were located south of the forty-ninth parallel at bargain prices, and so to secure control of the rich Minnesota territory. Fort Pembina was abandoned and the operations of the Canadian traders on the Red River of the North ceased. In 1821 the British government excluded American traders from the Canadian field, and international competition was transferred to the Columbia.

Even more bitter than the jealousy of foreign rivals was the opposition to government intervention, whether in the form of fees, bonds and penalties, or of official competition. The attack on the government trading houses was led by Thomas H. Benton, the newly elected senator from Missouri and the faithful ally of the St. Louis traders. Astor's influence also was actively hostile. The charges of inefficiency and corruption brought against the government factors were substantiated by such witnesses as Ramsay Crooks, Astor's right-hand man, and the agent for Indian Affairs on the Missouri, Benjamin O'Fallon, who owed his appointment to Astor's influence with the War Department. It was urged that the goods furnished the Indians were inferior to those offered by private traders, that the prices charged were exorbitant, that for these reasons the Indians had ceased to trade at the government factories, and finally, that the impression made on the savage mind by the official factors was far from contributing to the influence of the United States government on the frontier. The superintendent of Indian Trade,

Thomas L. McKinney, protested that the competition of private traders, not the disinclination of the Indians, thwarted the effort of his factors to further the humane purposes of the government and that the latter could not compete against the credit advances permitted the private trader and his clandestine sale of whiskey. The license fee, he argued, should be raised to $200 and the bond to $10,000 in order to eliminate the small trader who peddled whiskey and firearms and otherwise demoralized the trade. The superintendent made out a good case, but the importunities of the fur traders prevailed. The government factories were abolished (March, 1822) and the trade was thrown open to all American citizens who could secure a license, no endorsements being required. The system of fees and penalties was not revived, and the bond, fixed in proportion to capital invested, was never to exceed $5000. The result was a régime of cut-throat competition. The less scrupulous traders practised unblushing frauds upon the Indians and upon each other. The savages were incited to ignore the credit obligation and turn over the proceeds of the winter's hunt to the party first on the ground in the spring, a pernicious practice that was mutually destructive. The fur trade was given over to unbridled license.

Twenty years later (1842), Fremont described the conditions then prevailing at Fort Laramie. "The articles of trade consist, on the one side, almost entirely of buffalo robes; and, on the other, of blankets, calicoes, guns, powder, and lead, with

such cheap ornaments as glass beads, looking-
glasses, rings, vermilion for painting, tobacco, and
principally, and in spite of the prohibition, of
spirits, brought into the country in the form of
alcohol, and diluted with water before sold. While
mentioning this fact, it is but justice to the American Fur Company to state that, throughout the
country, I have always found them strenuously
opposed to the introduction of spirituous liquors.
But, in the present state of things, when the country is supplied with alcohol, when a keg of it will
purchase from an Indian everything he possesses —
his furs, his lodge, his horses, and even his wife and
children, — and when any vagabond who has money
enough to purchase a mule can go into a village and
trade against them successfully, without withdraw-
ing entirely from the trade, it is impossible for them
to discontinue its use. In their opposition to this
practice, the company is sustained, not only by
their obligation to the laws of the country and the
welfare of the Indians, but clearly, also, on grounds
of policy; for, with heavy and expensive outfits,
they contend at manifestly great disadvantage
against the numerous independent and unlicensed
traders, who enter the country from various avenues,
from the United States and from Mexico, having
no other stock in trade than some kegs of liquor,
which they sell at the modest price of thirty-six
dollars per gallon. The difference between the
regular trader and the *coureur de bois* (as the French
call the itinerant or peddling traders) with respect
to the sale of spirits, is here, as it always has been,

fixed and permanent, and growing out of the nature of their trade. The regular trader looks ahead, and has an interest in the preservation of the Indians, and in the regular pursuit of their business, and the preservation of their arms, horses, and everything necessary to their future and permanent success in hunting. The *coureur de bois* has no permanent interest, and gets what he can, and for what he can, from every Indian he meets, even at the risk of disabling him from doing anything more at hunting."[44]

The American Fur Company

Disinterested observers most conversant with the situation had repeatedly recommended that the Missouri River trade should be made over for a term of years to an exclusive corporation adequately financed, which, under suitable regulation, should be trusted to develop the region in the conservative fashion practised by the Hudson's Bay Company; but this proposal was regarded as antagonistic to the genius of American institutions and therefore unpatriotic. The only business organization equal to such an enterprise was the American Fur Company, and jealousy of the New York financier was so great that no congressman could be induced to propose so unprecedented a monopoly. Astor, however, had by no means abandoned his purpose of invading the Missouri territory, and in 1822 he established a branch of the American Fur Company at St. Louis. The opposition of his western competitors he overcame by joining forces with the most important of the old houses, *e.g.* Bernard

Pratte & Co., the Chouteaus, the Columbia Fur Company,—so that the ablest men in St. Louis were enlisted in the service of the new enterprise. Besides the old-time Astorians, Ramsay Crooks, Robert Stuart, Russell Farnham, several agents of the Canadian companies, Kenneth Mackenzie, Etienne Provost, Vanderburg, were enlisted. The fusion of the North West with the Hudson's Bay Company had thrown some nine hundred clerks, traders, and trappers out of employment, and these, Scotchmen for the most part, were glad to try their luck with the great American company. Fully conversant with the Missouri country and on excellent terms with the Assiniboins and the Blackfeet, they were able to secure the trade of the northern rivers for their new patron. The Western Department of the American Fur Company (the term Northern Department was henceforth applied to the business centring at Mackinaw) soon developed a trade that quite overshadowed its operations along the Great Lakes, and so far preëmpted the fur trade of the Missouri region that it was commonly known as "the Company," while all outside traders were designated collectively "the Opposition." A post, Fort Union, was built at the mouth of the Yellowstone to intercept the trade with the Assiniboins, which, since it commanded both routes to the beaver grounds, became the depository of the season's catch. Fort Piegan (later Fort Mackenzie and finally Fort Benton) was placed at the mouth of Maria's River to control the Blackfeet country, while Fort Cass, at the junction of the Big Horn, secured the adherence of the Crows.

The limitless resources of the parent company rendered possible experiments and losses which would have ruined any or all of the St. Louis houses. In 1830 a startling innovation was determined on. The keel boat was to be supplanted by steamers for the transportation of goods and furs. Steamboats had been used on the lower river since 1819, but no vessel of such proportions had ventured above the Kansas since the costly experiment of the government in the Aricara campaign. Pierre Chouteau contended, however, that the upper river could be successfully navigated by stern-wheelers, such as the Long party had used with entire success, and that the saving in time and in operating force would be great. Under his auspices, the *Yellowstone* made her virgin voyage in the spring of 1831, achieving the round trip from St. Louis to Fort Tecumseh, at the mouth of the Kansas, in three months, two months up-stream and one down. In the following year, the little craft ascended the river as far as Fort Union. The saving in time and labor was sufficient to justify the adoption of steam, but the impression produced upon the Indians was perhaps the most significant gain. They said that "the British might turn out their dogs and burn their sledges, as they would no longer be useful while the Fire Boat walked on the waters." [45] They began bringing their furs to the Americans by preference, and thenceforth the loss of trade from Hudson's Bay Company competition was no longer dreaded.

By these means the American Fur Company had succeeded in monopolizing the trade on the upper

The American Fur Company's S.S. "Yellowstone," on the Missouri.

Missouri, the Yellowstone, and their tributaries, — the apparently inexhaustible beaver meadows revealed by the Lewis and Clark expedition. Rivals were induced to combine forces, were bought off, or were driven from the field by craft or violence, as the situation might suggest. The methods used to crush out competitors were quite comparable to the practices of certain industrial combinations of to-day. The natives were incited to waylay, rob, and even murder trading parties who dared invade the territory covered by the operations of "the Company," prices of furs were advanced and prices of goods lowered when the presence of a rival threatened to seduce the Indians, agents being given *carte blanche* to depart from the established schedules in such business emergencies. Whiskey, though forbidden by law, was freely sold to the Indians in the contested districts, and when the difficulty in getting the contraband stuff up the river past the government inspector at Fort Leavenworth proved too serious, a distillery was set up at Fort Union, and fire-water, "as fine a liquor as need be drunk," was made from the corn grown by the natives. Mackenzie, Crooks, and Chouteau justified this practice on the ground that so long as their irresponsible rivals smuggled liquor into the territory and enticed the Indians away from their posts, they must offer whiskey in trade or abandon the field.[46]

The methods of the American Fur Company were no more reprehensible than those employed by its competitors, but, because of its greater resources,

the warfare waged by its agents was far more cruel
and effective. For this reason the sympathy of the
public was always with the independent trader.
Under Astor's shrewd management, the business was
highly systematized and placed on a basis that insured the principal against loss. The stock in trade,
whether imported or purchased in the home market,
was collected at New York and forwarded thence in
the early spring *via* New Orleans and the Mississippi.
From St. Louis the goods were despatched to the
interior posts by keel boat or steamer as the case
might be. The furs collected during the winter
hunt were returned over the same routes to New
York, the primary market, where they were as-
sorted, made up into bales, and shipped to Europe
and China. The resident agent at Kansas Post,
Fort Union, Fort Benton, or Fort Cass was charged
for his season's supplies at fixed prices that covered
the initial cost plus duties and transportation and
still allowed a considerable margin of profit, while
the price paid for furs was determined each season
by the conditions of the foreign market. Whether
the year's operations left the local trader with a surplus or a deficit depended on the terms he was able
to make with the Indians and trappers on whom he
relied to bring in the furs. The credit system still
held. In the autumn, after the corn was gathered
in, the native hunters came to the post for the supplies without which they could not live through the
winter, much less trap beaver. Taking advantage
of their necessity, the trader furnished blankets,
kettles, firearms, flints, powder and lead, beaver

and muskrat traps, needles, thread, and gewgaws at double the price charged to him. When the braves returned in the spring with the proceeds of the season's hunt, the situation was reversed, the trader was in straits, and the Indians paid as little as they dared of the accumulated debt. The customary rate of account was $2 a pound for beaver, $3 for a land otter skin, from $1 to $1.50 for a buffalo hide, one buckskin, two doeskins, four muskrat or raccoon skins for $1; [47] but often no more than one-half, one-third, or one-fourth the debt would be made good. Moreover, the prices the goods could command had dwindled to half those prevailing in the autumn, so that the trader was hard put to it to clear himself and rarely reaped any considerable profit. These spring settlements were accompanied by acrid altercations which not infrequently resulted in bloodshed, and many a trader lost his life in the service of the far-away commercial potentate popularly known as "Grandpapa."

The *engagés* and free trappers employed by "the Company" endured far more hardships and took greater risks, but their remuneration was hardly more secure. A free trapper on the Missouri contracted to furnish one man and one-half the supplies for the season's hunt. Mackenzie furnished on behalf of the Company two men and half the supplies, was entitled to half the catch, and expected to purchase the remainder, — beaver skins at from $3 to $4 per pound, " castorum " at $3 per pound. An account between Mackenzie and a free trapper,

John Gardner, cited by Chittenden,[48] gives the balance due for thirteen years' service, after supplies had been deducted from credits against beaver and otter skins brought in, as $930, — not a munificent reward for half a lifetime of strenuous labor. Ugly stories were current to the effect that even this pittance was sometimes withheld and that employees who ventured to St. Louis to present their claims had been murdered *en route*. The white trapper was hardly better off than the Indian, for he paid the same inflated prices for advances (*e.g.* one blanket $12, one axe $6, one kettle $5, the shoeing of a horse $3, etc.), and he, like the Indian, spent one-third his returns in liquor and feasting. The system was a demoralizing one to all concerned. The Indians were induced to abandon the occupations that had made them self-supporting, in order that they might devote their energies to the hunt. In fact, the advantage of the trader increased as his tribe became dependent upon the post for a livelihood. The white men employed earned a bare subsistence, while in the lonely life of the post or the inevitable brutalities of the hunt they degenerated to a status hardly to be distinguished from that of the savage.

Astor's contribution to the success of the American Fur Company was that of entrepreneur. The first financial genius of the age, he determined the markets in which to buy supplies and sell furs, and his world-wide commercial operations gave him every advantage. Supplies were sent out with unfailing regularity, and the disasters of one department were offset by the successes of another. In trade competition this plenitude of resources rendered victory sure, for the great Company could ruin a rival by the manipulation of prices. The influence Astor exercised at Washington was used unhesitatingly to promote favorable and defeat adverse legislation, as well as to protect his agents against the too zealous espionage of government officials. For example, the right of Astor's Mackinaw boats to descend the Mississippi was challenged by St. Louis traders on the ground that they were manned by Canadians. One boat was captured and the *bourgeois* arrested. Astor's influence secured the vindication of the right of the American Fur Company's agents to navigate the Mississippi rivers, and the appointment of an Indian agent (Benjamin O'Fallon) less amenable to the St. Louis houses. The same astute genius did much to placate public criticism by politic favors to scientists and men in position; *e.g.* Bradbury and Nuttall were carried up the Missouri by Hunt's party; Catlin, the painter, ascended the river in the Company's steamboat in 1832; and a similar service was rendered to Maximilien, Prince of Wied, in 1833.

The Rocky Mountain Fur Company

In 1821 a new company was organized by the St. Louis traders, Americans and pioneers all of them. General W. H. Ashley, the prime mover, was a Virginian who had come to Missouri in 1802 and borne a prominent part in the development of the territory. His second, Andrew Henry, was the fearless trapper who had crossed the continental divide and built a post on westward-flowing water in advance of Hunt's party. Returning from that disastrous experience, he had accumulated some property in the lead mines, but was now ready to join this new venture in the fur trade. With these veterans were associated on a profit-sharing basis a number of younger men, Jedidiah S. Smith (a New Yorker), William L. and Milton G. Sublette, Solomon P. Andrew (a Kentuckian), David E. Jackson, James Bridger (a Virginian), Thomas Fitzpatrick and Robert Campbell (Irishmen),—frontiersmen whose courage and resourcefulness no less than their unscrupulous daring recalled the best days of the North West Company. The first expeditions up the Missouri were unfortunate. Henry's party was robbed by the Assiniboins, and he pushed on to Great Falls only to be driven back by the Blackfeet (1822). The following year, Ashley's boats were attacked by the Aricaras and forced to retreat down the river. After the Leavenworth campaign, a more aggressive enterprise was projected, no less than the founding of a fort for protection of the trappers. Henry proceeded up the Yellowstone with a large party and built a post at its junction with the Big Horn; but a band of hostiles killed several of the trappers and carried off the horses.

In this same year, a more successful expedition under Henry, Bridger, and Etienne Provost followed the North Platte River to the South Pass and beyond to Green River. This, the easiest of all the passes across the Rockies, had been used for ages by the buffalo and the Indians, but was now for the first time utilized by the traders. It led to beaver-bearing streams hardly less profitable than those of the upper Missouri, and the party returned with a fine take of furs. The operations of the Rocky Mountain Fur Company were immediately transferred to this uncontested field. In 1824 Ashley went out in person to explore the new territory, followed the South Platte into the labyrinth of mountain ranges that make up western Colorado, and forced his way through to the Green River. In an attempt to follow down this dangerous stream his boat was wrecked, but the indomitable leader made his way on foot to Sevier Lake (called Ashley Lake by the traders) and, later, north to Great Salt Lake. The Hudson's Bay Company's trappers had come as far south as Bear Lake that year, and Peter Skeene Ogden, their patron, had cached his first season's take in a lovely mountain valley, long famous as Ogden's Hole. Ashley appropriated the furs as treasure trove and thereby recouped his desperate fortunes.[49]

For ten years, thereafter, the Rocky Mountain Fur Company justified its name, being in full control of the bleak desert between the Snake River and the Colorado. The Digger Indians could not be depended on to bring in furs, and Ashley was forced to rely on free trappers. Every stream and mountain park that harbored beaver was diligently searched out by the intrepid men who summered and wintered in this inhospitable region. Supplies were brought out by the spring brigade, up the North Platte and over the South Pass to the desig-

nated *rendezvous*. Ashley did not attempt to build
trading posts, but brought his whole force together
at an appointed time and place, where the trappers
exchanged their season's catch of furs for pork,
flour, sugar and tea, clothing, ammunition and
whiskey. Irving's description of the *rendezvous* at
Green River is too well known to require quoting
here.[50]   The return trip was made by pack train or,
when the rivers served, by boat.   From South Pass
the preferred route was by way of the Big Horn,
Yellowstone, and Missouri rivers, — streams always
navigable for the bull boats which the traders had
adopted.   The first wheeled vehicles to cross the
plains north of the Santa Fé Trail were sent to
Ashley's *rendezvous* on Lake Utah in 1826 or 1827.
Ashley's success in this unexploited country was immediate and highly satisfactory.   The return from
the hunt of 1824 was one hundred packs of beaver,
that of 1826, one hundred and twenty-three, that of
1827, one hundred and thirty.   In the latter year
he made over the business to Smith, Sublette, and
Jackson and settled at St. Louis, where he realized
a very comfortable income by supplying goods to
the traders in the field, receiving their furs in payment.

The new firm did not prosper financially, for the
heyday of the fur trade was past.   Their great
achievements were geographical, the unwitting result
of the search for fresh hunting-grounds.   An obscure
hunter, taking a daring wager, followed the circuitous
course of the Bear River and launched his canoe
on the treacherous waters of Salt Lake.   Etienne

Uintah Post, Robidoux' Headquarters among the Utes.

Provost rediscovered Utah Lake, coming in by way of the Provo River, to the north of Escallante's trail. In 1824 Jedidiah Smith, turning north from South Pass, followed up the Green River to the Snake and came upon the Hudson's Bay Company's post, Fort Boisé. In the summer of 1826 he set out from Salt Lake with a party of fifteen men to explore the country to the southwest. He ascended the Sevier valley to the mountainous land of the Pah Utes and thence followed the Virgin River to the Colorado, where he found Indians cultivating corn, beans, melons, and even cotton. Here he purchased fresh horses out of a herd stolen from the Spaniards and undertook to cross the desert that lay west of the Colorado. A runaway neophyte served as guide and brought the party after three weeks' desperate march to San Gabriel and San Diego. The alarm of the *commandante* at this undreamed of invasion had nearly thwarted Smith's hopes. He and his men were detained for a time and his journal was confiscated and despatched to the City of Mexico.[51] Forbidden to visit the Spanish settlements along the coast, the Americans turned directly north and crossed Tehatchepi Pass into the San Joaquin valley, where they found plenty of beaver. Here they trapped during the winter of 1826–1827, and in the spring the fearless leader set out with two men, seven horses, and two pack-mules loaded with hay and food, to seek fresh supplies at the *rendezvous*. He made his way over the Sierras by the Merced River and Sonora Pass. (Smith called the Sierra Range Mt. Joseph.) The snow lay in heavy drifts from four to eight feet deep and men and animals suffered severely, but the feat was accomplished in eight days. The march across the Great American Desert, a region "arid and without game or vegetation," was made in twenty days. From the rocky ridges that cross this waste of sand and sage-brush, rivulets of good water flowed, but only to be immediately sucked down by the thirsty earth. It was impossible to carry much luggage and the party was sometimes without water for two days' march. No help could be had from the Digger Indians, the most wretched of human beings, whose food was snakes and lizards taken with the hands and whose only shelter was the wickiup of sage-brush. When the daring party arrived at Salt Lake, but one horse and one mule remained alive, and the men were so exhausted that they could hardly stagger under the meagre remnant of their equipment. Stopping at Salt Lake only long enough to secure a new outfit, Smith again set out for California to recover his trappers and their accumulation of furs. While crossing the Virgin River the party was attacked by Indians, and ten of the men and all the supplies were lost; but this dauntless pathfinder made his way across the desert to San Gabriel Mission and, leaving there two wounded men, proceeded by ship to Monterey. He was again arrested as a dangerous character, and again American sea-captains were found to stand sponsor for his good intentions. He was released (November, 1827), on condition that he should withdraw from California within two months.

Smith was a man of his word; but instead of attempting to cross the Sierras, an impossible feat in midwinter, he went north to the first tributary of the Sacramento (thereafter called American Fork) and trapped along that valley until the floods had subsided. Then in April, 1828, the party followed an Indian trail up the Shasta River, over Siskyou Pass, and down Rogue River to the Umpqua. There, during Smith's absence, the party got into trouble with the Indians, the camp was attacked, the men killed, the horses stolen, and the luggage carried away. Smith and the two men with him found their way down the Willamette to Fort Vancouver. Dr. McLoughlin received the survivors with characteristic generosity, gave them quarters at the Fort, and despatched his stepson McKay with an adequate force to punish the Umpquas and recover the stolen property. With characteristic justice, he paid the American trader the current price for the furs, traps, and horses, deducting only the actual cost of the punitive expedition. With business shrewdness equally characteristic, the chief factor stipulated that one of Smith's men should remain to serve as guide to the beaver grounds of the Sacramento valley. In the autumn of 1828, McLeod was sent south to prosecute the trade in this promising district.

Smith remained at Fort Vancouver throughout the winter of 1828–1829 and accompanied the spring brigade to Spokane House and Flat Head Post; there, turning south, he followed the Indian trail to Henry's Fork of Snake River. By lucky chance, the *rendezvous* for that year was appointed at Pierre's Hole, and there the wanderers found Sublette and Jackson and the Rocky Mountain men in full force. Smith insisted that henceforth the hunt should be carried on east of the divide so that they should not trench upon the territory claimed by the Hudson's Bay Company. The operations of 1829–1830 were restricted to the Big Horn, Yellowstone, and upper Missouri valleys and were highly successful in spite of severe weather, hostile Blackfeet, and the jealous machinations of the American Fur Company. In the spring of 1830, Sublette went to St. Louis for supplies and returned in the following spring up the North Platte and over South Pass to the *rendezvous* on Green River with cattle and milch cows and a train of ten wagons. In the autumn of 1832, the partners came back to St. Louis with one hundred and ninety packs of beaver, worth $95,000, and realized a profit that enabled them to retire from the business. William Sublette followed Ashley's example and opened a wholesale supply business, while Jackson and Smith went into the Santa Fé trade, an enterprise that promised to realize better returns with less labor and risk to life and limb.

Younger men succeeded to the direction of the Rocky Mountain Fur Company. Milton G. Sublette, Thomas Fitzpatrick, and James Bridger led the brigades to the annual *rendezvous*, and their free trappers explored every beaver-bearing stream between Green River and the Missouri, overlapping the region claimed by the American Fur Company, and the Missouri River posts retaliated by sending their men to the Big Horn. The fame of Ashley's winnings attracted adventurers from the eastern states, who entered the arena hopefully, with little conception of its hazard. At the *rendezvous* held at Pierre's Hole in 1832, Fitzpatrick encountered Vanderburg and Drips — Astor's agents — Nathaniel J. Wyeth, who had brought out a band of raw recruits from New England, and Captain Bonneville, also a novice in the trade, whose elaborate equipment was highly amusing to the experienced men.[52]

The movements of mere adventurers could be ig-

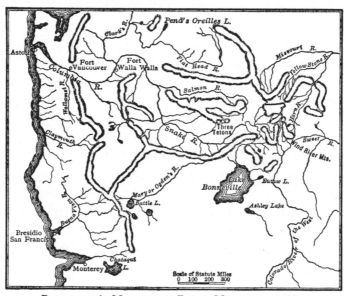

BONNEVILLE'S MAP OF THE ROCKY MOUNTAINS, 1837.

nored, and Wyeth and Bonneville were not molested; but the two great companies locked horns in a life and death combat. Vanderburg attempted to follow Fitzpatrick and find out his hunting-grounds, and the latter led him astray into the Blackfeet country where he and his party fell into an ambush and were destroyed. Fitzpatrick, in turn, was robbed by the Crows at the instigation of the American Fur Company's men, and his furs were restored to him only on payment of the price paid the Indians. The natives were demoralized by the unscrupulous methods of the whites, and the *engagés* were taught reckless knavery. The rival agents spied upon each other's business operations with all the zeal of a modern "trust," and a man transferring from one service to another ran the risk of persecution, even murder. In spite of its brilliant achievements and the superior calibre of the men in its service, the Rocky Mountain Fur Company was the loser in this cut-throat competition. Ashley had been the organizing genius of the business, and there was no one to take his place. The courage, resourcefulness and ingenuity of Smith, Fitzpatrick, Bridger, and other brave men could make little headway against the limitless financial resources of Astor's company. Losses which meant ruin to them were a negligible quantity in the balance-sheet of a great corporation whose deficits in one field were sure to be offset by gains in another.

Chittenden estimates that during the twelve years of its career the Rocky Mountain Fur Company shipped to St. Louis one thousand packs of beaver worth $500 a pack.[53] The losses in goods and furs and horses injured or stolen he estimates at $100,000, the human loss at one hundred lives. The bulk of the profits accrued to General Ashley and W. L. Sublette, even after they had withdrawn from the partnership, for they manipulated the prices of goods and furs so as to skim the cream off the returns. None of the other partners made money, and most of them, as well as the major part of the free trappers and *engagés*, were eventually wrecked in health and fortune.

The great and permanent achievements of the Rocky Mountain men were quite independent of financial success or failure. They opened up a new fur country at the head waters of the Snake, the Green, and the Big Horn rivers,—streams that, rising in the Wind River Mountains, the core of the continent, diverge to east, south, and west, and empty into the Pacific, the Gulf of California, and the Gulf of Mexico. They first explored that vast tract of mountain and desert, the Cordilleran area; they discovered the Great Salt, the Utah and Sevier lakes; they traced the Snake, the Green, and the Colorado rivers from mountain source to the sea; they demonstrated the practicability of the South Pass, Walker's Pass, and other routes over the Rockies and the Sierras. When the United States government undertook to explore the Far West, the topographical engineers were fain to enlist the services of "mountain men" like Kit Carson and James Bridger. Finally, the Rocky Mountain Fur Company cleared the way for settlers by the long and relentless warfare they carried on with the nomad Indian tribes, the Blackfeet, Aricaras, Crows, Comanches, and Pah Utes, between whom and the traders there was never a truce. Not the United States army nor the treaties so carefully negotiated by the Indian Department, but the trappers' rifles, taught the redman respect for the white man's capacity for self-defense.

Section VI

Decline of the Fur Trade

By 1840, all profit had vanished for the independent trader. The beaver dams were practically exhausted, and even the less important furs, as otter, mink, fox, and lynx, were hard to get. The buffalo herds, which had seemed limitless, were fast diminishing, yet they kept the fur trade alive for twenty years after the beaver were trapped out. The original range of the bison was from the Alleghanies to the Rocky Mountains, from the Great Lakes to the Gulf; but they had disappeared from the eastern side of the Mississippi by the end of the eighteenth century and were rarely found east of the Missouri after the first decade of the nineteenth. For fifty years thereafter, they ranged the Great Plains. They varied their feeding grounds with the season, pushing far to the north in the summer when the bunch grass was richest, retreating before the snows across the rolling prairies of the Platte and the Kansas, to winter on the "staked plains" of Texas. To the Indian the buffalo was the staff of life; to the white man he furnished important articles of commerce. The hide, the tongue, the tallow were in great demand, and the fur traders exercised their utmost ingenuity to supply the market. The annual yield for the decade from 1840 to 1850 was estimated at ninety thousand robes;

that from 1850 to 1860, at one hundred thousand. Not more than one-third the buffalo killed were represented in the trade, for there was enormous waste. The hides of the bulls were never used, and those of the cows were fit for dressing during the winter months only.

When Fremont crossed the Plains (1842), the buffalo range was confined to "the eastern base of the Rocky Mountains, sometimes extending at their southern extremity to a considerable distance into the plains between the Platte and Arkansas rivers, and along the eastern frontier of New Mexico as far south as Texas." Fitzpatrick told him that some twenty years before there were immense numbers of buffalo in the Green and Bear river valleys, but the hunters had driven them from this retreat to the upper reaches of Snake River. Fremont describes the "great highways, continuous for hundreds of miles, always several inches, and sometimes several feet in depth, which the buffalo have made in crossing from one river to another, or in traversing the mountain ranges." [54] Stansbury adds: "When the emigration first commenced, travelling trains were frequently detained for hours by immense herds crossing their track, and in such numbers that it was impossible to drive through them." [55] As white men increased, slaughter augmented with reckless glee. Burton, who followed the mail route in 1859, estimated that the annual destruction amounted to two or three hundred thousand. By that time the buffalo was rarely seen on the trail, and the hunters followed the herds into the wild country; but buffalo steaks, always regarded as more nutritious and wholesome than beef, were furnished at the wayside inns.

The annual take of the American Fur Company in 1832, according to Maximilien, Prince of Wied, was twenty-five thousand beaver skins worth $8 apiece, from forty to fifty thousand buffalo hides worth $4 each, from twenty to thirty thousand deerskins worth $1 each, from one to two thousand lynx, two thousand mink, two to three thousand fox, of which only the silver fox was valuable (twenty to thirty skins at $60 each), and as many muskrats as they chose to accept, from one thousand to one hundred thousand. The total value of the furs received amounted in the early thirties to $500,000 a year. It was evident to any one acquainted with the situation that this yield could not long be maintained. In 1834, John Jacob Astor, then in London looking into the European markets, became convinced that the profitable days of the fur trade were past. The beaver meadows were nearing exhaustion, and the market for the fur was declining. "It appears that they make hats of silk in place of beaver." He returned ready to sell his interest in the American Fur Company, and it was taken over by Ramsay Crooks, who had for some time been in charge of the New York department and was now backed by Pratte, Chouteau & Co., of St. Louis. The new firm bought out Fitzpatrick, Sublette, and Bridger this same year and the Union Fur Company in 1845.

Thenceforth the American Fur Company was in full control of the Rocky Mountain trade, but the industry was declining, as Astor had foreseen, and the ablest men of the frontier were turning to other pursuits. Even in the Hudson's Bay Company's territory beyond the divide, the receipts from the trapping expeditions were dwindling. According to N. J. Wyeth, the revenue from sales of peltry taken in the western district of the Hudson's Bay Company, the region between the forty-second and the forty-ninth parallel, the Rocky Mountains and the Pacific, did not amount to more than $138,000 a year, — not a large gross return considering the heavy expenditures (*e.g.* $20,000 on goods shipped from London, the vessels required to transport goods and furs, the services of three hundred and fifty employees, and two years' interest on the capital). The annual net profit of the Hudson Bay Company, did not, he believed, exceed $10,000. "My impression is, notwithstanding the great disparity of the money value of the objects exchanged in this trade, that it has been less profitable than any other in which as much danger of life and property is incurred." This experienced and disinterested observer anticipated a steady decline in revenue from this source. "The furs produced in this country have heretofore been of considerable value, and doubtless will furnish a means, to a small extent, for supplying the wants of a new country; but that business has been carried to its full limit; it may for a few years be kept up to its present point of production, but must soon decrease, especially if the country is thrown open to emigrants, most of whom will become dealers to a greater or less degree in it, and many will turn to the more exciting and immediate profits of the hunter, rather than to the slow labors of the farmer." [56] After visiting the posts in 1841 Governor Simpson wrote: "I am concerned to say the returns are gradually diminishing from year to year; this arises from no want of attention to the management of the district, but from the exhausted state of the country, which has been closely wrought for many years without any intermission." [57]

The trappers and traders were dying out quite as rapidly as the beaver. Exposure, drink, and the hostility of the Indians were destroying them one by one. Their wages were spent in the carouses that disgraced the *rendezvous* and the trading posts. Few had accumulated property enough to return to the civilized world. Alexander Ross, who had long experience with the Hudson's Bay Company and knew the American traders, estimates the comparative chances of success as follows: "In the fur trade of the north many have attained to a competency, not a few to independence, and many have realized fortunes after a servitude of years; but in the slippery and ruinous traffic of the south many fortunes have been lost, and an awful sacrifice made of human life; so that of all the adventurers engaged, for half a century past, in the fur trade of that licentious quarter, few, very few indeed, ever left it with even a bare competency." [58]

The best of the "mountain men" settled down in some fertile valley or mountain meadow, built a cabin for the Indian wife and half-breed children, and managed to provide food, clothing, and whiskey by trapping during the winter and farming during the summer months. Farnham describes such a man, one

Joseph Meek, whom he met on Bear River. "He came to the mountains many years ago — and has so long associated with Indians, that his manners much resemble theirs. The same wild, unsettled, watchful expression of the eyes; the same unnatural gesticulation in conversation, the same unwillingness to use words when a sign, a contortion of the face or body, or movement of the hand will manifest thought; in standing, walking, riding — in all but complexion he was an Indian. . . . Meek was evidently very poor. He had scarcely clothing enough to cover his body. And while talking with us the frosty winds which sucked up the valley, made him shiver like an aspen leaf. He reverted to his destitute situation, and complained of the injustice of his former employers; the little remuneration he had received for the toils and dangers he had endured on their account, &c.; a complaint which I had heard from every trapper whom I had met on my journey." [59]

In his *Forty Years of a Fur Trader*, Charles Larpenteur has given a graphic account of the vicissitudes of the life for a man distinctly above the average mentally and morally. A Frenchman of good birth, he went from Baltimore to Missouri to seek his fortune, and entered the service of Sublette & Co. in 1832, at a yearly salary of $296 and supplies. His description of the sufferings of horses and men on the long marches to the *rendezvous* bears internal evidence of authenticity. When his patron sold out to Fitzpatrick, Larpenteur found a berth with the American Fur Company and served under Kenneth Mackenzie, "the king of the Missouri," for the next fifteen years. He was assistant clerk at Fort Union at a salary of $350 a year, with food and living quarters and one suit of broadcloth furnished. Larpenteur was not only intelligent but temperate, and he won the confidence of his superiors mainly by his ability to keep sober during the wild carousals which left every other man, white and red, *engagé,* trapper, clerk, and factor, dead drunk for days at a time. Strong drink was, according to this Frenchman, the curse of the trade. Equally destructive from a business point of view was the competitive warfare waged by the upstart companies that endeavored to invade the territory long monopolized by the "big house." Fox, Livingstone & Co., of New York, set up a post, Fort Mortimer, on the Yellowstone in 1846, and for four years maintained a precarious existence through enticing the American Fur Company's trappers to desert by promises of higher wages, and secured first innings in the Indian trade by lavish dispensing of liquor. No sooner had this firm sold out than a new "opposition" arose, Harvey, Pruneau & Co., former clerks of the Great Company, and the business degenerated from bad to worse.

At forty years of age, Larpenteur, grown pigheaded and captious, quarrelled with his superiors and determined to quit the fur trade and take his Assiniboin wife and half-breed children to the Flathead mission of which Father de Smet had told him. In company with another trade-weary Frenchman (1847), he set out up the Missouri, meaning to cross the mountains by the Lewis and Clark Pass. The

FORT BRIDGER, 1849.

FORT LARAMIE, 1853.

little caravan of two wagons, two carts, and eight pack horses succeeded in reaching Sun River with no serious mishap, but there a brush with the Blackfeet and the approach of winter turned them back. The two families made a second attempt the following year, mounted this time on horseback, and got as far as Great Falls; but they were a second time forced back by hardships too severe for even Indian women to endure, and Larpenteur returned to the service of the American Fur Company. Two years' experience convinced him that "there was nothing more to be made in the Indian trade," [60] and he bought a claim on the Little Sioux River, meaning to "open a small farm." The place lay in the path of the Mormon migration, and realizing that "settlers were coming in fast," the old trader thought he saw a chance to make money more rapidly than by growing corn. He built a store and a blacksmith shop for the use of emigrants and ran a ferry across the river, borrowing heavily to finance these improvements. He might have succeeded had not the crisis of 1857 ruined his credit.

The resources of civilization having failed him, Larpenteur again turned to the wilderness and joined a party that proposed to hunt buffalo in the Assiniboin country. To avoid the hostile Sioux, the eight wagons and eleven men travelled far north by way of St. Paul and the Red River of the North, which they crossed on the bridge at Pembina, and so up the Souris River to the Missouri. The hunt was successful, and they were returning well satisfied, with two thousand robes, when the news that the outbreak of the Civil War had shut off the foreign market and halved the price of furs balked their expectations of profit. Turning again to his old employers, Larpenteur found the Great Company disintegrating. As a sympathizer with the Confederacy, Chouteau was refused a license to trade with the Indians and was obliged to sell his interests to a Chicago firm (Hulbard, Hawley & Co.; A. B. Smith, manager) which, under the title of the North West Company, carried on the languishing trade. All the old loyalty lost, Larpenteur worked first for this house and then for "the Opposition," and again on his own account, and finally died a pauper.

More fortunate were some of the traders who, by the aid of *engagés* and Indians, converted their posts into productive farms and raised supplies for the fast-coming emigrants. Colonel A. P. Chouteau had a large farm in the Osage country (1831), "where he raises every article of necessary food and in greater abundance than is necessary for himself, his very numerous family and followers." [61] Lupton's trading post at Fort Lancaster on the South Platte is described by Fremont. "His post was beginning to assume the appearance of a comfortable farm; stock, hogs, and cattle were ranging about on the prairie; there were different kinds of poultry; and there was the wreck of a promising garden, in which a considerable variety of vegetables had been in a flourishing condition, but it had been almost entirely ruined by the recent high waters." [62] The most important of these attempts of the fur traders to adjust themselves to the new order was Fort Bridger, the palisaded post built by James

Bridger on the Black Fork of Green River. This
famous frontiersman knew at first hand the vast
Cordilleran wilderness from the Missouri River to the
Rio Grande and from the Gila to the Columbia.
"With a buffalo-skin and a piece of charcoal, he will
map out any portion of this immense region, and
delineate mountains, streams, and the circular valleys
called 'holes,' with wonderful accuracy." [63]   Their
intimate knowledge of the Far West gave the "mountain men" an advantage in the selection of settlement
sites, and when the pioneer farmers arrived on the
ground they usually found some old trapper or trader
squatting on the most fertile and best watered land.

NOTES

VOLUME I

PART I

CHAPTER I

1 Humboldt, *New Spain*, II, 248.

2 Venegas, writing in 1758, is quite in doubt as to whether the straits of Anian are not "altogether imaginary" and concludes: "We must wait for the solution till the same spirit of discovery that brought us first acquainted with the Indies and with America, reveals to us with equal certainty, whether it is sea or land, or a mixture of both, that intervenes between these two mighty continents." Venegas, *History of California*, I, Preface A 4.

3 Edward Everett Hale first pointed out the relation between Montalvos' romance, the Deeds of Esplandian, and Cortès' discovery. In *Atlantic Monthly*, XIII, 265; cf. Bancroft, *California*, I, 66; Venegas, *California*, I, 131–132.

4 Lyman (*History of Oregon*, I, Chap. V) gives several Indian traditions of such wrecks that antedate Gray's discovery of the Columbia, *e.g.* A ship was driven ashore at Nehalem River, the crew saved their lives, but were later killed by the natives. The ship's cargo of beeswax drifted in and was scattered on the sands. Some of the cakes which were preserved showed the mark I. H. S., which indicated that they were intended for a mission church. From another vessel wrecked off the south shore, two men escaped and were hospitably received by the Clatsops. One of them, called Konapee by the Indians, fashioned iron knives from the wreckage and possessed bright pieces of silver like Chinese *cash*. One ship came close inshore and landed a boat bringing a box which was buried on the cliff.

Franchère, *Narrative*, 248, describes a man of Spanish antecedents whom the Astorians found on the Columbia.

"We found here an old blind man, who gave us a cordial reception. Our guide said that he was a white man, and that his name was *Soto*. We learned from the mouth of the old man himself that he was the son of a Spaniard who had been wrecked at the mouth of the river; that a part of the crew on this occasion got safe ashore, but were all massacred by the Clatsops, with the exception of four, who were spared and who married native women; that these four Spaniards, of whom his father was one, disgusted with the savage life, attempted to reach a settlement of their own nation toward the south, but had never been heard of since; and that when his father, with his companions, left the country, he himself was yet quite young."

379

⁵ Drake, *The World Encompassed*, 118.

⁶ Winship, *Journey of Coronado*, 11.

⁷ Winship, *Coronado*, 22.

⁸ The Spanish word *pueblo* means town.   In American parlance it has come to signify those peculiar "joint tenements" built by the Zuñi, Moqui, and Tigua Indians.

⁹ Winship, *Coronado*, 23.

¹⁰ Winship, *Coronado*, 26.

¹¹ Winship, *Coronado*, 30.   This may have been the *pitaya cocida*, a preserve still made by the Mexicans from the fruit of the *suharo* (giant cactus), or the *tulapai*, a fermented drink which the Apaches distil from the same luscious fruit.

¹² Winship, *Coronado*, 99.

¹³ The buffalo was first described by Nunez Cabeza de Vaca and was numerous to the east of the mountains. Cf. *Journey*, 94.

¹⁴ Winship, *Coronado*, 38.   The Pueblo Indians had no sheep before the Spanish conquest.   According to Bandelier, their blankets were probably made of strips of rabbit skin woven into a heavy fabric. — Bandelier, *Final Report*.

¹⁵ "This country was elevated and full of low twisted pines, very cold, and lying open towards the north, so that, this being the warm season, no one could live there on account of the cold.   They spent three days on this bank looking for a passage down to the river, which looked from above as if the water was six feet across, although the Indians said it was half a league wide.   It was impossible to descend, for after these three days Captain Melgosa and one Juan Galeras and another companion, who were the three lightest and most agile men, made an attempt to go down at the least difficult place, and went down until those who were above were unable to keep sight of them.   They returned about four o'clock in the afternoon, not having succeeded in reaching the bottom on account of the great difficulties which they found, because what seemed to be easy from above was not so, but instead very hard and difficult. They said that they had been down about a third of the way and that the river seemed very large from the place which they reached, and that from what they saw they thought the Indians had given the width correctly.   Those who stayed above had estimated that some huge rocks on the sides of the cliffs seemed to be about as tall as a man, but those who went down swore that when they reached these rocks they were bigger than the great tower of Seville.   They did not go farther up the river, because they could not get water." — Winship, *Coronado*, 35–36. ·¹

¹⁶ Winship, *Coronado*, 41.

¹⁷ Castañeda estimated that there were sixty-six villages "in the country of the terraced houses," twenty thousand fighting men, and some hundred thousand people.   Of the *pueblos* seen by Coronado's party, Acoma

alone remains standing. Full account, given in Winship, *Coronado*, Part III, Chap. VII ; Bandelier, *Final Report*, Part I, 34.

[18] Winship, *Coronado*, 43.

[19] Winship, *Coronado*, 139–140.

[20] Winship, *Coronado*, 75–76.

[21] Winship, *Coronado*, 66.

[22] These folks live in tents made of the tanned skins of the cows. They travel around near the cows, killing them for food. — Winship, *Coronado*, 65. Bandelier identifies these nomads of the plains with the Apaches.

[23] Rumors of the martyrdom of these missionaries of the faith filled the Franciscans with zeal to undertake the conversion of the northern heathen.

[24] Winship, *Coronado*, 115.

[25] Winship, *Coronado*, 146.

CHAPTER II

[1] The *encomienda* was an institution allied to the feudal practice of commendation. The viceroy and governors were empowered to assign the native villages or *rancherias* to the nearest landowners. The *encomendero* was under obligation to instruct, sustain, and protect his Indian vassals, to defend the province against attack, and render other military service at the summons of the governor. He was entitled to a certain amount of personal service from the people on his estate, but he might not legally extort tribute, sell or give away his dependents or take them out of the province, nor might they be forfeited in payment for debt. They might not be forced to work in mines or manufactures, and the viceroy was commanded to punish severely any maltreatment. In case of abuse an Indian had the right of appeal to the *Royal Audencia*. — *Leyes de las Indias*, Libro Sexto.

[2] The creole was of pure Spanish blood but born in the colony. The *mestizo* was of mixed blood.

[3] The Spanish explorers greatly exaggerated the population of the *pueblos*. Bandelier thinks it cannot have exceeded 25,000 at the time of the conquest. — *Final Report*, I, 121.

[4] Gregg, *Commerce of the Prairies*, I, 260.

[5] To every settler and his descendants was accorded by the king's command the status of *hidalgo* or nobleman. — Pedro Pino, *Noticias*, 3.

[6] "The village was very strong, because it was up on a rock out of reach, having steep sides in every direction, and so high that it was a very good musket that could throw a ball as high. There was a broad stairway for about 200 steps, then a stretch of about 100 narrower steps, and at the top they had to go up about three times as high as a man by means

of holes in the rock, in which they put the points of their feet, holding on at the same time by their hands. There was a wall of large and small stones at the top, which they could roll down without showing themselves, so that no army could possibly be strong enough to capture the village. On the top they had room to sow and store a large amount of corn, and cisterns to collect snow and water."—Winship, *Coronado*, 39.

[7] The term applied to an Indian village.

[8] Gregg, writing in 1839, says that the Pueblo Indians were then "considered the best horticulturists in the country, furnishing most of the fruits and a large portion of the vegetable supplies that are to be found in the markets. They were until very lately the only people in New Mexico who cultivated the grape. They also maintain at the present time considerable herds of cattle, horses, etc. They are, in short, a remarkably sober and industrious race, conspicuous for morality and honesty, and very little given to quarrelling or dissipation, except when they have had much familiar intercourse with the Hispano-Mexican population."—*Commerce of the Prairies*, II, 55. Cf. President's Message, 1854, 429.

[9] The decrees of Charles V (1523, 1533, 1551) dictated that each Indian village should be granted as much cultivated land as might be necessary for its sustenance, and that the mountain forests and pastures should be used in common by Indians and Spaniards. The extent of the *pueblo* lands was later defined (1682) as four square leagues for each community, but these grants were not formally assigned till the eighteenth century. This arable land was to remain a tribal possession, and no individual was at liberty to sell or alienate to outsiders except by express permission of the *Protectores de los Indios*.

[10] *Desordines que se advier en el Nuevo Mexico.* De Morfi seems to have been a man of affairs. He accompanied Croix to Texas in 1778 and wrote the *Diario*, also *Memorias para la Historia de Texas*.

[11] A *fanega*, the common measure for grain, is equivalent to two bushels.

[12] The organization of the caravan is thus described by a contemporary: "Forty leagues from Santa Fé in the parish called Joya de Sevilleta, all those participating come together in the last days of November, with freight, firearms, ammunition, arrows, shields, horses, etc. Everything is passed in review, and when the number of men (five hundred) for the trip is made up, they indicate those who are to take turns on the journey, in the vanguard, rear and centre; those who are to take care of the horses and mules; those who have to serve as sentinels (the number regularly exceeds one hundred); the night guards who must keep ears to the ground on dark nights to make sure whether they hear steps and avoid the surprises they are accustomed to suffer. As to the provisions which are necessary, they exceed six hundred *fanegas* of wheat flour made up into toasted bread which they call *biscochos*, more than one hundred steers converted into *tassago* (pemican), one hundred and fifty *fanegas* of *pinole* (parched corn), a corresponding quantity of *frijoles*, *garbanzos*, some mutton; also the barrels to carry the water in the deserts, like that called *Jornado del Muerto* (Journey of Death), where one must ride more

than thirty leagues without finding any water. All these preparations have been insufficient in some years to enable them to escape from the cunning of the *gentiles* (Apaches)." — Pino, *Noticias*, 71-72.

¹³ Coues, *Pike*, II, 563.

¹⁴ Coues, *Pike*, II, 606.

¹⁵ Coues, *Pike*, II, 607.

¹⁶ Coues, *Pike*, II, 608, 611.

¹⁷ Coues, *Pike*, II, 685.

¹⁸ Coues, *Pike*, II, 740.

¹⁹ Coues, *Pike*, II, 740-741.

²⁰ Coues, *Pike*, II, 656.

²¹ Coues, *Pike*, II, 675.

Pedro Pino, *Noticias historicas y estadísticas de la antigua provincia del Nuevo Mexico.*

²³ Gregg, *Commerce of the Prairies*, I, 333.

²⁴ That this was an Indian contrivance is proved by the discovery of the *uso* in the extinct villages of the Gila River valley.

²⁵ Gregg, *Commerce of the Prairies*, I, 338.

²⁶ Pattie, *Personal Narrative*, 145.

²⁷ Gregg, *Commerce of the Prairies*, I, 289.

²⁸ Gregg, *Commerce of the Prairies*, I, 322-324.

²⁹ The first census taken in New Mexico, that of 1827, reported a population of 43,433, and the following category of occupations: agricultural laborers, 6588; day laborers, 2475; artisans, 1237; merchants, 93; schoolmasters, 17; scholars, 18.
    The wealth of the province was estimated in its cattle as follows: cattle, 5000, valued at $40,000; sheep and goats, 240,000, valued at $120,000; horses, 550, value $5500; mules 2150, value $53,750; mares, 300, value $2400.
    In 1840 the population was reckoned at 55,403. — Pino, *Revised Noticias.*

³⁰ Shea, *Discovery and Exploration*, 26, 28.

³¹ Joliet's journal was lost by shipwreck as he descended the St. Lawrence.

³² Cox, *La Salle*, I, 26.

³³ The king's commission empowered La Salle to explore "the western part of New France," "through which it was probable a road may be found to penetrate to Mexico." The ultimate aim of the expedition may have been the silver mines of New Biscay (Nueva Vizcaya).

[34] Cox, *La Salle*, II, 47.

[35] The stream and bay are still known as Lavaca, from the Spanish equivalent.

[36] Cox, *La Salle*, II, 66.

[37] Cox, *La Salle*, II, 69.

[38] Cox, *La Salle*, II, 94.

[39] Cox, *La Salle*, II, 95.

[40] Cox, *La Salle*, II, 95.

[41] Cox, *La Salle*, II, 101.

[42] Cox, *La Salle*, II, 128.

[43] Duhaut and Liotot were later shot by Hiens, with whom they had quarrelled over the distribution of the scanty stock of food.

[44] Cox, *La Salle*, II, 151.

[45] Cox, *La Salle*, II 185.

[46] Cox, *La Salle*, II, 127–128.

[47] Du Pratz, *Louisiana*, London Edition, 198–200.

[48] These common fields were donated to every colony by both French and Spanish governments, the grants were confirmed by the United States Congress, and this primitive system of land tenure has been perpetuated to the present day. Edward Flagg, who visited several of these villages in 1838, noted that "A single enclosure was erected and kept in repair at the expense of the villages, and the lot of every individual was separated from his neighbor's by a double furrow." — Flagg, *Far West*, Pt. I, 96. Cf. Bradbury, *Travels*, 259–261.

[49] Pike found him still at work there in 1805, when his annual output was from twenty to forty thousand pounds. The ore was easily smelted, and yielded seventy-five per cent metallic lead. After Dubuque's death, in 1810, the works were abandoned.

[50] Culbert and Magilhay, who were established near Cottonwood Creek.

[51] L'année des Batteaux.

[52] Bradbury, *Travels in the Interior of America*, 269–270.

[53] The term *presidio* is applied to any fortified post. Its garrison served as a guard to the missions.

[54] For first hand account of the mission of La Conception, San Antonio, see the report of 1762 quoted in Garrison's *Texas*, 56–60.

[55] The *metate*, the stone mortar in universal use among the aborigines of the southwest.

[56] *Reducidos*, the term used to designate the converted or subjugated Indians.

NOTES

[57] Altamira estimated in 1744 that the colonization of Texas had cost 3,000,000 *pesos* up to that date, and that the annual charge must continue at 63,000 *pesos*.

[58] The number of savages was estimated at fourteen thousand.

[59] Coues, *Pike*, II, 783.

[60] Pike found one of Nolan's men (Solomon Colly) imprisoned at Santa Fé and another (David Ferro) at Chihuahua, and he vainly interceded with Salcedo on their behalf.

[61] Coues, *Pike*, II, 785.

[62] Bastrop was a French émigré who had been sent to Texas by the Spanish government on a secret mission. He had been recompensed by a land grant of thirty square miles between the Mississippi and Red rivers.

[63] The term was applied to all baptized Indians dependent on the missions.

[64] Costanzó, *Historical Journal, Out West*, 14 : 488.

[65] Costanzó, the scientist of the party, carried Venega's *Noticias de las Californias* and a manual of navigation by the experienced pilot, Cabrera Bueno.

[66] Crespi, *Journal*.

[67] Costanzó, *Journal, Out West*, 15 : 39.

[68] Costanzó, *Journal, Out West*, 15 : 45.

[69] The revenue from the salt works at San Blas was devoted to this purpose.

[70] Palou, *Noticias*, IV, 103.

[71] Bancroft assumes that Anza entered the San Gabriel Valley by San Gorgonio Pass, following the present route of the Southern Pacific Railway, but recent researches favor the pass west of the San Jacinto Mountains. The trail was rough and steep, but there was abundant water. — Z. S. Eldridge, in *Journal of American History*, 1908.

[72] In 1774, roused by the rumor that they were all to be forcibly baptized, the Indians had attacked the mission buildings and murdered Father Jaime and some of the garrison. All the force Alta California could muster was required to suppress the revolt.

[73] Anza, *Journal*.

[74] *Reglamento de Neve*, Section V, in Rockwell's *Spanish and Mexican Law*, I, 445. Cf. *Recopilacion de Leyes*, Lib. IV, Tit. V, Ley VI. Philip II.

[75] The *vara* (33⅓ inches) was the universal unit of survey.

[76] "The new colonists shall enjoy, for the purpose of maintaining their cattle, the common privilege of the water and the pasturage, firewood and timber, of the common forest and pasture lands [*ejidos*], to be designated according to law to each new *pueblo* . . . and it not being pos-

sible that each one can dedicate himself to the taking care of the small stock consigned to them — as by so doing they would be unable to attend to agriculture and the public works — for the present, the small cattle, and the sheep and goats of the community, must feed together, and the shepherd must be paid by such community." — Rockwell, *Spanish and Mexican Law*, I, 448.

[77] "No colonist is to possess more than fifty head of the same kind of cattle, so that the utility produced by cattle be distributed amongst the whole of them, and that the true riches of the pueblo be not monopolized by a few inhabitants."

[78] The schedule of prices fixed by Governor Fages (1782–1791) was as just as de Neve could have desired ; viz. horses, $9 each ; mule, $14–20 ; ox or cow, $5 ; heifer or steer, $4 ; sheep, $1–2 ; an *arroba* (25 lb.) of wool, $2 ; ox-hide, 37½¢ ; *fanega* of wheat, $2 ; *fanega* of peas, $3. — Hittell, *History of California*, I, 534.

[79] The teachers at San Francisco and Monterey rendered voluntary service.

[80] Hogs and goats did not flourish under the new conditions.

[81] Costanzó, *Informe*, 1794.

[82] Vancouver, *Voyage of Discovery*, II, 501.

[83] Bacon, *Essay on Plantation*, 1625.

[84] Garcés left a full account of his journey up the Colorado, and it has been carefully edited by Elliott Coues, *On the Trail of a Spanish Pioneer*. Escallante's briefer journal has never found a publisher.

[85] In 1785 the French government ordained an exploration of the northwest coast of America with a view to "opening a communication with some part of Hudson's Bay" and ascertaining whether France might profitably establish a trading post to the north of the Spanish dominions. Comte de la Perouse reconnoitered the coast from the Fairweather Mountains to Monterey, where he spent sixteen days. The expedition was wrecked off the New Hebrides on the homeward voyage, and all hands perished. Perouse's journals, which were forwarded to Paris from Petropaulovski, are all that remain to us of his gallant adventure.

[86] De la Perouse, *Voyage autour du Monde*, II, 288–289.

[87] Between the years 1769 and 1797, 21,853 Indians had been baptized, and of these 10,437 had died at the missions.

[88] In 1806 the herds of the San Francisco neighborhood had become so numerous that the governor ordered 20,000 killed, lest the pastures should be exhausted.

[89] Von Langsdorff was the journalist of the expedition of de Resanoff, who visited the Pacific coast (1803–1806) in the interest of the Russian-American Fur Company.

[90] Kotzebue, *Voyage of Discovery*, I, 283.

[91] Humboldt, *New Spain*, II, 239.

[92] Sola (1818) reckoned the Spanish population of Upper California at three thousand. In 1841 (according to de Mofras), there were four thousand four hundred and fifty Indians and seven thousand whites.

[93] Vancouver, II, 27.

[94] Von Langsdorff, *Voyages and Travels*, II, 187.

[95] Von Langsdorff, II, 207.

[96] The fortress built by Borica on the bluff selected by Anza.

[97] All ports of California were thrown open to Mexican vessels in 1822, and customs duties imposed averaging 25 per cent. The four presidial ports were "open" to foreign vessels in 1829, and this favor was sometimes extended to San Pedro. Later Monterey and San Diego were the only open ports, and the duties were raised to 42.5 per cent.

[98] Tallow was in requisition for lighting the mines of Peru.

[99] The tariff of prices fixed by the governor: Hides, $1 each; wheat, $3 per *fanega;* tallow, $2 per *arroba;* soap, $16 per *cental;* pickled beef, $4 per *cental.*

[100] Drogher was the West India term applied to these slow and clumsy coasting vessels.

[101] Beechey, II, *Voyage to the Pacific,* 60.

[102] Beechey, II, 68.

[103] Beechey, II, 68.

[104] Beechey, II, 69.

[105] Beechey, II, 66–67.

[106] The Pious Fund was estimated at this time to amount to $500,000 with an annual revenue of $50,000. It was finally confiscated by Santa Anna in 1842, when the value was estimated at $2,000,000.

[107] Echeandia is known in the annals of the Franciscans as the "scourge of the missions." He proposed a plan of secularization which was adopted by the Territorial Deputation (1830), but never carried into execution. The several missions were to be converted into *pueblos* and the land distributed to the neophytes (one *solar* and one *suerte* to each), and they were to be supplied, acording to the *reglamento*, with live stock and tools. The *padres* might remain as curates, but it was hoped they would go to the Tulares to found new missions among the *gentiles*. The church and its furnishings and the residence of the missionary were reserved, but all other buildings were to be devoted to the uses of the *pueblos* for schools, hospitals, and so forth. Mills, orchards, vineyards, and gardens were to be administered by the *ayuntamientos* (councils) for the public benefit. Echeandia was superseded, before this scheme was put into operation, by Victoria, a reactionary goyernor; but secularization was soon given the sanction of the Mexican government.

[108] Quoted by Richman, *California under Spain and Mexico.*

[109] Hittell, II, 205–207.

[110] 1841 was a year of drought.

[111] Simpson, *Journey round the World*, I, 294–295.

[112] According to William C. Jones, the disposition of the remnant of the mission property was as follows: —

San Diego, sold to Santiago Arguello, June 18, 1846.

San Luis Rey, sold to Antonio Cot and Andres Pico, May 13, 1846.

San Juan Capristrano, sold to John Foster and James McKinley, December, 1845.

San Gabriel, sold to Julian Workman and Hugo Reid, June, 1846.

San Fernando, rented to Andres Pico for nine years, but sold to Juan Celis, 1846.

San Buenaventura, sold to Josef Armaz.

Santa Barbara, rented to Nicholas Den for nine years.

Santa Inez, rented to Joaquin Carrelo.

La Purissima, sold to John Temple, December, 1846.

San Luis Obispo, made over to *pueblo.*

San Miguel, sold to Captain Cooke, an Englishman, for $300. (According to Jules Remy.)

San Antonio and Santa Cruz, vacant.

Soledad, sold to Sobranes, January, 1846.

Carmel, San Juan Bautista, and Dolores made over to *pueblos.*

Santa Clara, San José, and San Francisco Solano ; missions in charge of priest, but property made over to the Valléjos.

[113] See Richman, *California under Spain and New Mexico*, for a full account of the ultimate destination of the mission property.

[114] *Alfileria*, a species of herb robert brought to California in the fleece of sheep imported from Spain. It still grows luxuriantly on mountain slopes and is popularly known as "filaree."

[115] De Mofras found a Frenchman, M. Barie, working a placer there. He was taking out one ounce of pure gold per day.

[116] In 1841 these items amounted to $265,000 out of a total of $280,000 (de Mofras), although the export of hides had dwindled to 30,000 per year.

[117] The contrivance is described by Wilkes and is still used in Lower California.

PART II

CHAPTER I

[1] The *bidarka* was a canoe constructed of whale bones and covered with walrus skin. Only a man-hole was left for the bodies of the two hunters, and they were tied in with oilskins so that the boat would not leak if capsized.

NOTES

389

[2] Von Langsdorff, *Voyages and Travels,* II, 228–229.

[3] De Resanoff projected an agricultural colony on the Columbia River, but his ship was driven off the entrance by adverse winds. His untimely death prevented the execution of this and other purposes he had in hand.

[4] Von Langsdorff, II, 180.

[5] Greenhow, 432–433.

[6] The charts and log-books of Bodega Quadra proved of great use to Captain James Cook and also to Von Humboldt.

[7] Cook also hoped to reach the eighty-ninth degree north latitude and so to win the prize offered for the identification of the North Pole!

[8] "We can now with safety assert that no such river as that of St. Roc exists, as laid down in the Spanish charts." (Lyman, *Oregon,* I, 271.)

[9] The *Columbia,* the *Washington,* the *Hancock,* the *Jefferson,* and the *Hope* from Boston: the *Eleanora,* the *Fair American,* the *Margaret* from New York.

[10] The publication of Cook's own *Journal* was delayed until 1784.

[11] This little schooner of thirty tons was the first ship built on the west coast.

[12] "They discovered a harbor in latitude 46° 53′ and longitude 122° 51′. This is Gray's Harbor. Here they were attacked by the natives, and the savages had a considerable slaughter among them. They next entered the Columbia River, and went up it about thirty miles and doubted not that it was navigable upwards of a hundred. Besides sea-otter skins, they purchased a great number of land furs of very considerable value." — Haswell, *Logbook,* printed as appendix to Bancroft, *Northwest Coast.*

[13] Vancouver, I, 210.

[14] Vancouver, I, 215.

[15] Vancouver, I, 420.

[16] Vancouver, II, 66.

[17] Narrative of the Adventures and Sufferings of John R. Jewitt.

CHAPTER II

[1] Carver, *Travels,* 102.

[2] "The cheapness and ease with which any quantity of it may be procured, will make up for the length of way that is necessary to transport it before it reaches the sea-coast, and enable the proprietors to send it to foreign markets on as good terms as it can be exported from other countries." — Carver, *Travels,* 139–140.

[3] Carver, *Travels*, 76.

[4] Thwaites, *Lewis and Clark*, VII, 193.

[5] Quoted by Laut, *Vikings of the Pacific*, 359.

[6] Mackay's map of the Missouri was evidently familiar to Lewis and Clark, and his instructions to John Evans for the tour of exploration bear a marked similarity both in spirit and in detail to the instructions Jefferson sent to Meriwether Lewis. Cf. Teggart, Notes Supplementary to any Edition of Lewis and Clark.

[7] Thwaites, *Lewis and Clark*, VII, 208.

[8] In a letter to Lewis (from Louisville, July 24, 1803) Clark writes : "Several young men (gentlemen's sons) have applyed to accompany us. As they are not accustomed to labour and as that is a verry essential part of the services required of the party, I am cautious in giving them any encouragement." — Thwaites, *Lewis and Clark*, VII, 263.

[9] Thwaites, *Lewis and Clark*, VII, 210.

[10] The ménu was thus set forth by Captain's orders : "The day after to-morrow lyed corn and grece will be issued to the party, the next day Poark and flour, and the day following indian meal and poark ; and in conformity to that rotiene, provisions will continue to be issued to the party untill further orders. . . . No poark is to be issued when we have fresh meat on hand." — Thwaites, *Lewis and Clark*, I, 33.

[11] Sergeant C. Floyd died of a sudden chill contracted after unusually violent exercise (August 16, 1804).

[12] Thwaites, *Lewis and Clark*, I, 145.

[13] Masson, *Bourgeois de la Compagnie du Nord-Ouest*, I, 307–308.

[14] Thwaites, *Lewis and Clark*, I, 240.

[15] Thwaites, *Lewis and Clark*, I, 330.

[16] Harmon, of the North West Company, records the arrival at the Mandan villages of Lewis and Clark and the reception of their letter of October 31. Also that M. Chaboillez writes him that "they behave honorably toward his people, who are there to trade with the natives."

[17] Masson, *Bourgeois de la Compagnie du Nord-Ouest*, I, 336.

[18] Thwaites, *Lewis and Clark*, I, 248. (This post was projected at Turtle Mt. on the forty-ninth parallel, and hence on the boundary line.)

[19] Thwaites, *Lewis and Clark*, VII, 320.

[20] Thwaites, *Lewis and Clark*, VII, 320, 321.

[21] Thwaites, *Lewis and Clark*, I, 322.

[22] Thwaites, *Lewis and Clark*, II, 14.

[23] Thwaites, *Lewis and Clark*, II, 14.

[24] Thwaites, *Lewis and Clark*, II, 17.

[25] Thwaites, *Lewis and Clark*, II, 100.

²⁶ Thwaites, *Lewis and Clark* , II, 113.

²⁷ Thwaites, *Lewis and Clark*, II, 147.

²⁸ Thwaites, *Lewis and Clark*, II, 149-150.

²⁹ Thwaites, *Lewis and Clark*, II, 209.

³⁰ There were no wild horses in this region. The few which seemed masterless bore marks of having been trained to the saddle, some of them showing the brand of the Spanish ranchman from whom they were bought or stolen. Spanish bits, bridles, and saddles were not uncommon among the Shoshones, though saddles and stirrups were reserved for the use of women and old men. A halter of twisted hair and a small leather pad secured by a leather girth were sufficient equipment for a warrior.

³¹ Thwaites, *Lewis and Clark*, II, 380.

³² Thwaites, *Lewis and Clark*, III, 73, 74.

³³ Thwaites, *Lewis and Clark*, III, 78.

³⁴ Thwaites, *Lewis and Clark*, IV, 192-193. An Indian, Hunter John, who remembered seeing the Lewis and Clark party, lived near Port Angeles until 1912.

³⁵ Thwaites, *Lewis and Clark*, IV, 176-177.

³⁶ Thwaites, *Lewis and Clark*, IV, 238.

³⁷ Thwaites, *Lewis and Clark*, V, 390.

³⁸ Thwaites, *Lewis and Clark*, V, 394.

³⁹ Clark's description of a Schenectady boat, *i.e.* bateau: Length, thirty feet, width eight feet, pointed bow and stern, flat bottom, rowed by six oars only. "Being wide and flat they are not Subject to the dangers of roleing Sands." — Thwaites, *Lewis and Clark*, V, 390.

⁴⁰ Coues, *Pike*, I, 202.

⁴¹ Coues, *Pike*, I, 133.

⁴² Coues, *Pike*, I, 156.

⁴³ Coues, *Pike*, I, 156.

⁴⁴ Coues, *Pike*, I, 247-254.

CHAPTER III

¹ *E.g.* Auguste Chouteau of St. Louis was granted exclusive right to trade with the Osages, and built a post on the Missouri in 1796 which he called Carondelet.

² Biddle, *Lewis and Clark*, III, 290.

³ Chittenden, III, Appendix B, 902.

⁴ He argued that this flourishing commerce should not be "left to the adventurers of the United States, acting without regularity or capital or the desire of conciliating future confidence, and looking only to the interest of the moment." See also Archibald Campbell, "A Voyage round the World" (1806-1812), *London Quarterly Review*, October, 1816.

⁵ Masson, I, 331.

⁶ Gregg, *Commerce of the Prairies*, II, 264. Cf. Burton's *City of the Saints*, 52.

⁷ Washington Irving (*Captain Bonneville* I, 31) estimated that three-fifths of the men pursuing this dangerous trade met with unnatural death.

⁸ Irving's phrase.

⁹ Brackenridge, *Journal*, 31-32.

¹⁰ Brackenridge, 66.

¹¹ Chittenden, III, Appendix B, 901.

¹² The Scotch partners were McKay, Mackenzie, McDougal, David and Robert Stuart, and Ramsay Crooks. The Americans were Hunt, Miller, McLellan, and Clark.

¹³ Franchère, Narrative, 230.

¹⁴ Ross, *First Settlers in Oregon*, 89.

¹⁵ Franchère, *Narrative*, 259.

¹⁶ Ross, *First Settlers in Oregon*, 161.

¹⁷ Ross, 101. Cf. Franchère, 253.

¹⁸ In 1807, Thompson crossed the mountains by Saskatchewan Pass and ascended the Columbia River to its source. In 1810, he attempted to descend this river to the sea, but the project, which if successful might have given Great Britain title to the whole course of the River of the West, was delayed till the following year when the Astorians had gained possession. The two or three years subsequent Thompson devoted to the production of that *Map of the North West Territory of the Province of Canada* which has furnished the basis of all later cartography in this region. In 1813, David Thompson was the official surveyor of the British government for the determination of the boundary line between the United States and Canada. J. J. Bigsby of the International Boundary Commission wrote of Thompson, " No living person possesses a tithe of his information respecting the Hudson's bay countries, which from 1793 to 1820 he was constantly traversing." Lieutenant Pike refers to the exploration of the source of the Mississippi, undertaken by the North West Company, " They have had a gentleman by the name of Thompson making a geographical survey of the northwest part of the continent ; who for three years with an astonishing spirit of enterprise and perseverance, passed over all that extensive and unknown country." Coues, *Pike*, I, 279.

¹⁹ "Mr. Thompson kept a regular journal, and travelled, I thought, more like a geographer than a fur-trader. He was provided with a sextant, chronometer, and barometer, and during a week's sojourn which he made at our place, had an opportunity to make several astronomical observations." — Franchère, 254.

[20] That these assurances were not to be relied upon is clear from the fact later discovered, that on his return journey, Thompson placed a British flag at the junction of Lewis' or Snake River with the Columbia, together with a legend forbidding the subjects of other powers to trade north of that point. The legend read: "Know hereby that this country is claimed by Great Britain as part of its Territories, & that the N. W. Company of Merchants from Canada, finding the Factory for this People inconvenient for them, do intend to erect a Factory in this Place for the Commerce of the Country around. — D. Thompson."— Ross, 138.

[21] The Spokanes traded the goods purchased from the traders for horses from the Nez Perces.

[22] Ross, 174.

[23] Ross, 181.

[24] Ross, 178.

[25] Ross, 179.

[26] Brackenridge, 72.

[27] At Henry's Fort and lower down the river two parties of trappers were left: one under A. Carson, the other under J. Miller. The latter had announced his intention of abandoning the expedition.

[28] Caldron Linn has been identified with the rapids at Milburn, Idaho.

[29] Franchère, 269–270.

[30] Ross, 188, 189.

[31] Ross, 187.

[32] Ross, 227.

[33] Ross, 228.

[34] Franchère, 280–281.

[35] Cf. Astor's letter to J. Q. Adams, quoted by Lyman, *History of Oregon*, II, 298.

[36] Ross Cox, *Adventures on the Columbia*, I, 276.

[37] Astor's enterprise seemed pursued by misfortune. The *Pedler* was wrecked off the coast of California, and the men made their way with great difficulty through Mexico to the United States. Hunt recovered his fortunes and became a prosperous merchant at St. Louis. Russell Farnham and Alfred Seton attained distinction, the one as traveller and writer, the other as a New York financier.

[38] Franchère, 303.

[39] Ross, 279, states the loss of life as follows: On the bar of the Columbia, eight; on the overland expedition, five; on the *Tonquin*, twenty-seven; on the *Lark*, eight; in the Snake country, nine; at Astoria, three; at the final departure, one.

[40] Coues, *Greater Northwest*, II, 889.

⁴¹ Dunn, *Oregon*, 108–109.

⁴² Citation by A. C. Laut from the Ms. journals of Alexander Ross.

⁴³ Manuel Lisa died in 1820, and no successor was found to equal him in daring or resource. The affairs of the Missouri Fur Company were not wound up until 1830.

⁴⁴ Fremont, *First Expedition*, 39–40.

⁴⁵ Chittenden, I, 341, quoted from the *Missouri Republican*.

⁴⁶ Wyeth learned of Mackenzie's distillery when he visited Fort Union (1833). He reported to General Clark at St. Louis, who promptly reported to Washington. It was proposed to withdraw the license of the offending company, and but for Benton's good offices the operations of the American Fur Company might have been brought to a halt. As it was, Mackenzie, the offending agent, was obliged to withdraw from its service.

⁴⁷ Buffalo hides, scraped and softened and ready for use, were sold on the Plains at from $1 to $1.50 each; at from $5 to $10 in the States. When elaborately decorated with paint and porcupine quills, a robe brought $35.

⁴⁸ Chittenden, *Fur Trade*, Vol. III, 944.

⁴⁹ Some accounts indicate that Ashley found his British competitor out of supplies and was therefore able to purchase his furs for a song; others, that he enticed his men away by the lure of whiskey and then made advantageous terms with the helpless leader. In either case Ogden could not complain, for his own stern maxim was "Necessity knows no law." Ogden was trapped a second time at this same spot by Fitzpatrick five years later and relieved of all his furs. — Ross Cox, II, 243; Elliott, *Peter Skeene Ogden*, 20. Cf. Chittenden, I, 277, 293. Wyeth; *History of Oregon*, I, 74.

⁵⁰ *Adventures of Captain Bonneville*, Ch. V. Cf. Appendix D, Chittenden.

⁵¹ So Bancroft, but the effort to find it made by the Academy of Pacific Coast History was fruitless. Portions of the later journals are in the possession of Smith's descendants and may soon be published.

⁵² Captain Bonneville was an officer in the United States army who secured permission from the War Department to explore the Far West and report on the Indian tribes, economic resources, etc. The expedition was financed by Alfred Seton of the Astorian party and other New York merchants who hoped for a rich return in furs. During his three years in the west (1832–1835) Bonneville explored Salt Lake and the Wind River Mountains more thoroughly than had yet been undertaken. He followed the Snake and Salmon Rivers to the Columbia and made two bootless attempts to establish a trading station in Hudson's Bay Company territory. Joseph Walker, who was sent on a trapping expedition to California (1833), crossed the desert to Humboldt Sink and thence by

Sonora Pass and the Merced River made his way to the Pacific. The furs taken in Bonneville's various expeditions were not sufficient to pay the wages of his men and he presented no report to the War Department. He made no discoveries, since the country he traversed was well known to the fur traders; but his map of the Rocky Mountains, while not so accurate as that already published by Gallatin, is of great interest and far better known. Bonneville's chief claim to fame is the delightful and sympathetic account of his wanderings transcribed for the press by Washington Irving.

[53] A pack was made up of sixty pelts and weighed approximately one hundred pounds. The fur sold for $5 a pound in St. Louis and $7 to $8 in New York.

[54] Fremont, *Second Expedition*, 144–145.

[55] Stansbury, *Expedition to Great Salt Lake*, 35.

[56] N. J. Wyeth, *Report on the Fur Trade*, 1839.

[57] *American Historical Review*, 14 : 73.

[58] Ross, *First Settlers in Oregon*, 177–178.

[59] Farnham, *Travels in the Great Western Prairies*, 69.

[60] Larpenteur, *Journal*, II, 289.

[61] Forsythe, *Letter to Lewis Cass*, Chittenden; III, 933–934.

[62] Fremont, *Second Expedition*, 111.

[63] Gunnison, *Valley of the Great Salt Lake*, 151.

BIBLIOGRAPHY

VOLUME I

PART I

CHAPTER I. — THE EXPLORERS

Bandelier, A. F.
Contributions to the History of the Southwestern Portion of the United States.
Cambridge, 1890.

Papers of the Archæological Institute. American Series, V. Explorations of Nuñez Cabeza de Vaca, Fray Marcos, Villagra.

—— Final Rept. of Investigations among the Indians of the south-western United States, carried on mainly in the years from 1880–1885.
Cambridge, 1890.

Papers of the Archæological Institute of America. American Series, III, IV.

Castañeda, Pedro de.
The Journey of Coronado, 1540–42. Edited by George Parker Winship.
A. S. Barnes. Trail Makers Series.

Coronado, Francesco Vasquez de.
Journey, as told by Pedro de Castañeda. Edited by George Parker Winship.
A. S. Barnes. Trail Makers Series.

Cox, I. J.
Joutel's Journal of La Salle's Journeyings.
A. S. Barnes, 1905. Trail Makers Series.

Davidson, George.
Drake's Anchorage on the Coast of California.
Calif. Hist. Soc. Pubs., 1888.

—— Discovery of San Francisco Bay.
Proceedings Geog. Soc. of Pacific, 1907.

Drake, Sir Francis.
The World Encompassed, collated with an unpublished manuscript of Francis Fletcher, chaplain to the Expedition.
Hakluyt Society, I, 115–133, 1854.
The Earliest Texas.
Am. Hist. Ass. Pubs., An. Rept., 1891, 199–205.
Harby, Mrs. Lee.
—— The Tehas.
Am. Hist. Ass. Pubs., An. Rept., 1894, 6–82.
Humboldt, Alexander von.
Political Essay on the Kingdom of New Spain. 4 vols.
London, 1814.

New California, Vol. II, 289–308.

Joutel, Henri.
Journal of La Salle's Last Voyage. Edited by H. R. Stiles.
McDonough, Albany, 1906.

Reprint of the original with full introduction.

—— The Journeyings of La Salle. Edited by I. J. Cox.
A. S. Barnes, 1905. Trail Makers Series.
Nuñez Cabeza de Vaca.
Journey from Florida to the Pacific (1582–36), together with the report of Fr. Marcos de Nizza.
A. S. Barnes, 1905. Trail Makers Series.

Translated by Fanny Bandelier from the Spanish *Naufragios y relacion de la jornada* de Nuñez Cabeza de Vaca. This extraordinary journey is represented in Purchas' Pilgrims, Vol. IX, also in *Narrative of Alva Nuñez Cabeza de Vaca*, translated by Buckingham Smith.

Washington, 1851.
Shea, J. S.
Discovery and Exploration of the Mississippi.
New York, 1852.

The history in brief, accompanied by the original Narratives of Marquette, Hennepin, etc.

De Soto, Hernando.
Narrative of the Career of, in the Conquest of Florida. 1539–1542. Edited by Ed. G. Bourne, in 2 volumes.
A. S. Barnes. Trail Makers Series.

Venegas, Fray Miguel.
Noticia de la California y de su conquesta.
Madrid, 1757. Translation, London, 1759.
Winship, George Parker.
The Coronado Expedition.

Castañeda's Journal in the original Spanish and in translation, with notes and illustrations. Bureau of American Ethnology, Report 14, Part I, 329.

——— Why Coronado went to New Mexico.
Am. Hist. Ass., An. Rept., 1894, 83–92.

CHAPTER II. — THE COLONIZERS

NEW MEXICO

Bancroft, H. H.
History of the Pacific Coast States of North America.
San Francisco, 1882–91.

Vol. XVII. Arizona and New Mexico.

Brackenridge, H. M.
Early Discoveries by Spaniards in New Mexico.
Pittsburg, 1857.
Coues, Elliott.
On the Trail of a Spanish Pioneer. The Diary of Fray Francisco Garcés, 1775–76.
Francis P. Harper, 1900.
Davis, W. H. H.
Spanish Conquest of New Mexico, 1527–1703.
Doylestown, Pa., 1869.
Donaldson, T.
Moqui Pueblo Indians of Arizona and Pueblo Indians of New Mexico.
Washington, 1893. Extra bulletin of eleventh census.
Garcés, Fray Francisco.
Diary of, 1775–76. Edited by Elliott Coues. (On the Trail of a Spanish Pioneer.)
Francis P. Harper, 1900.

Helps, Sir Arthur.
The Spanish Conquest and its Relation to the History of Slavery.
London, 1855–61. 4 vols.

Vol. III, Bk. XIV; valuable discussion of encomiendas — origin and influence.

Hodge, Frederick W.
Spanish Explorers in the Southern United States.
Charles Scribner's Sons, 1907.

Excellent maps.

Holmes, Geo. K.
Agriculture of the Pueblo Indians in Bailey's Cyclopædia of Agriculture, Vol. IV, Ch. 2.

Lowery, W.
Spanish Settlements in the United States, 1513–61.
G. P. Putnam's Sons, 1901.

Lummis, C. F.
Mining Three Hundred and Fifty Years Ago.
Out West, Vol. XX, 3, 111, 223.

Illustrated with numerous cuts from Agricola's *De Re Metallica*, 1550.

Morfi, Fray J. A. de.
Desordines que se advierten en el Nuevo Mexico, 1778.

MS. in Bancroft Collection.

Pattie, J. O.
Personal Narrative during an Expedition from St. Louis, through the Vast Regions between that place and the Pacific Ocean and thence back through the City of Mexico to Vera Cruz, during journeying of six years (1824–30); in which he and his father, who accompanied him, suffered unheard of Hardships and Dangers, had Various Conflicts with the Indians, and were made Captives (at San Diego) in which Captivity his Father died; together with a Description of the country and the Various Nations through which they passed. Edited by Timothy Flint, 1831. Reëdited by Reuben Thwaites. Vol. XVIII, Early Western Travels, 1905.

Pike, Zebulon M.
The Expeditions of, Edited by Elliott Coues. 3 vols.
Francis P. Harper, 1895.

Pike, Z. M.

Papers confiscated at Chihuahua. Collected by Prof. Bolton, of University of Texas.

Reported upon in Am. Hist. Rev., July, 1908.

Pino, Fray Pedro.

Noticias historicas y estadisticas de la antigua provincia del Nuevo Mexico.

City of Mexico, 1849.

Powell, J. W.

Exploration of the Colorado River of the West, 1869–72. Edited by Elliott Coues.

Washington, 1875. (Under direction of the Smithsonian Institution, Government Printing Office.)

Prince, L. Bradford.

Historical Sketches of New Mexico.

Kansas City, 1883.

Recopilacion de Leyes de los Regnos de las Indias.

In four quarto volumes. Madrid, 1774.

Libro VI. Encomiendas, obligations of encomenderos, limitations on labor service.

Libro IX. Regulations affecting the fleet, exclusion of foreigners, etc.

Shea, John G.

Catholic Missions Among the Indian Tribes of the United States.

New York, 1855.

California Missions, Ch. VI.
New Mexico Missions, Ch. IV.
Texas Missions, Ch. V.

Simpson, J. H.

Journal of a Reconnoissance from Santa Fé, New Mexico, to the Navajo country in 1849.

Philadelphia, 1852.

Villagra, Capitan Gaspar de.

Historia de la Nueva Mexico.

A rhyming chronicle of the deeds of Don Juan de Oñate which narrates the conquest of New Mexico to the siege of Acoma, with much spirit and with surprising accuracy. Used by Bancroft as basis for his narrative, Vol. XVII, 112–115.

Wilkinson, General James.

Memories of my own Times.

Philadelphia, 1816.

TEXAS

Almonte, Juan N.
Noticia Estadistica sobre Tejas.
City of Mexico, 1835.

Bancroft, H. H.
History of the Pacific Coast States of North America.
San Francisco, 1882–91.
Vols. XV, XVI. North Mexican States and Texas.

Bean, Ellis P.
Account of Philip Nolan's Texas Expedition. Printed in Yoakum's History of Texas, I, Appendix I.

Cox, I. J.
Joutel's Journal of La Salle's Journeyings.
A. S. Barnes, 1905. Trail Makers Series.

Garrison, George P.
Texas, a Contest of Civilizations.
Houghton Mifflin Co., 1903. American Commonwealth Series.

Morfi, Fray J. A. de.
Memorias para la Historia de Texas, 1783.
Vols. XXVII and XXVIII of the Archivo General de Mexico. Still unpublished, according to George P. Garrison of the Texas Hist. Society, 1902.

Rockwell, John A.
Spanish and Mexican Law.
Voorhees, Albany, N.Y., 1851.
p. 451. Mexican law of 1824, offering land to foreigners.
p. 453. Mexican Law of 1828, defining terms for land grants.

Venegas, Fray Miguel.
History of California, Translated from the Madrid edition of 1758.
London, 1759.
Vol. I, Pt. II. Explorations in New Mexico and California.
Cortés, Coronado, Cabrillo, Vizcaino.

LOUISIANA

Brackenridge, H. M.
Recollections of Persons and Places in the West.
Philadelphia, 1834.
—— Views of Louisiana, together with Journal.
Pittsburg, 1834.

Bradbury, John.
Travels into the Interior of North America.
Early Western Travels, Vol. V.

Cable, George W.
The Creoles of Louisiana.
Charles Scribner's Sons, 1884.

Cox, Isaac J.
Exploration of Louisiana Frontier, 1803.
Am. Hist. Ass. Rept., 1904, 150–174.

Fortier, Alcée.
History of Louisiana in 4 vols. Edition de luxe.
Manzi, Joyant & Co. New York, 1904.

Freeman, Thos.
An Account of the Red River in Louisiana.
Washington, 1806?
Rept. of Expedition of Freeman and Custis up the Red River in 1806.

French, B. F.
Historical Collections of Louisiana. 3 vols.
New York, 1851.
La Salle's Memoir, Journals of Tonty, Joutel, Hennepin, Papers of Crosat, La Harpe, etc.

Gayarré, Charles.
History of Louisiana, 1539–1816, in 4 vols.
New Orleans, 1885.

Heinrich, Pierre.
La Louisiane sous la compagnie des Indes (1717–31).
Paris, 1907.

Hosmer, J. K.
The Louisiana Purchase.
D. Appleton & Co., 1902.

Houck, Louis.
Boundaries of the Louisiana Purchase, a Monograph.
St. Louis, 1901.

Le Gac, Charles.
Sur la Louisiane; sa géographie, la situation de la colonie française du 26 Aoust 1718 au 5 Mars 1721 et de Moyens de l'améliorer.

Le Page Du Pratz.
Histoire de la Louisiane. 3 vols.
Paris, 1758.

Le Page Du Pratz.
Louisiana under the Company of the West. Translation.
London, 1774.

The translation published in London in 1763 in two vols. is the better book.

Mascrier, M. L. L.
Mémoires historiques sur la Louisiane — composés sur les mémoires de M. Dumont.
Paris, 1753.

Robertson, J. A.
Louisiana under the Rule of Spain, France, and the United States, 1785–1807. 2 vols. A. H. Clark & Co., Cleveland.

Documents in translation, political in the main, with interesting sidelights on social and economic conditions.

Stoddart, Amos M.
Sketches of Louisiana.
Philadelphia, Carey, 1812.

Vaudreuil, P. S.
Letters on the Trade of Louisiana.
London, 1744.

Wallace, Joseph.
Illinois and Louisiana under the French Rule.
Cincinnati, 1893.

From original narratives.

CALIFORNIA

Adam, Rev. J.
Life of Padre Junipero Serra.
San Francisco, 1884.

An abridgement of Palou's Vida.

Anza, Juan Bautista.
Diario de una expedicion desde Sonora a San Francisco, 1775–1776. Ms. in Bancroft Collection. Publications of the Academy of Pacific Coast History. Vol. VI in preparation.

Bancroft, H. H.
Pacific Coast States.
San Francisco, 1882–91.

Vols. XVIII–XX. California, 1542–1840.

Beechey, Captain F. W.
Voyage to the Pacific, in 2 vols.
London, 1831.

Vol. II. Chs. I, II, III. California.

Belcher, Sir Edward.
Voyage Round the World, in 2 vols.
London, 1843.

Vol. I. California.

Blackmar, F. W.
Spanish Institutions of the Southwest.
Johns Hopkins University Series, 1891.

Choris, Louis.
Voyage Pittoresque autour du Monde.
Paris, 1822.

Cleveland, R. J.
Narrative of Voyages and Commercial Enterprises.
Cambridge, 1842.

Costanzó, Miguel.
Historical Journal of the Expedition by sea and land to Northern California, 1768, 1769, 1770.
Dalrymple, London, 1790. (Scarce.)
Publications of the Academy of Pacific Coast History.
Vol. VII. In preparation.

Crespi, Fray.
Letter to Costanzó, May 2, 1772.
Out West, Vol. XVII, 56–59.

Dana, Richard H.
Two Years Before the Mast. (1835–36.)
Houghton Mifflin Co., 1911.

Davis, Wm. Heath.
Sixty Years in California.
A. J. Leary. San Francisco, 1889.

Dwinelle, John W.
Colonial History of San Francisco.
San Francisco, 1863.

Eldridge, Zoeth S.
Journal of Anza's First Expedition.
Journal of American History, Vol. II, Nos. 1, 2, 3.

Eldridge, Zoeth S.
The March of Postola.   San Francisco, 1910.
Engelhardt, Father Z.
The Franciscans in California.
Harbor Springs, Mich., 1897.
—— Missions and Missionaries of California.
San Francisco, 1908.

Vol. I. Lower California. Pt. III, Chs. 2, 3, Galvez. Ch. 9, Echeandia.
Ch. 10, Pious Fund.
Vol. II. Upper California in preparation.

Font, Padre Pedro.
Diary of Expedition to California.
Publications of Academy of Pacific Coast History, Vol. 6.
In preparation.
Forbes, Alexander.
History of California, Upper and Lower.
London, 1839.
Hall, Frederick.
History of San José and Surroundings.
San Francisco, 1871.
Hittell, John S.
History of San Francisco.
San Francisco, 1878.
Hittell, T. H.
History of California, in 4 vols.
Occidental Publishing Co.   San Francisco, 1885.

The first two volumes of Hittell's History have a unique value, since
they are based on the California archives, 300 volumes of documentary
material, all of which perished in the San Francisco fire.   There are
considerable transcripts in the Bancroft Library.

Kotzebue, Otto von.
Voyage of Discovery into the South Sea and Behring Straits,
for the purpose of exploring a Northeast passage, at the ex-
pense of Count Romanzoff, in the ship *Rurik*, 1815–18, in
3 vols.
London, 1821.
La Perouse, J. F. de G.
Voyage Round the World, 1785–88, in 4 vols.
London, 1779.

Vol. I, 437–456. California.

Langsdorf, G. von.
Voyages and Travels, 1803–07.
London, 1813.   Philadelphia, 1817.
Lévy, Daniel.
Les Français en Californie.
San Francisco, 1884.
Mofras, Duflot de.
Exploration au Territoire de l'Oregon, des Californies, et de
la Mer Vermeille.
Paris, 1844.
Palou, Fray.
Vida de Padre Junipero Serra.   1787.
P. E. Dougherty & Co.   San Francisco, 1884.
Portolá, Gaspar de.
Diary — during the California Expedition of 1769–70; also,
Official Account of the Expedition.
Publications of the Academy of Pacific Coast History,
Vol. I, Nos. 2 and 3.

Original text and translation.

Richman, I. B.
California under Spain and Mexico.
Houghton Mifflin Co., 1911
Robinson, Alfred.
Life in California, 1829–46.
Putnams, N.Y., 1846.   San Francisco, 1891.
Rockwell, John A.
Spanish and Mexican Law.
Voorhees.   Albany, N.Y., 1851.

p. 445.   Reglamento of de Neve.
p. 455.   Law of 1833 for secularization of missions.
p. 456.   Provisions imposed by Figueroa.

Serra, Fray Junipero.
Diary of, March 28–June 30, 1769.
Translated in Out West, Vol. XVI, 293, 399, 513, 635;
Vol. XVII, 69.
Shaler, Captain of the *Lelia Byrd.*
Journal of a Voyage between China and the Northwestern
Coast of America.
American Register, III, 137–175, 1809.

Simpson, Sir George.
Journey Round the World, 1841–42. 2 vols.
London, 1847.

Torres Campos, D. Rafael.
España en California y en el Noroeste de America.
Ateneo de Madrid, 1892.

Vancouver, George.
Voyage of Discovery.
London, 1801. First edition, London, 1798.

Vol. III, 8–400. California.

Wilkes, Charles.
Exploring Expedition, 1833–42, in 5 vols.
Philadelphia, 1845.

Vol. V, Ch. V. California.

PART II

EXPLORATION AND THE FUR TRADE

CHAPTER I. — THE NORTHWEST COAST

Bancroft, H. H.
The Northwest Coast, Vols. XXVII, XXVIII.
Bancroft & Co. San Francisco, 1891.
History of the Hudson's Bay Company.
Sampson, Low, Marston & Co. London, 1900.

Bryce, George.
—— Lord Selkirk's Colonists.
Sampson, Low, Marston & Co. — London, 1910 (?)

Cook, Captain James.
Three Voyages to the Pacific Ocean.
Boston, 1797.
—— A Voyage to the Pacific Ocean, 1776–80. 4 vols.
London, 1784.

Coues, Elliott.
The Greater Northwest. Manuscript Journals of Alexander
Henry and David Thompson, 1799–1814. 3 vols.
Francis P. Harper, 1897.

Coxe, Wm.
Discoveries of the Russians between Asia and America.
London, 1787.

Discoveries since 1745 and commerce with China, Pt. III, Ch. III.

Douglas, Sir James.
Journal, 1840–41.
Ms. in Bancroft Collection.

Interesting information on H. B. C. operations in Oregon and California.

Dunn, John.
Oregon and the History of the British North American Fur Trade.
Philadelphia, 1846.

Franchère, Gabriel.
Narrative of the Voyage to the Northwest Coast of America, 1811–14.
Translated by J. V. Huntingdon. Redfield, New York, 1854.
Early Western Travels, Vol. VI.

Greenhow, Robert.
History of Oregon and California.
Boston, 1845.

See appendices for Michael Lock's account of the voyage of Juan de Fuca, Haceta's report on San Roque River, 430–433; Gray's Logbook, 434–436.

Haswell's Log Book.
Printed as appendix to Bancroft's North-west Coast, 1–729.

Henry, Alexander (the younger), and *Thompson, David.*
Manuscript Journals, edited by Elliott Coues as "The Greater Northwest."
Francis P. Harper, 1897.

Vol. III, Pt. III. The Columbia, Nov. and Dec., 1813.

Jewitt, John R.
Narrative of the Adventures and Sufferings of the only survivors of the crew of the Ship *Boston* (1803).
Ithaca, N.Y., 1849.

Kotzebue, Otto von.
Voyage of Discovery. 3 vols.
London, 1821.

Langsdorf, G. von.
  Voyages and Travels, 1803–07.
    Philadelphia, 1817.
Laut, Agnes C.
  The Conquest of the Great Northwest. 2 vols.
  "Being the story of the Adventurers of England known as The Hudson's Bay Company. New pages in the history of the Canadian Northwest and Western States." The Outing Publishing Company, New York, 1908.
—— Vikings of the Pacific.
    The Macmillan Co., 1905.
Lewis, Meriwether.
  Report on Louisiana, 1808.

  Interesting though unfinished account of the fur trade under Spanish auspices. Reprinted in Biddle's Journal of Lewis and Clark.

Ledyard, John.
  Journal of Cook's Last Voyage.
    Hartford, 1783.

  The original journal was confiscated on the return of the expedition as precaution against misrepresentation, and was never recovered. Ledyard wrote a short account of the voyage two years after.

Lyman, H. S.
  History of Oregon in 4 vols.
  Edited by H. W. Scott, Chas. B. Billinger and Frederick G. Young.
  North Pacific Pub. Society. New York, 1903.
Manning, W. R.
  The Nootka Sound Controversy. University of Chicago dissertation.
    Printed by Government, Washington, 1905.
Tikhmeneff.
  Historical Review of the Russian American Fur Company.
    St. Petersburg, 1861.
    Translation by Ivan Petrof.
Vancouver, George.
  Voyage of Discovery. Vol. III.
    London, 1801.

CHAPTER II. — OVERLAND SEARCH FOR THE
WESTERN SEA

Biddle, Nicolas.
Lewis and Clark Expedition.
Philadelphia, 1814.
Carver, Jonathan.
Travels in North America.
London, 1777.
Elliott, T. C.
David Thompson, Pathfinder.
Walla Walla, 1912.
Gass, Patrick.
A Journal of the Voyages and Travels of a Corps of Discovery.
Matthew Carey. Philadelphia, 1810.
Harmon, Daniel Williams.
Voyages of a Partner in the Northwest Company, 1800–05.
A. S. Barnes. New York. Trail Makers Series.
Hennepin's New Discovery.
Edited by R. G. Thwaites in 2 vols.
A. C. McClurg & Co., 1903.
Laut, Agnes C.
Pathfinders of the West.
The Macmillan Co. New York, 1904.
Ledyard, John.
Travels and Adventures.
London, Second Edition, 1834.

Biography with full quotations from Ledyard's letters and Journal.

Lewis and Clark.
Journals, edited by R. G. Thwaites, 1904.
Arthur H. Clark, Cleveland, in 7 vols.

Comprises all the original journals of Lewis, Clark, Pryor, Ordway,
Floyd, together with many reproductions of maps, sketches, etc., and
much valuable editorial matter.

—— Journals, edited by Elliott Coues. 3 vols.
Francis P. Harper.

An ably edited reprint of the Biddle Edition.

Lewis and Clark.
  Journals.
    A. S. Barnes. New York. 2 vols. Trail Makers Series.
    A reprint of the Biddle Edition.
Lewis, Meriwether.
  Report addressed to President Jefferson from the Mandan
Villages, March, 1805.
    American State Papers — Indian Affairs, I, 706–707.
Mackenzie, Alexander.
  Voyages from Montreal through the continent of North
America to the frozen and Pacific oceans in 1789 and 1793.
    London, 1802.   New Amsterdam Book Co., N. Y., 1902.
    Also Trail Makers Series.
Masson.
  Bourgeois de la Compagnie du Nord-Ouest. 2 vols.
    Quebec, 1889.
Nicollet, J. N.
  Report on Exploration of the Mississippi and Missouri rivers.
    Washington, 1843.
Parkman, Francis.
  Discoveries of the Great West.
    Little, Brown, & Co. Boston, 1880.
Radisson, Pierre.
  Voyages, 1652–1684. Edited by G. D. Scull.
    Prince Society, Boston, 1805.
Schoolcraft, H. R.
  Narrative of an Expedition through the Upper Mississippi
Valley to Itasca Lake, 1820. New York, 1854.
Sparks, Jared.
  Life of John Ledyard, in Spark's Library of American Biography.
    Cambridge, 1829.
Teggart, F. J.
  Notes Supplementary to any Edition of Lewis and Clarke.
    Am. Hist. Ass. An. Rept., 1908, I, 183–195.
    Careful examination of the operation of the Spanish *Compania de
descubridores del Misuri.* Relation of achievements of Mackay and Evans
to the later explorations of Lewis and Clark.
Thompson, David.
  Journals.
    In preparation by the Champlain Society of Canada.

Thwaites, R. G.
Lewis and Clark, Journals.
Cleveland, 1904.
—— William Clark; Soldier, Explorer, Statesman.
Missouri Historical Society Collections, Vol. II, No. 7.
—— Father Marquette.
D. Appleton & Co., 1902.
—— Rocky Mountain Exploration.
D. Appleton & Co., 1904.
Tyrrell, J. B.
David Thompson.
Canadian Institute Proceedings. Toronto, 1888.
—— - David Thompson, a Great Geographer. In Geographical
Journals, 1911, 37, 49.
The Royal Geographical Society.
Wheeler, Olin D.
Trail of Lewis and Clark. 2 vols.
G. P. Putnam's Sons, 1904.
Whiting, Henry.
Life of Z. M. Pike. Spark's Lib. of Am. Biog., Vol. V, 219–317.
Little, Brown, & Co. Boston, 1848.

CHAPTER III. — THE FUR TRADE

American State Papers.
Indian Affairs.

Vols. I and II under titles "Indian trade," "Factories," "Agents" —
for government factories and opposition of private traders, 1796–1822.
Vol. II, 54–66, Schoolcraft's report on fur trade on Missouri, 1815–1830.
Public Lands, Vol. III — see index for salt mines, lead mines, etc.

Beckworth, James P.
Life and Adventures of, as dictated to S. D. Bonner.
New York, 1856.

First hand account of adventures of a trapper who became a guide and
a pioneer settler. Reëdited by C. S. Leland. New York, 1892.

Bilson, B.
The Hunters of Kentucky.
New York, 1847.

A poor reproduction of Pattie's Narrative, but more widely read than
the original.

Brackenridge, H. M.
Journal of a Voyage up the River Missouri, 1811.
Early Western Travels, Vol. VI.
Bradbury, John.
Travels into the Interior of America.
Early Western Travels, Vol. V.
Chittenden, H. M.
History of the Early Western Fur Trade. 3 vols. and map.
Francis P. Harper, New York, 1902.
Coman, Katherine.
The Government Factory: an Attempt to regulate Competition in the Fur Trade.
American Economic Association. Pubs., 1911.
Cox, Ross.
Adventures on the Columbia River.
London, 1831.
Vol. I, Chs. IV, X. Oregon.

Crooks, Ramsay.
Letters. Printed in the Wisconsin Historical Publications with letters of other fur traders in chronological order.
Elliott, T. C.
David Thompson, Pathfinder, and the Columbia River.
Kettle Falls, Wash., 1911.
—— Peter Skene Ogden.
Portland, Oregon, 1910.
A memoir based on original documents of Ms. journals furnished by the family, the Hudson's Bay Company's records, etc.

Farnham, T. J.
Travels in the Great Western Prairies, the Anahuac and Rocky Mountains and in Oregon Territory, 1839.
Early Western Travels, Vol. XXVIII.
Forsyth, Thomas.
Report to Lewis Cass, Sec. of War, on the State of the Fur Trade in 1831.
Ms. Letter in the Manuscript Dept. State Historical Society, Wisconsin, reprinted in Chittenden, Vol. III, 926–946.

Franchère, Gabriel.
Narrative of a Voyage to the Northwest Coast, 1811–1814.
Huntington's Translation, New York, 1854.
Early Western Travels, Vol. VI.

Fremont, J. C.
  Journal of the Second Expedition.
    Washington, 1845.
Irving, Washington.
  Adventures of Captain Bonneville.
    Philadelphia, 1837.
—— Astoria.
    G. P. Putnam's Sons, 1867.   Philadelphia, 1836–37.

  A new edition of this admirable account, with historical and geographical notes, is now needed.

—— Scenes in the Rocky Mountains.
    Philadelphia, 1837.
Larpenteur, Charles.
  Forty years of a Fur Trader on the Upper Missouri, 1833–72.
  Edited by Elliott Coues.
    Francis P. Harper.
Laut, Agnes C.
  Story of the Trapper.
    D. Appleton & Co.
Maximilien, Prince of Wied.
  Travels in the Interior of North America, 1832–34.
    English edition, 1843.
    Early Western Travels, Vols. XXII, XXIII, XXIV, and atlas.
Morgan, Lewis H.
  The American Beaver.
    Philadelphia, 1868.
Peters, De Witt C.
  Life and Adventures of Kit Carson.   New York, 1859.
Ross, Alexander.
  Adventures of the First Settlers on the Oregon.
    Early Western Travels, Vol. VII.
Scharf, J. T.
  History of St. Louis.
    Philadelphia, 1883.
Schoolcraft, H. B.
  Report on Fur Trade on the Missouri, 1815–30.
    Senate Doc. No. 90, 22d Cong. First Series.
Smith, Jedidiah S.
  Letter of Oct. 11, 1827, describing traverse of Mohave Desert.
    Nouvelles Annales des Voyages, Tome XXXVII.

Switzler, Wm. F.
  Kit Carson.
  Missouri Historical Society Collections, Vol. II, No. 1, 35–45.
Thompson, David.
  Journals.
  Pub. by the Champlain Society of Canada. (In preparation.)
Willson, Beckles.
  The Great Company (H. B. C.).
  Dodd, Mead & Co., 1900.
Youngman, Anna.
  Fortune of John Jacob Astor, The Fur Trade.
  Journal of Pol. Econ., XVI, 345–368.

XIII.   Timothy Pitkin, A STATISTICAL VIEW OF THE COM-
         MERCE OF THE UNITED STATES OF AMERICA.

XIV.   Katherine Coman, ECONOMIC BEGINNINGS OF THE
         FAR WEST, 2 volumes.

XV.   William R. Bagnall, THE TEXTILE INDUSTRIES OF
         THE UNITED STATES.

XVI.   Witt Bowden, THE INDUSTRIAL HISTORY OF THE
         UNITED STATES.

XVII.   Melvin T. Copeland, THE COTTON MANUFACTURING
         INDUSTRY OF THE UNITED STATES.

XVIII.   Blanche E. Hazard, THE ORGANIZATION OF THE BOOT
         AND SHOE INDUSTRY IN MASSACHUSETTS BE-
         FORE 1875.

XIX.   Albert Gallatin, REPORT OF THE SECRETARY OF THE
         TREASURY ON THE SUBJECT OF ROADS AND
         CANALS, 1807.

XX.   Henry S. Tanner, A DESCRIPTION OF THE CANALS
         AND RAILROADS OF THE UNITED STATES.

XXI.   J. Warren Stehman, THE FINANCIAL HISTORY OF
         THE AMERICAN TELEPHONE AND TELEGRAPH
         COMPANY.

XXII.   Kathleen Bruce, VIRGINIA IRON MANUFACTURE IN
         THE SLAVE ERA.

XXIII.   Abraham Gesner, A PRACTICAL TREATISE ON COAL,
         PETROLEUM AND OTHER DISTILLED OILS, revised
         and enlarged by George W. Gesner.

XXIV.   Alexander Hamilton, INDUSTRIAL AND COMMERCIAL
         CORRESPONDENCE OF ALEXANDER HAMILTON
         ANTICIPATING HIS REPORT ON MANUFACTURES,
         edited by Arthur H. Cole. With a Preface by Prof. Edwin
         F. Gay.